WRITING AN INTERPRETER IN GO

THORSTEN BALL

CONTENTS

ACKNOWLEDGMENTS

I want to use these lines to express my gratitude to my wife for supporting me. She's the reason you're reading this. This book wouldn't exist without her encouragement, faith in me, assistance and her willingness to listen to my mechanical keyboard clacking away at 6am.

Thanks to my friends Christian, Felix and Robin for reviewing early versions of this book and providing me with invaluable feedback, advice and cheers. You improved this book more than you can imagine.

INTRODUCTION

The first sentence of this introduction was supposed to be this one: "Interpreters are magical". But one of the earliest reviewers, who wishes to remain anonymous, said that "sounds super stupid". Well, Christian, I don't think so! I still think that interpreters *are* magical! Let me tell you why.

On the surface they look deceptively simple: text goes in and something comes out. They are programs that take other programs as their input and produce something. Simple, right? But the more you think about it, the more fascinating it becomes. Seemingly random characters - letters, numbers and special characters - are fed into the interpreter and suddenly become **meaningful**. The interpreter gives them meaning! It makes sense out of nonsense. And the computer, a machine that's built on understanding ones and zeroes, now understands and acts upon this weird language we feed into it - thanks to an interpreter that translates this language while reading it.

I kept asking myself: *how does this work?* And the first time this question began forming in my mind, I already knew that I'll only be satisfied with an answer if I get to it by writing my own interpreter. So I set out to do so.

A lot of books, articles, blog posts and tutorials on interpreters exist. Most of the time, though, they fall into one of two categories. Either they are huge, incredibly heavy on theory and more targeted towards people who already have a vast understanding of the topic, or they are really short, provide just a small introduction to the topic, use external tools as black boxes and only concern themselves with "toy interpreters".

One of the main sources of frustration was this latter category of resources, because the interpreters they explain only interpret languages with a really simple syntax. I didn't want to take a shortcut! I truly wanted to understand how interpreters work and that included understanding how lexers and parsers work. Especially with a C-like language and its curly braces and semicolons, where I didn't even know how to start parsing them. The academic textbooks had the answers I was looking for, of course. But rather inaccessible to me, behind their lengthy, theoretical explanations and mathematical notation.

What I wanted was something between the 900 page book on compilers and the blog post that explains how to write a Lisp interpreter in 50 lines of Ruby code.

So I wrote this book, for you and me. This is the book I wish I had. This is a book for people who love to look under the hood. For people that love to learn by understanding how something really works.

In this book we're going to write our own interpreter for our own programming language - from scratch. We won't be using any 3rd party tools and libraries. The result won't be production-ready, it won't have the performance of a fully-fledged interpreter and, of course, the language it's built to interpret will be missing features. But we're going to learn a lot.

It's difficult to make generic statements about interpreters since the variety is so high and none are alike. What can be said is that the one fundamental attribute they all share is that they take source code and evaluate it without producing some visible, intermediate result that can later be executed. That's in contrast to compilers, which take source code and produce output in another language that the underlying system can understand.

Some interpreters are really small, tiny, and do not even bother with a parsing step. They just interpret the input right away. Look at one of the many Brainfuck interpreters out there to see what I mean.

On the other end of the spectrum are much more elaborate types of interpreters. Highly optimized and using advanced parsing and evaluation techniques. Some of them don't just evaluate their input, but compile it into an internal representation called bytecode and then evaluate this. Even more advanced are JIT interpreters that compile the input just-in-time into native machine code that gets then executed.

But then, in between those two categories, there are interpreters that parse the source code, build an abstract syntax tree (AST) out of it and then evaluate this tree. This type of interpreter is sometimes called "tree-walking" interpreter, because it "walks" the AST and interprets it.

What we will be building in this book is such a tree-walking interpreter.

We're going to build our own lexer, our own parser, our own tree representation and our own evaluator. We'll see what "tokens" are, what an abstract syntax tree is, how to build such a tree, how to evaluate it and how to extend our language with new data structures and built-in functions.

THE MONKEY PROGRAMMING LANGUAGE & INTERPRETER

Every interpreter is built to interpret a specific programming language. That's how you "implement" a programming language. Without a compiler or an interpreter a programming language is nothing more than an idea or a specification.

We're going to parse and evaluate our own language called Monkey. It's a language specifically designed for this book. Its only implementation is the one we're going to build in this book - our interpreter.

Expressed as a list of features, Monkey has the following:

- C-like syntax
- variable bindings
- integers and booleans
- arithmetic expressions
- built-in functions
- first-class and higher-order functions
- closures
- a string data structure
- an array data structure
- a hash data structure

We're going to take a detailed look at and implement each of these features in the rest of this book. But for now, let's see what Monkey looks like.

Here is how we bind values to names in Monkey:

```
let age = 1;
let name = "Monkey";
let result = 10 * (20 / 2);
```

Besides integers, booleans and strings, the Monkey interpreter we're going to build will also support arrays and hashes. Here's what binding an array of integers to a name looks like:

```
let myArray = [1, 2, 3, 4, 5];
```

And here is a hash, where values are associated with keys:

```
let thorsten = {"name": "Thorsten", "age": 28};
```

Accessing the elements in arrays and hashes is done with index expressions:

```
myArray[0]       // => 1
thorsten["name"] // => "Thorsten"
```

The `let` statements can also be used to bind functions to names. Here's a small function that adds two numbers:

```
let add = fn(a, b) { return a + b; };
```

But Monkey not only supports `return` statements. Implicit return values are also possible, which means we can leave out the `return` if we want to:

```
let add = fn(a, b) { a + b; };
```

And calling a function is as easy as you'd expect:

```
add(1, 2);
```

A more complex function, such as a `fibonacci` function that returns the Nth Fibonacci number, might look like this:

```
let fibonacci = fn(x) {
  if (x == 0) {
    0
  } else {
    if (x == 1) {
      1
    } else {
      fibonacci(x - 1) + fibonacci(x - 2);
    }
  }
};
```

Note the recursive calls to `fibonacci` itself!

Monkey also supports a special type of functions, called higher order functions. These are functions that take other functions as arguments. Here is an example:

```
let twice = fn(f, x) {
  return f(f(x));
};

let addTwo = fn(x) {
  return x + 2;
};

twice(addTwo, 2); // => 6
```

Here `twice` takes two arguments: another function called `addTwo` and the integer `2`. It calls `addTwo` two times with first `2` as argument and then with the return value of the first call. The last line produces `6`.

Yes, we can use functions as arguments in function calls. Functions in Monkey are just values, like integers or strings. That feature is called "first class functions".

The interpreter we're going to build in this book will implement all these features. It will tokenize and parse Monkey source code in a REPL, building up an internal representation of the code called abstract syntax tree and then evaluate this tree. It will have a few major parts:

- the lexer
- the parser
- the Abstract Syntax Tree (AST)
- the internal object system
- the evaluator

We're going to build these parts in exactly this order, from the bottom up. Or better put: starting with the source code and ending with the output. The drawback of this approach is that it won't produce a simple "Hello World" after the first chapter. The advantage is that it's easier to understand how all the pieces fit together and how the data flows through the program.

But why the name? Why is it called "Monkey"? Well, because monkeys are magnificent, elegant, fascinating and funny creatures. Exactly like our interpreter.

And why the name of the book?

WHY GO?

If you read this far without noticing the title and the words "in Go" in it, first of all: congratulations, that's pretty remarkable. And second: we will write our interpreter in Go. Why Go?

I like writing code in Go. I enjoy using the language, its standard library and the tools it provides. But other than that I think that Go is in possession of a few attributes that make it a great fit for this particular book.

Go is really easy to read and subsequently understand. You won't need to decipher the Go code I present to you in this book. Even if you are not an experienced Go programmer. I'd bet that you can follow this book along even if you've never written a single line of Go in your life.

Another reason is the great tooling Go provides. The focus of this book is the interpreter we are writing - the ideas and concepts behind it and its implementation. With Go's universal formatting style thanks to `gofmt` and a testing framework built-in, we can concentrate on our interpreter and not worry about 3rd party libraries, tools and dependencies. We won't be using any other tools in this book other than the ones provided by the Go programming language.

But I think much more important is that the Go code presented in this book maps closely to other and possibly more low-level languages, like C, C++ and Rust. Maybe the reason for this is Go itself, with its focus on simplicity, its stripped-down charm and lack of programming language constructs that are absent in other languages and hard to translate. Or maybe it's because of the way I chose to write Go for this book. Either way, there won't be any meta-programming tricks to take a shortcut that nobody understands anymore after two weeks and no grandiose object-oriented designs and patterns that need pen, paper and the sentence "actually, it's pretty easy" to explain.

All of these reasons make the code presented here easy to understand (on a conceptual as well as a technical level) and reusable for you. And if you, after reading this book, choose to write your own interpreter in another language this should come in handy. With this book I want to provide a starting point in your understanding and construction of interpreters and I think the code reflects that.

HOW TO USE THIS BOOK

This book is neither a reference, nor is it a theory-laden paper describing concepts of interpreter implementation with code in the appendix. This book is meant to be read from start to finish and I recommend that you follow along by reading, typing out and modifying the presented code.

Each chapter builds upon its predecessor - in code and in prose. And in each chapter we build another part of our interpreter, piece by piece. To make it easier to follow along, the book comes with a folder called `code`, that contains, well, code. If your copy of the book came without the folder, you can download it here:

https://interpreterbook.com/waiig_code_1.4.zip

The `code` folder is divided into several subfolders, with one for each chapter, containing the final result of the corresponding chapter.

Sometimes I'll only allude to something being in the code, without showing the code itself (because either it would take up too much space, as is the case with the test files, or it is just some detail) - you can find this code in the folder accompanying the chapter, too.

Which tools do you need to follow along? Not much: a text editor and the Go programming language. Any Go version above 1.0 should work, but just as a disclaimer and for future generations: at the time of writing I'm using Go 1.7.

I also recommend using direnv[1], which can change the environment of your shell

[1] http://direnv.net/

according to an `.envrc` file. Each sub-folder in the code folder accompanying this book contains such an `.envrc` file that sets the `GOPATH` correctly for this sub-folder. That allows us to easily work with the code of different chapters.

And with that out of the way, let's get started!

CHAPTER 1

LEXING

1.1 - LEXICAL ANALYSIS

In order for us to work with source code we need to turn it into a more accessible form. As easy as plain text is to work with in our editor, it becomes cumbersome pretty fast when trying to interpret it in a programming language as another programming language.

So, what we need to do is represent our source code in other forms that **are** easier to work with. We're going to change the representation of our source code two times before we evaluate it:

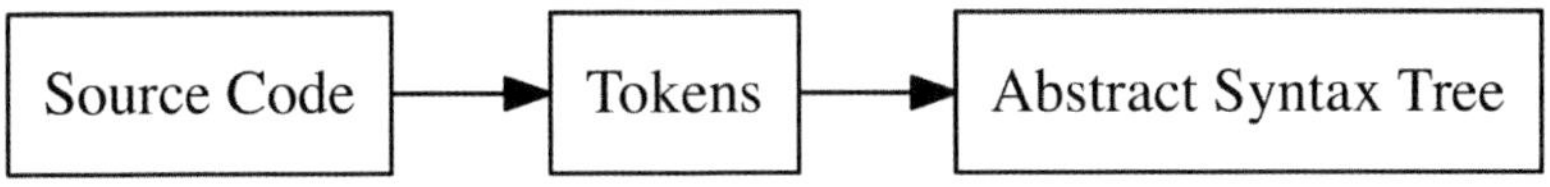

The first transformation, from source code to tokens, is called "lexical analysis", or "lexing" for short. It's done by a lexer (also called tokenizer or scanner – some use one word or the other to denote subtle differences in behaviour, which we can ignore in this book).

Tokens itself are small, easily categorizable data structures that are then fed to the parser, which does the second transformation and turns the tokens into an "Abstract Syntax Tree".

Here's an example. This is the input one gives to a lexer:

```
"let x = 5 + 5;"
```

And what comes out of the lexer looks kinda like this:

```
[
  LET,
  IDENTIFIER("x"),
  EQUAL_SIGN,
  INTEGER(5),
  PLUS_SIGN,
  INTEGER(5),
  SEMICOLON
]
```

All of these tokens have the original source code representation attached. `"let"` in the case of `LET`, `"+"` in the case of `PLUS_SIGN`, and so on. Some, like `IDENTIFIER` and `INTEGER` in our example, also have the concrete values they represent attached: `5` (not `"5"`!) in the case of `INTEGER` and `"x"` in the case of `IDENTIFIER`. But what exactly constitutes a "token" varies between different lexer implementations. As an example, some lexers only convert the `"5"` to an integer in the parsing stage, or even later, and not when constructing tokens.

A thing to note about this example: whitespace characters don't show up as tokens. In our case that's okay, because whitespace length is not significant in the Monkey language. Whitespace merely acts as a separator for other tokens. It doesn't matter if we type this:

```
let x = 5;
```

Or if we type this:

```
let   x   =   5;
```

In other languages, like Python, the length of whitespace *is* significant. That means the lexer can't just "eat up" the whitespace and newline characters. It has to output the whitespace characters as tokens so the parser can later on make sense of them (or output an error, of course, if there are not enough or too many).

A production-ready lexer might also attach the line number, column number and filename to a token. Why? For example, to later output more useful error messages in the parsing stage. Instead of `"error: expected semicolon token"` it can output:

```
"error: expected semicolon token. line 42, column 23, program.monkey"
```

We're not going to bother with that. Not because it's too complex, but because it would take away from the essential simpleness of the tokens and the lexer, making it harder to understand.

1.2 - DEFINING OUR TOKENS

The first thing we have to do is to define the tokens our lexer is going to output. We're going to start with just a few token definitions and then add more when extending the lexer.

The subset of the Monkey language we're going to lex in our first step looks like this:

```
let five = 5;
let ten = 10;

let add = fn(x, y) {
  x + y;
};

let result = add(five, ten);
```

Let's break this down: which types of tokens does this example contain? First of all, there are the numbers like `5` and `10`. These are pretty obvious. Then we have the variable names `x`, `y`, `add` and `result`. And then there are also these parts of the language that are not numbers, just words, but no variable names either, like `let` and `fn`. Of course, there are also a lot of special characters: `(`, `)`, `{`, `}`, `=`, `,`, `;`.

The numbers are just integers and we're going to treat them as such and give them a separate type. In the lexer or parser we don't care if the number is `5` or `10`, we just want to know if it's a number. The same goes for "variable names": we'll call them "identifiers" and treat them the same. Now, the other words, the ones that look like identifiers, but aren't really identifiers, since they're part of the language, are called "keywords". We won't group these together since it **should** make a difference in the parsing stage whether we encounter a `let` or a `fn`. The same goes for the last category we identified: the special characters. We'll treat each of them separately, since it is a big difference whether or not we have a `(` or a `)` in the source code.

Let's define our `Token` data structure. Which fields does it need? As we just saw, we definitely need a "type" attribute, so we can distinguish between "integers" and "right bracket" for example. And it also needs a field that holds the literal value of the token, so we can reuse it later and the information whether a "number" token is a `5` or a `10` doesn't get lost.

In a new `token` package we define our `Token` struct and our `TokenType` type:

```go
// token/token.go

package token
```

```go
type TokenType string

type Token struct {
    Type    TokenType
    Literal string
}
```

We defined the `TokenType` type to be a `string`. That allows us to use many different values as `TokenType`s, which in turn allows us to distinguish between different types of tokens. Using `string` also has the advantage of being easy to debug without a lot of boilerplate and helper functions: we can just print a `string`. Of course, using a `string` might not lead to the same performance as using an `int` or a `byte` would, but for this book a `string` is perfect.

As we just saw, there is a limited number of different token types in the Monkey language. That means we can define the possible `TokenType`s as constants. In the same file we add this:

```go
// token/token.go

const (
    ILLEGAL = "ILLEGAL"
    EOF     = "EOF"

    // Identifiers + literals
    IDENT = "IDENT" // add, foobar, x, y, ...
    INT   = "INT"   // 1343456

    // Operators
    ASSIGN   = "="
    PLUS     = "+"

    // Delimiters
    COMMA     = ","
    SEMICOLON = ";"

    LPAREN = "("
    RPAREN = ")"
    LBRACE = "{"
    RBRACE = "}"

    // Keywords
    FUNCTION = "FUNCTION"
    LET      = "LET"
)
```

As you can see there are two special types: `ILLEGAL` and `EOF`. We didn't see them in the example above, but we'll need them. `ILLEGAL` signifies a token/character we don't know about and `EOF` stands for "end of file", which tells our parser later on that it can stop.

So far so good! We are ready to start writing our lexer.

1.3 - The Lexer

Before we start to write code, let's be clear about the goal of this section. We're going to write our own lexer. It will take source code as input and output the tokens that represent the source code. It will go through its input and output the next token it recognizes. It doesn't need to buffer or save tokens, since there will only be one method called `NextToken()`, which will output the next token.

That means, we'll initialize the lexer with our source code and then repeatedly call `NextToken()` on it to go through the source code, token by token, character by character. We'll also make life simpler here by using `string` as the type for our source code. Again: in a production environment it makes sense to attach filenames and line numbers to tokens, to better track down lexing and parsing errors. So it would be better to initialize the lexer with an `io.Reader` and the filename. But since that would add more complexity we're not here to handle, we'll start small and just use a `string` and ignore filenames and line numbers.

Having thought this through, we now realize that what our lexer needs to do is pretty clear. So let's create a new package and add a first test that we can continuously run to get feedback about the working state of the lexer. We're starting small here and will extend the test case as we add more capabilities to the lexer:

```
// lexer/lexer_test.go

package lexer

import (
    "testing"

    "monkey/token"
)

func TestNextToken(t *testing.T) {
    input := `=+(){},;`

    tests := []struct {
        expectedType    token.TokenType
        expectedLiteral string
    }{
```

```go
        {token.ASSIGN, "="},
        {token.PLUS, "+"},
        {token.LPAREN, "("},
        {token.RPAREN, ")"},
        {token.LBRACE, "{"},
        {token.RBRACE, "}"},
        {token.COMMA, ","},
        {token.SEMICOLON, ";"},
        {token.EOF, ""},
    }

    l := New(input)

    for i, tt := range tests {
        tok := l.NextToken()

        if tok.Type != tt.expectedType {
            t.Fatalf("tests[%d] - tokentype wrong. expected=%q, got=%q",
                i, tt.expectedType, tok.Type)
        }

        if tok.Literal != tt.expectedLiteral {
            t.Fatalf("tests[%d] - literal wrong. expected=%q, got=%q",
                i, tt.expectedLiteral, tok.Literal)
        }
    }
}
```

Of the course, the tests fail – we haven't written any code yet:

```
$ go test ./lexer
# monkey/lexer
lexer/lexer_test.go:27: undefined: New
FAIL    monkey/lexer [build failed]
```

So let's start by defining the `New()` function that returns `*Lexer`.

```go
// lexer/lexer.go
package lexer

type Lexer struct {
    input        string
    position     int  // current position in input (points to current char)
    readPosition int  // current reading position in input (after current char)
    ch           byte // current char under examination
}

func New(input string) *Lexer {
    l := &Lexer{input: input}
```

```go
    return l
}
```

Most of the fields in Lexer are pretty self-explanatory. The ones that might cause some confusion right now are position and readPosition. Both will be used to access characters in input by using them as an index, e.g.: l.input[l.readPosition]. The reason for these two "pointers" pointing into our input string is the fact that we will need to be able to "peek" further into the input and look after the current character to see what comes up next. readPosition always points to the "next" character in the input. position points to the character in the input that corresponds to the ch byte.

A first helper method called readChar() should make the usage of these fields easier to understand:

```go
// lexer/lexer.go

func (l *Lexer) readChar() {
    if l.readPosition >= len(l.input) {
        l.ch = 0
    } else {
        l.ch = l.input[l.readPosition]
    }
    l.position = l.readPosition
    l.readPosition += 1
}
```

The purpose of readChar is to give us the next character and advance our position in the input string. The first thing it does is to check whether we have reached the end of input. If that's the case it sets l.ch to 0, which is the ASCII code for the "NUL" character and signifies either "we haven't read anything yet" or "end of file" for us. But if we haven't reached the end of input yet it sets l.ch to the next character by accessing l.input[l.readPosition].

After that l.position is updated to the just used l.readPosition and l.readPosition is incremented by one. That way, l.readPosition always points to the next position where we're going to read from next and l.position always points to the position where we last read. This will come in handy soon enough.

While talking about readChar it's worth pointing out that the lexer only supports ASCII characters instead of the full Unicode range. Why? Because this lets us keep things simple and concentrate on the essential parts of our interpreter. In order to fully support Unicode and UTF-8 we would need to change l.ch from a byte to rune and change the way we read the next characters, since they could be multiple bytes wide now. Using l.input[l.readPosition] wouldn't work anymore. And then we'd also need to change a few other methods and functions we'll see later on. So it's left as an exercise to the reader to fully support Unicode (and emojis!) in Monkey.

Let's use `readChar` in our `New()` function so our `*Lexer` is in a fully working state before anyone calls `NextToken()`, with `l.ch`, `l.position` and `l.readPosition` already initialized:

```go
// lexer/lexer.go

func New(input string) *Lexer {
    l := &Lexer{input: input}
    l.readChar()
    return l
}
```

Our tests now tell us that calling `New(input)` doesn't result in problems anymore, but the `NextToken()` method is still missing. Let's fix that by adding a first version:

```go
// lexer/lexer.go

import "monkey/token"

func (l *Lexer) NextToken() token.Token {
    var tok token.Token

    switch l.ch {
    case '=':
        tok = newToken(token.ASSIGN, l.ch)
    case ';':
        tok = newToken(token.SEMICOLON, l.ch)
    case '(':
        tok = newToken(token.LPAREN, l.ch)
    case ')':
        tok = newToken(token.RPAREN, l.ch)
    case ',':
        tok = newToken(token.COMMA, l.ch)
    case '+':
        tok = newToken(token.PLUS, l.ch)
    case '{':
        tok = newToken(token.LBRACE, l.ch)
    case '}':
        tok = newToken(token.RBRACE, l.ch)
    case 0:
        tok.Literal = ""
        tok.Type = token.EOF
    }

    l.readChar()
    return tok
```

```go
}

func newToken(tokenType token.TokenType, ch byte) token.Token {
    return token.Token{Type: tokenType, Literal: string(ch)}
}
```

That's the basic structure of the `NextToken()` method. We look at the current character under examination (`l.ch`) and return a token depending on which character it is. Before returning the token we advance our pointers into the input so when we call `NextToken()` again the `l.ch` field is already updated. A small function called `newToken` helps us with initializing these tokens.

Running the tests we can see that they pass:

```
$ go test ./lexer
ok      monkey/lexer 0.007s
```

Great! Let's now extend the test case so it starts to resemble Monkey source code.

```go
// lexer/lexer_test.go

func TestNextToken(t *testing.T) {
    input := `let five = 5;
let ten = 10;

let add = fn(x, y) {
  x + y;
};

let result = add(five, ten);
`

    tests := []struct {
        expectedType    token.TokenType
        expectedLiteral string
    }{
        {token.LET, "let"},
        {token.IDENT, "five"},
        {token.ASSIGN, "="},
        {token.INT, "5"},
        {token.SEMICOLON, ";"},
        {token.LET, "let"},
        {token.IDENT, "ten"},
        {token.ASSIGN, "="},
        {token.INT, "10"},
        {token.SEMICOLON, ";"},
        {token.LET, "let"},
        {token.IDENT, "add"},
        {token.ASSIGN, "="},
```

```
        {token.FUNCTION, "fn"},
        {token.LPAREN, "("},
        {token.IDENT, "x"},
        {token.COMMA, ","},
        {token.IDENT, "y"},
        {token.RPAREN, ")"},
        {token.LBRACE, "{"},
        {token.IDENT, "x"},
        {token.PLUS, "+"},
        {token.IDENT, "y"},
        {token.SEMICOLON, ";"},
        {token.RBRACE, "}"},
        {token.SEMICOLON, ";"},
        {token.LET, "let"},
        {token.IDENT, "result"},
        {token.ASSIGN, "="},
        {token.IDENT, "add"},
        {token.LPAREN, "("},
        {token.IDENT, "five"},
        {token.COMMA, ","},
        {token.IDENT, "ten"},
        {token.RPAREN, ")"},
        {token.SEMICOLON, ";"},
        {token.EOF, ""},
    }
// [...]
}
```

Most notably the `input` in this test case has changed. It looks like a subset of the Monkey language. It contains all the symbols we already successfully turned into tokens, but also new things that are now causing our tests to fail: identifiers, keywords and numbers.

Let's start with the identifiers and keywords. What our lexer needs to do is recognize whether the current character is a letter and if so, it needs to read the rest of the identifier/keyword until it encounters a non-letter-character. Having read that identifier/keyword, we then need to find out if it is a identifier or a keyword, so we can use the correct `token.TokenType`. The first step is extending our switch statement:

```
// lexer/lexer.go

import "monkey/token"

func (l *Lexer) NextToken() token.Token {
    var tok token.Token

    switch l.ch {
```

```go
// [...]
    default:
        if isLetter(l.ch) {
            tok.Literal = l.readIdentifier()
            return tok
        } else {
            tok = newToken(token.ILLEGAL, l.ch)
        }
    }
// [...]
}

func (l *Lexer) readIdentifier() string {
    position := l.position
    for isLetter(l.ch) {
        l.readChar()
    }
    return l.input[position:l.position]
}

func isLetter(ch byte) bool {
    return 'a' <= ch && ch <= 'z' || 'A' <= ch && ch <= 'Z' || ch == '_'
}
```

We added a `default` branch to our switch statement, so we can check for identifiers whenever the `l.ch` is not one of the recognized characters. We also added the generation of `token.ILLEGAL` tokens. If we end up there, we truly don't know how to handle the current character and declare it as `token.ILLEGAL`.

The `isLetter` helper function just checks whether the given argument is a letter. That sounds easy enough, but what's noteworthy about `isLetter` is that changing this function has a larger impact on the language our interpreter will be able to parse than one would expect from such a small function. As you can see, in our case it contains the check `ch == '_'`, which means that we'll treat _ as a letter and allow it in identifiers and keywords. That means we can use variable names like `foo_bar`. Other programming languages even allow `!` and `?` in identifiers. If you want to allow that too, this is the place to sneak it in.

`readIdentifier()` does exactly what its name suggests: it reads in an identifier and advances our lexer's positions until it encounters a non-letter-character.

In the `default:` branch of the switch statement we use `readIdentifier()` to set the `Literal` field of our current token. But what about its `Type`? Now that we have read identifiers like `let`, `fn` or `foobar`, we need to be able to tell user-defined identifiers apart from language keywords. We need a function that returns the correct `TokenType` for the token literal we have. What better place than the `token` package to add such a function?

```go
// token/token.go

var keywords = map[string]TokenType{
    "fn":  FUNCTION,
    "let": LET,
}

func LookupIdent(ident string) TokenType {
    if tok, ok := keywords[ident]; ok {
        return tok
    }
    return IDENT
}
```

`LookupIdent` checks the `keywords` table to see whether the given identifier is in fact a keyword. If it is, it returns the keyword's `TokenType` constant. If it isn't, we just get back `token.IDENT`, which is the `TokenType` for all user-defined identifiers.

With this in hand we can now complete the lexing of identifiers and keywords:

```go
// lexer/lexer.go

func (l *Lexer) NextToken() token.Token {
    var tok token.Token

    switch l.ch {
// [...]
    default:
        if isLetter(l.ch) {
            tok.Literal = l.readIdentifier()
            tok.Type = token.LookupIdent(tok.Literal)
            return tok
        } else {
            tok = newToken(token.ILLEGAL, l.ch)
        }
    }
// [...]
}
```

The early exit here, our `return tok` statement, is necessary because when calling `readIdentifier()`, we call `readChar()` repeatedly and advance our `readPosition` and `position` fields past the last character of the current identifier. So we don't need the call to `readChar()` after the switch statement again.

Running our tests now, we can see that `let` is identified correctly but the tests still fail:

```
$ go test ./lexer
--- FAIL: TestNextToken (0.00s)
```

```
    lexer_test.go:70: tests[1] - tokentype wrong. expected="IDENT", got="ILLEGAL"
FAIL
FAIL    monkey/lexer 0.008s
```

The problem is the next token we want: a `IDENT` token with `"five"` in its `Literal` field. Instead we get an `ILLEGAL` token. Why is that? Because of the whitespace character between "let" and "five". But in Monkey whitespace only acts as a separator of tokens and doesn't have meaning, so we need to skip over it entirely:

```go
// lexer/lexer.go

func (l *Lexer) NextToken() token.Token {
    var tok token.Token

    l.skipWhitespace()

    switch l.ch {
// [...]
}

func (l *Lexer) skipWhitespace() {
    for l.ch == ' ' || l.ch == '\t' || l.ch == '\n' || l.ch == '\r' {
        l.readChar()
    }
}
```

This little helper function is found in a lot of parsers. Sometimes it's called `eatWhitespace` and sometimes `consumeWhitespace` and sometimes something entirely different. Which characters these functions actually skip depends on the language being lexed. Some language implementations do create tokens for newline characters for example and throw parsing errors if they are not at the correct place in the stream of tokens. We skip over newline characters to make the parsing step later on a little easier.

With `skipWhitespace()` in place, the lexer trips over the `5` in the `let five = 5;` part of our test input. And that's right, it doesn't know yet how to turn numbers into tokens. It's time to add this.

As we did previously for identifiers, we now need to add more functionality to the `default` branch of our switch statement.

```go
// lexer/lexer.go

func (l *Lexer) NextToken() token.Token {
    var tok token.Token

    l.skipWhitespace()
```

```go
    switch l.ch {
// [...]
    default:
        if isLetter(l.ch) {
            tok.Literal = l.readIdentifier()
            tok.Type = token.LookupIdent(tok.Literal)
            return tok
        } else if isDigit(l.ch) {
            tok.Type = token.INT
            tok.Literal = l.readNumber()
            return tok
        } else {
            tok = newToken(token.ILLEGAL, l.ch)
        }
    }
// [...]
}

func (l *Lexer) readNumber() string {
    position := l.position
    for isDigit(l.ch) {
        l.readChar()
    }
    return l.input[position:l.position]
}

func isDigit(ch byte) bool {
    return '0' <= ch && ch <= '9'
}
```

As you can see, the added code closely mirrors the part concerned with reading identifiers and keywords. The `readNumber` method is exactly the same as `readIdentifier` except for its usage of `isDigit` instead of `isLetter`. We could probably generalize this by passing in the character-identifying functions as arguments, but won't, for simplicity's sake and ease of understanding.

The `isDigit` function is as simple as `isLetter`. It just returns whether the passed in byte is a Latin digit between `0` and `9`.

With this added, our tests pass:

```
$ go test ./lexer
ok      monkey/lexer 0.008s
```

I don't know if you noticed, but we simplified things a lot in `readNumber`. We only read in *integers*. What about floats? Or numbers in hex notation? Octal notation? We ignore them and just say that Monkey doesn't support this. Of course, the reason for this is again the educational aim and limited scope of this book.

It's time to pop the champagne and celebrate: we successfully turned the small subset of the Monkey language we used in the our test case into tokens!

With this victory under our belt, it's easy to extend the lexer so it can tokenize a lot more of Monkey source code.

1.4 - EXTENDING OUR TOKEN SET AND LEXER

In order to eliminate the need to jump between packages when later writing our parser, we need to extend our lexer so it can recognize more of the Monkey language and output more tokens. So in this section we will add support for ==, !, !=, -, /, *, <, > and the keywords `true`, `false`, `if`, `else` and `return`.

The new tokens we will need to add, build and output can be classified as one of these three: one-character token (e.g. -), two-character token (e.g. ==) and keyword token (e.g. `return`). We already know how to handle one-character and keyword tokens, so we add support for these first, before extending the lexer for two-character tokens.

Adding support for -, /, *, < and > is trivial. The first thing we need to do, of course, is modify the input of our test case in `lexer/lexer_test.go` to include these characters. Just like we did before. In the code accompanying this chapter you can also find the extended `tests` table, which I won't show in the remainder of this chapter, in order to save space and to keep you from getting bored.

```
// lexer/lexer_test.go

func TestNextToken(t *testing.T) {
    input := `let five = 5;
let ten = 10;

let add = fn(x, y) {
  x + y;
};

let result = add(five, ten);
!-/*5;
5 < 10 > 5;
`

// [...]
}
```

Note that although the input looks like an actual piece of Monkey source code, some lines don't really make sense, with gibberish like `!-/*5`. That's okay. The lexer's job is not to tell us whether code makes sense, works or contains errors. That comes in a later stage. The lexer should only turn this input into tokens. For that reason the test cases I write for lexers cover all tokens and also try to provoke off-by-one errors, edge cases at end-of-file, newline handling, multi-digit number parsing and so on. That's why the "code" looks like gibberish.

Running the test we get `undefined:` errors, because the tests contain references to undefined `TokenTypes`. To fix them we add the following constants to `token/token.go`:

```
// token/token.go

const (
// [...]

    // Operators
    ASSIGN   = "="
    PLUS     = "+"
    MINUS    = "-"
    BANG     = "!"
    ASTERISK = "*"
    SLASH    = "/"

    LT = "<"
    GT = ">"

// [...]
)
```

With the new constants added, the tests still fail, because we don't return the tokens with the expected `TokenTypes`.

```
$ go test ./lexer
--- FAIL: TestNextToken (0.00s)
  lexer_test.go:84: tests[36] - tokentype wrong. expected="!", got="ILLEGAL"
FAIL
FAIL    monkey/lexer 0.007s
```

Turning these tests from failing to passing requires us to extend our switch statement in the `NextToken()` method of `Lexer`:

```
// lexer/lexer.go

func (l *Lexer) NextToken() token.Token {
// [...]
    switch l.ch {
    case '=':
        tok = newToken(token.ASSIGN, l.ch)
    case '+':
```

```
            tok = newToken(token.PLUS, l.ch)
        case '-':
            tok = newToken(token.MINUS, l.ch)
        case '!':
            tok = newToken(token.BANG, l.ch)
        case '/':
            tok = newToken(token.SLASH, l.ch)
        case '*':
            tok = newToken(token.ASTERISK, l.ch)
        case '<':
            tok = newToken(token.LT, l.ch)
        case '>':
            tok = newToken(token.GT, l.ch)
        case ';':
            tok = newToken(token.SEMICOLON, l.ch)
        case ',':
            tok = newToken(token.COMMA, l.ch)
    // [...]
    }
```

The tokens are now added and the cases of the switch statement have been reordered to reflect the structure of the constants in `token/token.go`. This small change makes our tests pass:

```
$ go test ./lexer
ok      monkey/lexer 0.007s
```

The new one-character tokens have been successfully added. Next step: add the new keywords `true`, `false`, `if`, `else` and `return`.

Again, the first step is to extend the input in our test to include these new keywords. Here is what the `input` in `TestNextToken` looks like now:

```
// lexer/lexer_test.go

func TestNextToken(t *testing.T) {
    input := `let five = 5;
let ten = 10;

let add = fn(x, y) {
  x + y;
};

let result = add(five, ten);
!-/*5;
5 < 10 > 5;

if (5 < 10) {
    return true;
```

```
} else {
    return false;
}`
// [...]
}
```

The tests do not even compile since the references in the test expectations to the new keywords are undefined. Fixing that, again, means just adding new constants and in this case, adding the keywords to the lookup table for `LookupIdent()`.

```go
// token/token.go

const (
// [...]

    // Keywords
    FUNCTION = "FUNCTION"
    LET      = "LET"
    TRUE     = "TRUE"
    FALSE    = "FALSE"
    IF       = "IF"
    ELSE     = "ELSE"
    RETURN   = "RETURN"
)

var keywords = map[string]TokenType{
    "fn":     FUNCTION,
    "let":    LET,
    "true":   TRUE,
    "false":  FALSE,
    "if":     IF,
    "else":   ELSE,
    "return": RETURN,
}
```

And it turns out that we not only fixed the compilation error by fixing references to undefined variables, we even made the tests pass:

```
$ go test ./lexer
ok      monkey/lexer 0.007s
```

The lexer now recognizes the new keywords and the necessary changes were trivial, easy to predict and easy to make. I'd say a pat on the back is in order. We did a great job!

But before we can move onto the next chapter and start with our parser, we still need to extend the lexer so it recognizes tokens that are composed of two characters. The tokens we want to support look like this in the source code: `==` and `!=`.

At first glance you may be thinking: "why not add a new case to our switch statement and be done with it?" Since our switch statement takes the current character `l.ch` as the expression to compare against the cases, we can't just add new cases like `case "=="` - the compiler won't let us. We can't compare our `l.ch` byte with strings like `"=="`.

What we can do instead is to reuse the existing branches for `'='` and `'!'` and extend them. So what we're going to do is to look ahead in the input and then determine whether to return a token for = or ==. After extending `input` in `lexer/lexer_test.go` again, it now looks like this:

```
// lexer/lexer_test.go

func TestNextToken(t *testing.T) {
    input := `let five = 5;
let ten = 10;

let add = fn(x, y) {
  x + y;
};

let result = add(five, ten);
!-/*5;
5 < 10 > 5;

if (5 < 10) {
    return true;
} else {
    return false;
}

10 == 10;
10 != 9;
`

// [...]
}
```

Before we start working on the switch statement in `NextToken()`, we need to add a new helper method defined on `*Lexer` called `peekChar()`:

```
// lexer/lexer.go

func (l *Lexer) peekChar() byte {
    if l.readPosition >= len(l.input) {
        return 0
    } else {
        return l.input[l.readPosition]
    }
```

```
}
```

`peekChar()` is really similar to `readChar()`, except that it doesn't increment `l.position` and `l.readPosition`. We only want to "peek" ahead in the input and not move around in it, so we know what a call to `readChar()` would return. Most lexers and parser have such a "peek" function that looks ahead and most of the time it only returns the immediately next character. The difficulty of parsing different languages often comes down to how far you have to peek ahead (or look backwards!) in the source code to make sense of it.

With `peekChar()` added, the code with the updated test input doesn't compile. Of course, since we're referencing undefined token constants in the tests. Fixing that, again, is easy:

```go
// token/token.go

const (
// [...]

    EQ     = "=="
    NOT_EQ = "!="

// [...]
)
```

With the references to `token.EQ` and `token.NOT_EQ` in the tests for the lexer fixed, running `go test` now returns the correct failure message:

```
$ go test ./lexer
--- FAIL: TestNextToken (0.00s)
  lexer_test.go:118: tests[66] - tokentype wrong. expected="==", got="="
FAIL
FAIL    monkey/lexer 0.007s
```

When the lexer comes upon a `==` in the input it creates two `token.ASSIGN` tokens instead of one `token.EQ` token. The solution is to use our new `peekChar()` method. In the branches of the switch statement for `'='` and `'!'` we "peek" ahead. If the next token is also a `=` we create either a `token.EQ` or a `token.NOT_EQ` token:

```go
// lexer/lexer.go

func (l *Lexer) NextToken() token.Token {
// [...]
    switch l.ch {
    case '=':
        if l.peekChar() == '=' {
            ch := l.ch
            l.readChar()
            literal := string(ch) + string(l.ch)
```

```
            tok = token.Token{Type: token.EQ, Literal: literal}
        } else {
            tok = newToken(token.ASSIGN, l.ch)
        }
// [...]
    case '!':
        if l.peekChar() == '=' {
            ch := l.ch
            l.readChar()
            literal := string(ch) + string(l.ch)
            tok = token.Token{Type: token.NOT_EQ, Literal: literal}
        } else {
            tok = newToken(token.BANG, l.ch)
        }
// [...]
}
```

Note that we save `l.ch` in a local variable before calling `l.readChar()` again. This way we don't lose the current character and can safely advance the lexer so it leaves the `NextToken()` with `l.position` and `l.readPosition` in the correct state. If we were to start supporting more two-character tokens in Monkey, we should probably abstract the behaviour away in a method called `makeTwoCharToken` that peeks and advances if it found the right token. Because those two branches look awfully similar. For now though `==` and `!=` are the only two-character tokens in Monkey, so let's leave it as it is and run our tests again to make sure it works:

```
$ go test ./lexer
ok      monkey/lexer 0.006s
```

They pass! We did it! The lexer can now produce the extended set of tokens and we're ready to write our parser. But before we do that, let's lay another ground stone we can build upon in the coming chapters...

1.5 - Start of a REPL

The Monkey language needs a REPL. REPL stands for "Read Eval Print Loop" and you probably know what it is from other interpreted languages: Python has a REPL, Ruby has one, every JavaScript runtime has one, most Lisps have one and a lot of other languages too. Sometimes the REPL is called "console", sometimes "interactive mode". The concept is the same: the REPL reads input, sends it to the interpreter for evaluation, prints the result/output of the interpreter and starts again. Read, Eval, Print, Loop.

We don't know how to fully "Eval" Monkey source code yet. We only have one part of the process that hides behind "Eval": we can tokenize Monkey source code.

But we also know how to read and print something, and I don't think looping poses a problem.

Here is a REPL that tokenizes Monkey source code and prints the tokens. Later on, we will expand on this and add parsing and evaluation to it.

```go
// repl/repl.go

package repl

import (
    "bufio"
    "fmt"
    "io"
    "monkey/lexer"
    "monkey/token"
)

const PROMPT = ">> "

func Start(in io.Reader, out io.Writer) {
    scanner := bufio.NewScanner(in)

    for {
        fmt.Printf(PROMPT)
        scanned := scanner.Scan()
        if !scanned {
            return
        }

        line := scanner.Text()
        l := lexer.New(line)

        for tok := l.NextToken(); tok.Type != token.EOF; tok = l.NextToken() {
            fmt.Printf("%+v\n", tok)
        }
    }
}
```

This is all pretty straightforward: read from the input source until encountering a newline, take the just read line and pass it to an instance of our lexer and finally print all the tokens the lexer gives us until we encounter EOF.

In a `main.go` file (which we've been missing until now!) we welcome the user of the REPL and start it:

```go
// main.go

package main
```

```go
import (
	"fmt"
	"os"
	"os/user"
	"monkey/repl"
)

func main() {
	user, err := user.Current()
	if err != nil {
		panic(err)
	}
	fmt.Printf("Hello %s! This is the Monkey programming language!\n",
		user.Username)
	fmt.Printf("Feel free to type in commands\n")
	repl.Start(os.Stdin, os.Stdout)
}
```

And with that we can now interactively produce tokens:

```
$ go run main.go
Hello mrnugget! This is the Monkey programming language!
Feel free to type in commands
>> let add = fn(x, y) { x + y; };
{Type:let Literal:let}
{Type:IDENT Literal:add}
{Type:= Literal:=}
{Type:fn Literal:fn}
{Type:( Literal:(}
{Type:IDENT Literal:x}
{Type:, Literal:,}
{Type:IDENT Literal:y}
{Type:) Literal:)}
{Type:{ Literal:{}
{Type:IDENT Literal:x}
{Type:+ Literal:+}
{Type:IDENT Literal:y}
{Type:; Literal:;}
{Type:} Literal:}}
{Type:; Literal:;}
>>
```

Perfect! And **now** it's time to start parsing these tokens.

CHAPTER 2

PARSING

2.1 - PARSERS

Everyone who has ever programmed has probably heard about parsers, mostly by encountering a "parser error". Or maybe heard or even said something like "we need to parse this", "after it's parsed", "the parser blows up with this input". The word "parser" is as common as "compiler", "interpreter" and "programming language". Everyone knows that parsers *exist*. They have to, right? Because who else would be responsible for "parser errors"?

But what is a parser exactly? What is its job and how does it do it? This is what Wikipedia has to say[1]:

> A parser is a software component that takes input data (frequently text) and builds a data structure – often some kind of parse tree, abstract syntax tree or other hierarchical structure – giving a structural representation of the input, checking for correct syntax in the process. [...] The parser is often preceded by a separate lexical analyser, which creates tokens from the sequence of input characters;

For a Wikipedia article about a computer science topic this excerpt is remarkably easy to understand. We can even recognize our lexer in there!

A parser turns its input into a data structure that represents the input. That sounds pretty abstract, so let me illustrate this with an example. Here is a little bit of JavaScript:

```
> var input = '{"name": "Thorsten", "age": 28}';
> var output = JSON.parse(input);
```

[1]https://en.wikipedia.org/wiki/Parsing#Parser

```
> output
{ name: 'Thorsten', age: 28 }
> output.name
'Thorsten'
> output.age
28
>
```

Our `input` is just some text, a string. We then pass it to a parser hidden behind the `JSON.parse` function and receive an output value. This output is the data structure that represents the input: a JavaScript object with two fields named `name` and `age`, their values also corresponding to the input. We can now easily work with this data structure as demonstrated by accessing the `name` and `age` fields.

"But", I hear you say, "a JSON parser isn't the same as a parser for a programming language! They're different!" I can see where you're coming from with this, but no, they are not different. At least not on a conceptual level. A JSON parser takes text as input and builds a data structure that represents the input. That's exactly what the parser of a programming language does. The difference is that in the case of a JSON parser you can *see* the data structure when looking at the input. Whereas if you look at this

```
if ((5 + 2 * 3) == 91) { return computeStuff(input1, input2); }
```

it's not immediately obvious how this could be represented with a data structure. This is why, at least for me, they seemed different on a deeper, conceptional level. My guess is that this perception of conceptional difference is mainly due to a lack of familiarity with programming language parsers and the data structures they produce. I have a lot more experience with writing JSON, parsing it with a parser and inspecting the output of the parser than with parsing programming languages. As users of programming languages we seldom get to see or interact with the parsed source code, with its internal representation. Lisp programmers are the exception to the rule – in Lisp the data structures used to represent the source code are the ones used by a Lisp user. The parsed source code is easily accessible as data in the program. "Code is data, data is code" is something you hear a lot from Lisp programmers.

So, in order to bring our conceptual understanding of programming language parsers up to the level of our familiarity and intuitiveness with parsers of serialization languages (like JSON, YAML, TOML, INI, and so on) we need to understand the data structures they produce.

In most interpreters and compilers the data structure used for the internal representation of the source code is called a "syntax tree" or an "abstract syntax tree" (AST for short). The "abstract" is based on the fact that certain details visible in the source code are omitted in the AST. Semicolons, newlines, whitespace, comments, braces, bracket and parentheses – depending on the language and the parser these details are not represented in the AST, but merely guide the parser when constructing it.

A fact to note is that there is not one true, universal AST format that's used by every parser. Their implementations are all pretty similar, the concept is the same, but they differ in details. The concrete implementation depends on the programming language being parsed.

A small example should make things clearer. Let's say that we have the following source code:

```
if (3 * 5 > 10) {
  return "hello";
} else {
  return  "goodbye";
}
```

And let's say we are using JavaScript, have a `MagicLexer`, a `MagicParser` and the AST is built out of JavaScript objects, then the parsing step might produce something like this:

```
> var input = 'if (3 * 5 > 10) { return "hello"; } else { return "goodbye"; }';
> var tokens = MagicLexer.parse(input);
> MagicParser.parse(tokens);
{
  type: "if-statement",
  condition: {
    type: "operator-expression",
    operator: ">",
    left: {
      type: "operator-expression",
      operator: "*",
      left: { type: "integer-literal", value: 3 },
      right: { type: "integer-literal", value: 5 }
    },
    right: { type: "integer-literal", value: 10 }
  },
  consequence: {
    type: "return-statement",
    returnValue: { type: "string-literal", value: "hello" }
  },
  alternative: {
    type: "return-statement",
    returnValue: { type: "string-literal", value: "goodbye" }
  }
}
```

As you can see, the output of the parser, the AST, *is* pretty abstract: there are no parentheses, no semicolons and no braces. But it does represent the source code pretty accurately, don't you think? I bet that you can now "see" the AST structure when looking back at the source code!

So, this is what parsers do. They take source code as input (either as text or tokens) and produce a data structure which represents this source code. While building up the data structure, they unavoidably analyse the input, checking that it conforms to the expected structure. Thus the process of parsing is also called syntactic analysis.

In this chapter, we're going to write our parser for the Monkey programming language. Its input will be the tokens we defined in the previous chapter, produced by the lexer we already wrote. We will define our own AST, suited to our needs as interpreters of the Monkey programming language, and construct instances of this AST while recursively parsing tokens.

2.2 - Why not a Parser Generator?

Maybe you've already heard about parser generators, like the tools yacc, bison or ANTLR. Parser generators are tools that, when fed with a formal description of a language, produce parsers as their output. This output is code that can then be compiled/interpreted and itself fed with source code as input to produce a syntax tree.

There are a lot of parser generators, differing in the format of the input they accept and the language of the output they produce. The majority of them use a *context-free grammar* (CFG) as their input. A CFG is a set of rules that describe how to form correct (valid according to the syntax) sentences in a language. The most common notational formats of CFGs are the Backus-Naur Form (BNF) or the Extended Backus-Naur Form (EBNF).

```
PrimaryExpression ::= "this"
                    | ObjectLiteral
                    | ( "(" Expression ")" )
                    | Identifier
                    | ArrayLiteral
                    | Literal
Literal ::= ( <DECIMAL_LITERAL>
            | <HEX_INTEGER_LITERAL>
            | <STRING_LITERAL>
            | <BOOLEAN_LITERAL>
            | <NULL_LITERAL>
            | <REGULAR_EXPRESSION_LITERAL> )
Identifier ::= <IDENTIFIER_NAME>
ArrayLiteral ::= "[" ( ( Elision )? "]"
```

```
                  | ElementList Elision "]"
                  | ( ElementList )? "]" )
ElementList ::= ( Elision )? AssignmentExpression
                ( Elision AssignmentExpression )*
Elision ::= ( "," )+
ObjectLiteral ::= "{" ( PropertyNameAndValueList )? "}"
PropertyNameAndValueList ::= PropertyNameAndValue ( "," PropertyNameAndValue
                                                  | "," )*
PropertyNameAndValue ::= PropertyName ":" AssignmentExpression
PropertyName ::= Identifier
               | <STRING_LITERAL>
               | <DECIMAL_LITERAL>
```

This is part of a full description[2] of the EcmaScript syntax, in BNF. A parser generator would take something like this and turn it into compilable C code, for example.

Maybe you've also heard that you should use a parser generator instead of writing a parser by hand. "Just skip this part", they say, "it's a solved problem." The reason for this recommendation is that parsers are exceptionally well suited to being automatically generated. Parsing is one of the most well-understood branches of computer science and really smart people have already invested a lot of time into the problems of parsing. The results of their work are CFG, BNF, EBNF, parser generators and advanced parsing techniques used in them. Why shouldn't you take advantage of that?

I don't think that learning to write your own parser is a waste of time. I actually think it's immensely valuable. Only after having written your own parser, or at least attempted to, will you see the benefits parser generators provide, the drawbacks they have and the problems they solve. For me the concept of a parser generator only "clicked" after I wrote my first parser. I looked at it and only then really and truly understood how it's possible to generate this code automatically.

Most people, that recommend using a parser generator, when others want to get started with interpreters and compilers only do so because they've written a parser themselves before. They've seen the problems and solutions available and decided it's better to use an existing tool for the job. And they're correct - when you want to get something done and are in a production environment, where correctness and robustness are priorities. Of course you shouldn't try to write your own parser then, especially not if you've never written one before.

But we are here to learn, we want to understand how parsers work. And it's my opinion that the best way to do that is by getting our hands dirty and writing a parser ourselves. Also, I think it's immense fun.

[2]http://tomcopeland.blogs.com/EcmaScript.html

2.3 - Writing a Parser for the Monkey Programming Language

There are two main strategies when parsing a programming language: top-down parsing or bottom-up parsing. A lot of slightly different forms of each strategy exist. For example, "recursive descent parsing", "Early parsing" or "predictive parsing" are all variations of top down parsing.

The parser we are going to write is a recursive descent parser. And in particular, it's a "top down operator precedence" parser, sometimes called "Pratt parser", after its inventor Vaughan Pratt.

I won't go into the details of different parsing strategies here, because this is neither the place nor am I qualified enough to accurately describe them. Instead, let me just say, that the difference between top down and bottom up parsers is that the former starts with constructing root node of the AST and then descends while the latter does it the other way around. A recursive descent parser, which works from the top down, is often recommended for newcomers to parsing, since it closely mirrors the way we think about ASTs and their construction. I personally found the recursive approach starting at the root node really nice, even though it took writing some code before the concept really clicked. Which is another reason to get started with the code instead of delving into parsing strategies.

Now, when writing a parser ourselves, we have to make some trade-offs, yes. Our parser won't be the fastest of all time, we won't have formal proof of its correctness and its error-recovery process and detection of erroneous syntax won't be bullet proof. The last one is especially hard to get right without extensive study of the theory surrounding parsing. But what we're going to have is a fully working parser for the Monkey programming language that's open for extensions and improvements, easy to understand and a great start to further dive into the topic of parsing, if one were so inclined.

We're going to start by parsing statements: let and return statements. When we can parse statements and the basic structure of our parser stands, we will look at expressions and how to parse these (this is where Vaughan Pratt will come into play). Afterwards we extend the parser to make it capable of parsing a large subset of the Monkey programming language. As we go along we build up the necessary structures for our AST.

2.4 - Parser's First Steps: Parsing Let Statements

In Monkey, variable bindings are statements of the following form:

```
let x = 5;
let y = 10;
let foobar = add(5, 5);
let barfoo = 5 * 5 / 10 + 18 - add(5, 5) + multiply(124);
let anotherName = barfoo;
```

These statements are called "let statements" and bind a value to the given name. `let x = 5;` binds the value `5` to the name `x`. Our job in this section is to parse let statements correctly. For now we're going to skip parsing the expressions that produce the value of a given variable binding and come back to this later - as soon as we know how to parse expressions on their own.

What does it mean to parse let statements correctly? It means that the parser produces an AST that accurately represents the information contained in the original let statement. That sounds reasonable, but we don't have an AST yet, nor do we know what it should look like. So our first task is to take a close look at Monkey source code and see how it's structured, so that we can define the necessary parts of an AST that's able to accurately represent let statements.

Here is a fully valid program written in Monkey:

```
let x = 10;
let y = 15;

let add = fn(a, b) {
  return a + b;
};
```

Programs in Monkey are a series of statements. In this example we can see three statements, three variable bindings - let statements - of the following form:

```
let <identifier> = <expression>;
```

A let statement in Monkey consists of two changing parts: an identifier and an expression. In the example above `x`, `y` and `add` are identifiers. `10`, `15` and the function literal are expressions.

Before we go on, a few words about the difference between statements and expressions are needed. Expressions produce values, statements don't. `let x = 5` doesn't produce a value, whereas `5` does (the value it produces is `5`). A `return 5;` statement doesn't produce a value, but `add(5, 5)` does. This distinction - expressions produce values, statements don't - changes depending on who you ask, but it's good enough for our needs.

What exactly an expression is or a statement, what produces values and what doesn't, depends on the programming language. In some languages function literals (e.g.: `fn(x, y) { return x + y; }`) are expressions and can be used in any place where any other expression is allowed. In other programming languages though function literals can only be part of a function declaration statement, in the top level of the program. Some languages also have "if expressions", where conditionals are expressions and produce a value. This is entirely dependent on the choices the language designers made. As you'll see, a lot of things in Monkey are expressions, including function literals.

Back to our AST. Looking at the example above, we can see that it needs two different types of nodes: expressions and statements. Take a look at the start of our AST:

```go
// ast/ast.go

package ast

type Node interface {
    TokenLiteral() string
}

type Statement interface {
    Node
    statementNode()
}

type Expression interface {
    Node
    expressionNode()
}
```

Here we have three interfaces called `Node`, `Statement` and `Expression`. Every node in our AST has to implement the `Node` interface, meaning it has to provide a `TokenLiteral()` method that returns the literal value of the token it's associated with. `TokenLiteral()` will be used only for debugging and testing. The AST we are going to construct consists solely of `Node`s that are connected to each other - it's a tree after all. Some of these nodes implement the `Statement` and some the `Expression` interface. These interfaces only contain dummy methods called `statementNode` and `expressionNode` respectively. They are not strictly necessary but help us by guiding the Go compiler and possibly causing it to throw errors when we use a `Statement` where an `Expression` should've been used, and vice versa.

And here is our first implementation of `Node`:

```go
// ast/ast.go

type Program struct {
    Statements []Statement
}

func (p *Program) TokenLiteral() string {
    if len(p.Statements) > 0 {
        return p.Statements[0].TokenLiteral()
    } else {
        return ""
    }
}
```

This `Program` node is going to be the root node of every AST our parser produces. Every valid Monkey program is a series of statements. These statements are contained in the `Program.Statements`, which is just a slice of AST nodes that implement the `Statement` interface.

With these basic building blocks for our AST construction defined, let's think about what a node for a variable binding in the form of `let x = 5;` might look like. Which fields should it have? Definitely one for the name of the variable. And it also needs a field that points to the expression on the right side of the equal sign. It needs to be able to point to any expression. It can't just point to a literal value (the integer literal `5` in this case), since every expression is valid after the equal sign: `let x = 5 * 5` is as valid as `let y = add(2, 2) * 5 / 10;`. And then the node also needs to keep track of the token the AST node is associated with, so we can implement the `TokenLiteral()` method. That makes three fields: one for the identifier, one for the expression that produces the value in the let statement and one for the token.

```go
// ast/ast.go

import "monkey/token"

// [...]

type LetStatement struct {
    Token token.Token // the token.LET token
    Name  *Identifier
    Value Expression
}

func (ls *LetStatement) statementNode()       {}
func (ls *LetStatement) TokenLiteral() string { return ls.Token.Literal }

type Identifier struct {
```

```go
    Token token.Token // the token.IDENT token
    Value string
}

func (i *Identifier) expressionNode()      {}
func (i *Identifier) TokenLiteral() string { return i.Token.Literal }
```

LetStatement has the fields we need: Name to hold the identifier of the binding and Value for the expression that produces the value. The two methods statementNode and TokenLiteral satisfy the Statement and Node interfaces respectively.

To hold the identifier of the binding, the x in `let x = 5;`, we have the Identifier struct type, which implements the Expression interface. But the identifier in a let statement doesn't produce a value, right? So why is it an Expression? It's to keep things simple. Identifiers in other parts of a Monkey program **do** produce values, e.g.: `let x = valueProducingIdentifier;`. And to keep the number of different node types small, we'll use Identifier here to represent the name in a variable binding and later reuse it, to represent an identifier as part of or as a complete expression.

With Program, LetStatement and Identifier defined this piece of Monkey source code

```
let x = 5;
```

could be represented by an AST looking like this:

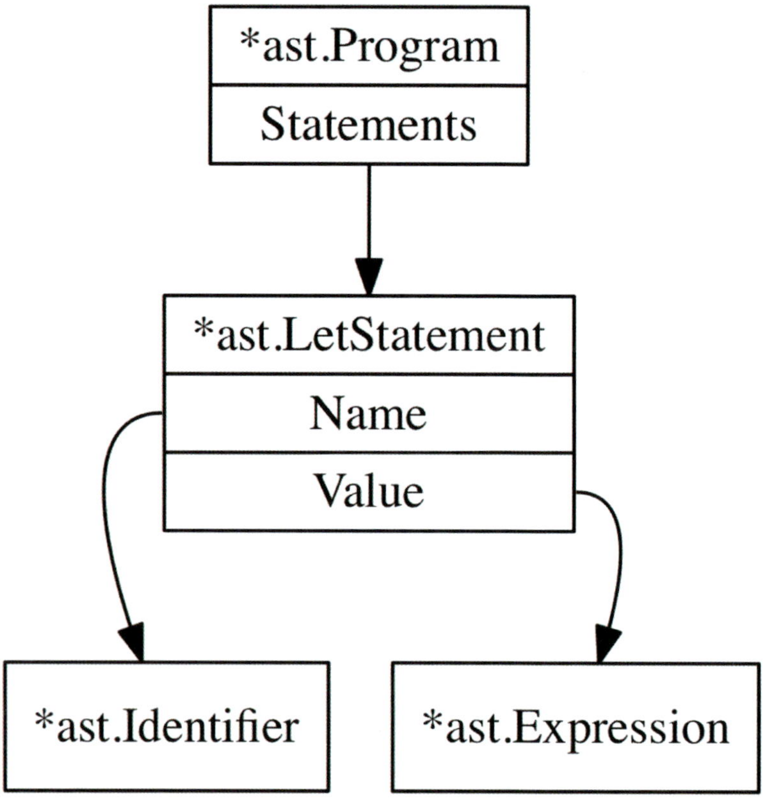

Now that we know what it's supposed to look like, the next task is to construct such an AST. So, without further ado here is the beginning of our parser:

```go
// parser/parser.go

package parser

import (
    "monkey/ast"
    "monkey/lexer"
    "monkey/token"
)

type Parser struct {
    l *lexer.Lexer

    curToken  token.Token
    peekToken token.Token
}
```

```go
func New(l *lexer.Lexer) *Parser {
    p := &Parser{l: l}

    // Read two tokens, so curToken and peekToken are both set
    p.nextToken()
    p.nextToken()

    return p
}

func (p *Parser) nextToken() {
    p.curToken = p.peekToken
    p.peekToken = p.l.NextToken()
}

func (p *Parser) ParseProgram() *ast.Program {
    return nil
}
```

The `Parser` has three fields: `l`, `curToken` and `peekToken`. `l` is a pointer to an instance of the lexer, on which we repeatedly call `NextToken()` to get the next token in the input. `curToken` and `peekToken` act exactly like the two "pointers" our lexer has: `position` and `readPosition`. But instead of pointing to a character in the input, they point to the current and the next token. Both are important: we need to look at the `curToken`, which is the current token under examination, to decide what to do next, and we also need `peekToken` for this decision if `curToken` doesn't give us enough information. Think of a single line only containing `5;`. Then `curToken` is a `token.INT` and we need `peekToken` to decide whether we are at the end of the line or if we are at just the start of an arithmetic expression.

The `New` function is pretty self-explanatory and the `nextToken` method is a small helper that advances both `curToken` and `peekToken`. But `ParseProgram` is empty, for now.

Now before we start writing tests and filling out the `ParseProgram` method I want to show you the basic idea and structure behind a recursive descent parser. That makes it a lot easier to understand our own parser later on. What follows are the major parts of such a parser in pseudocode. Read this carefully and try to understand what happens in the `parseProgram` function:

```
function parseProgram() {
  program = newProgramASTNode()

  advanceTokens()

  for (currentToken() != EOF_TOKEN) {
```

```
    statement = null

    if (currentToken() == LET_TOKEN) {
      statement = parseLetStatement()
    } else if (currentToken() == RETURN_TOKEN) {
      statement = parseReturnStatement()
    } else if (currentToken() == IF_TOKEN) {
      statement = parseIfStatement()
    }

    if (statement != null) {
      program.Statements.push(statement)
    }

    advanceTokens()
  }

  return program
}

function parseLetStatement() {
  advanceTokens()

  identifier = parseIdentifier()

  advanceTokens()

  if currentToken() != EQUAL_TOKEN {
    parseError("no equal sign!")
    return null
  }

  advanceTokens()

  value = parseExpression()

  variableStatement = newVariableStatementASTNode()
  variableStatement.identifier = identifier
  variableStatement.value = value
  return variableStatement
}

function parseIdentifier() {
  identifier = newIdentifierASTNode()
  identifier.token = currentToken()
  return identifier
}
```

```
function parseExpression() {
  if (currentToken() == INTEGER_TOKEN) {
    if (nextToken() == PLUS_TOKEN)  {
      return parseOperatorExpression()
    } else if (nextToken() == SEMICOLON_TOKEN) {
      return parseIntegerLiteral()
    }
  } else if (currentToken() == LEFT_PAREN) {
    return parseGroupedExpression()
  }
// [...]
}

function parseOperatorExpression() {
  operatorExpression = newOperatorExpression()

  operatorExpression.left = parseIntegerLiteral()
  operatorExpression.operator = currentToken()
  operatorExpression.right = parseExpression()

  return operatorExpression()
}
// [...]
```

Since this is pseudocode there are a lot of omissions, of course. But the basic idea behind recursive-descent parsing is there. The entry point is `parseProgram` and it constructs the root node of the AST (`newProgramASTNode()`). It then builds the child nodes, the statements, by calling other functions that know which AST node to construct based on the current token. These other functions call each other again, recursively.

The most recursive part of this is in `parseExpression` and is only hinted at. But we can already see that in order to parse an expression like `5 + 5`, we need to first parse `5 +` and then call `parseExpression()` again to parse the rest, since after the `+` might be another operator expression, like this: `5 + 5 * 10`. We will get to this later and look at expression parsing in detail, since it's probably the most complicated but also the most beautiful part of the parser, making heavy use of "Pratt parsing".

But for now, we can already see what the parser has to do. It repeatedly advances the tokens and checks the current token to decide what to do next: either call another parsing function or throw an error. Each function then does its job and possibly constructs an AST node so that the "main loop" in `parseProgram()` can advance the tokens and decide what to do again.

If you looked at that pseudocode and thought "Well, that's actually pretty easy to understand" I have great news for you: our `ParseProgram` method and the parser will look pretty similar! Let's get to work!

Again, we're starting with a test before we flesh out `ParseProgram`. Here is a test case to make sure that the parsing of let statements works:

```
// parser/parser_test.go

package parser

import (
    "testing"
    "monkey/ast"
    "monkey/lexer"
)

func TestLetStatements(t *testing.T) {
    input := `
let x = 5;
let y = 10;
let foobar = 838383;
`

    l := lexer.New(input)
    p := New(l)

    program := p.ParseProgram()
    if program == nil {
        t.Fatalf("ParseProgram() returned nil")
    }
    if len(program.Statements) != 3 {
        t.Fatalf("program.Statements does not contain 3 statements. got=%d",
            len(program.Statements))
    }

    tests := []struct {
        expectedIdentifier string
    }{
        {"x"},
        {"y"},
        {"foobar"},
    }

    for i, tt := range tests {
        stmt := program.Statements[i]
        if !testLetStatement(t, stmt, tt.expectedIdentifier) {
            return
        }
    }
}
```

```go
func testLetStatement(t *testing.T, s ast.Statement, name string) bool {
    if s.TokenLiteral() != "let" {
        t.Errorf("s.TokenLiteral not 'let'. got=%q", s.TokenLiteral())
        return false
    }

    letStmt, ok := s.(*ast.LetStatement)
    if !ok {
        t.Errorf("s not *ast.LetStatement. got=%T", s)
        return false
    }

    if letStmt.Name.Value != name {
        t.Errorf("letStmt.Name.Value not '%s'. got=%s", name, letStmt.Name.Value)
        return false
    }

    if letStmt.Name.TokenLiteral() != name {
        t.Errorf("s.Name not '%s'. got=%s", name, letStmt.Name)
        return false
    }

    return true
}
```

The test case follows the same principle as the test for our lexer and pretty much every other unit test we're going to write: we provide Monkey source code as input and then set expectations on what we want the AST - that's produced by the parser - to look like. We do this by checking as many fields of the AST nodes as possible to make sure that nothing is missing. I found that a parser is a breeding ground for off-by-one bugs and the more tests and assertions it has the better.

I choose not to mock or stub out the lexer and provide source code as input instead of tokens, since that makes the tests much more readable and understandable. Of course there's the problem of bugs in the lexer blowing up tests for the parser and generating unneeded noise, but I deem the risk too minimal, especially judged against the advantages of using readable source code as input.

There are two noteworthy things about this test case. The first one is that we ignore the `Value` field of the `*ast.LetStatement`. Why don't we check if the integer literals (`5`, `10`, ...) are parsed correctly? Answer: we're going to! But first we need to make sure that the parsing of let statements works and ignore the `Value`.

The second one is the helper function `testLetStatement`. It might seem like over-engineering to use a separate function, but we're going to need this function soon enough. And then it's going to make our test cases a lot more readable than lines and lines of type conversions strewn about.

As an aside: we won't look at all of the parser tests in this chapter, since they are just too long. But the code provided with the book contains all of them.

That being said, the tests fail as expected:

```
$ go test ./parser
--- FAIL: TestLetStatements (0.00s)
  parser_test.go:20: ParseProgram() returned nil
FAIL
FAIL    monkey/parser    0.007s
```

It's time to flesh out the `ParseProgram()` method of the `Parser`.

```go
// parser/parser.go

func (p *Parser) ParseProgram() *ast.Program {
    program := &ast.Program{}
    program.Statements = []ast.Statement{}

    for p.curToken.Type != token.EOF {
        stmt := p.parseStatement()
        if stmt != nil {
            program.Statements = append(program.Statements, stmt)
        }
        p.nextToken()
    }

    return program
}
```

Doesn't this look really similar to the `parseProgram()` pseudocode function we saw earlier? See! I told you! And what it does is the same too.

The first thing `ParseProgram` does is construct the root node of the AST, an `*ast.Program`. It then iterates over every token in the input until it encounters an `token.EOF` token. It does this by repeatedly calling `nextToken`, which advances both `p.curToken` and `p.peekToken`. In every iteration it calls `parseStatement`, whose job it is to parse a statement. If `parseStatement` returned something other than `nil`, a `ast.Statement`, its return value is added to `Statements` slice of the AST root node. When nothing is left to parse the `*ast.Program` root node is returned.

The `parseStatement` method looks like this:

```go
// parser/parser.go

func (p *Parser) parseStatement() ast.Statement {
    switch p.curToken.Type {
    case token.LET:
```

```
        return p.parseLetStatement()
    default:
        return nil
    }
}
```

Don't worry, the switch statement will get more branches. But for now, it only calls `parseLetStatement` when it encounters a `token.LET` token. And `parseLetStatement` is the method where we turn our tests from red to green:

```
// parser/parser.go

func (p *Parser) parseLetStatement() *ast.LetStatement {
    stmt := &ast.LetStatement{Token: p.curToken}

    if !p.expectPeek(token.IDENT) {
        return nil
    }

    stmt.Name = &ast.Identifier{Token: p.curToken, Value: p.curToken.Literal}

    if !p.expectPeek(token.ASSIGN) {
        return nil
    }

    // TODO: We're skipping the expressions until we
    // encounter a semicolon
    for !p.curTokenIs(token.SEMICOLON) {
        p.nextToken()
    }

    return stmt
}

func (p *Parser) curTokenIs(t token.TokenType) bool {
    return p.curToken.Type == t
}

func (p *Parser) peekTokenIs(t token.TokenType) bool {
    return p.peekToken.Type == t
}

func (p *Parser) expectPeek(t token.TokenType) bool {
    if p.peekTokenIs(t) {
        p.nextToken()
        return true
    } else {
        return false
```

```
    }
}
```

It works! The tests are green:

```
$ go test ./parser
ok      monkey/parser   0.007s
```

We can parse let statements! That's amazing! But, wait, how?

Let's start with `parseLetStatement`. It constructs an `*ast.LetStatement` node with the token it's currently sitting on (a `token.LET` token) and then advances the tokens while making assertions about the next token with calls to `expectPeek`. First it expects a `token.IDENT` token, which it then uses to construct an `*ast.Identifier` node. Then it expects an equal sign and finally it jumps over the expression following the equal sign until it encounters a semicolon. The skipping of expressions will be replaced, of course, as soon as we know how to parse them.

The `curTokenIs` and `peekTokenIs` methods do not need much of an explanation. They are useful methods that we will see again and again when fleshing out the parser. Already, we can replace the `p.curToken.Type != token.EOF` condition of the for-loop in `ParseProgram` with `!p.curTokenIs(token.EOF)`.

Instead of dissecting these tiny methods, let's talk about `expectPeek`. The `expectPeek` method is one of the "assertion functions" nearly all parsers share. Their primary purpose is to enforce the correctness of the order of tokens by checking the type of the next token. Our `expectPeek` here checks the type of the `peekToken` and only if the type is correct does it advance the tokens by calling `nextToken`. As you'll see, this is something a parser does a lot.

But what happens if we encounter a token in `expectPeek` that's not of the expected type? At the moment, we just return `nil`, which gets ignored in `ParseProgram`, which results in entire statements being ignored because of an error in the input. Silently. You can probably imagine that this makes debugging really tough. And since nobody likes tough debugging we need to add error handling to our parser.

Thankfully, the changes we need to make are minimal:

```
// parser/parser.go

type Parser struct {
// [...]
    errors []string
// [...]
}

func New(l *lexer.Lexer) *Parser {
    p := &Parser{
```

```go
        l:      l,
        errors: []string{},
    }
// [...]
}

func (p *Parser) Errors() []string {
    return p.errors
}

func (p *Parser) peekError(t token.TokenType) {
    msg := fmt.Sprintf("expected next token to be %s, got %s instead",
        t, p.peekToken.Type)
    p.errors = append(p.errors, msg)
}
```

The `Parser` now has an `errors` field, which is just a slice of strings. This field gets initialized in `New` and the helper function `peekError` can now be used to add an error to `errors` when the type of `peekToken` doesn't match the expectation. With the `Errors` method we can check if the parser encountered any errors.

Extending the test suite to make use of this is as easy as you'd expect:

```go
// parser/parser_test.go

func TestLetStatements(t *testing.T) {
// [...]

    program := p.ParseProgram()
    checkParserErrors(t, p)

// [...]
}

func checkParserErrors(t *testing.T, p *Parser) {
    errors := p.Errors()
    if len(errors) == 0 {
        return
    }

    t.Errorf("parser has %d errors", len(errors))
    for _, msg := range errors {
        t.Errorf("parser error: %q", msg)
    }
    t.FailNow()
}
```

The new `checkParserErrors` helper function does nothing more than check the parser for errors and if it has any it prints them as test errors and stops the execution of the current test. Pretty straightforward.

But nothing in our parser creates errors yet. By changing `expectPeek` we can automatically add an error every time one of our expectations about the next token was wrong:

```
// parser/parser.go

func (p *Parser) expectPeek(t token.TokenType) bool {
    if p.peekTokenIs(t) {
        p.nextToken()
        return true
    } else {
        p.peekError(t)
        return false
    }
}
```

If we now change our test case input from this

```
input := `
let x = 5;
let y = 10;
let foobar = 838383;
`
```

to this invalid input where tokens are missing

```
    input := `
let x 5;
let = 10;
let 838383;
`
```

we can run our tests to see our new parser errors:

```
$ go test ./parser
--- FAIL: TestLetStatements (0.00s)
  parser_test.go:20: parser has 3 errors
  parser_test.go:22: parser error: "expected next token to be =,\
    got INT instead"
  parser_test.go:22: parser error: "expected next token to be IDENT,\
    got = instead"
  parser_test.go:22: parser error: "expected next token to be IDENT,\
    got INT instead"
FAIL
FAIL    monkey/parser   0.007s
```

As you can see, our parser showcases a neat little feature here: it gives us errors for each erroneous statement it encounters. It doesn't exit on the first one, potentially saving us the grunt work of rerunning the parsing process again and again to catch all of the syntax errors. That's pretty helpful - even with line and column numbers missing.

2.5 - Parsing Return Statements

I said earlier that we're going to flesh out our sparse looking `ParseProgram` method. Now's the time. We're going to parse return statements. And the first step, as with let statements before them, is to define the necessary structures in the `ast` package with which we can represent return statements in our AST.

Here is what return statements look like in Monkey:

```
return 5;
return 10;
return add(15);
```

Experienced with let statements, we can easily spot the structure behind these statements:

```
return <expression>;
```

Return statements consist solely of the keyword `return` and an expression. That makes the definition of `ast.ReturnStatement` really simple:

```
// ast/ast.go

type ReturnStatement struct {
    Token       token.Token // the 'return' token
    ReturnValue Expression
}

func (rs *ReturnStatement) statementNode()       {}
func (rs *ReturnStatement) TokenLiteral() string { return rs.Token.Literal }
```

There is nothing about this node that you haven't seen before: it has a field for the initial token and a `ReturnValue` field that will contain the expression that's to be returned. We will again skip the parsing of the expressions and the semicolon handling for now, but will come back to this later. The `statementNode` and `TokenLiteral` methods are there to fulfill the `Node` and `Statement` interfaces and look identical to the methods defined on `*ast.LetStatement`.

The test we write next also looks pretty similar to the one for let statements:

```
// parser/parser_test.go

func TestReturnStatements(t *testing.T) {
```

```
    input := `
return 5;
return 10;
return 993322;
`
    l := lexer.New(input)
    p := New(l)

    program := p.ParseProgram()
    checkParserErrors(t, p)

    if len(program.Statements) != 3 {
        t.Fatalf("program.Statements does not contain 3 statements. got=%d",
            len(program.Statements))
    }

    for _, stmt := range program.Statements {
        returnStmt, ok := stmt.(*ast.ReturnStatement)
        if !ok {
            t.Errorf("stmt not *ast.returnStatement. got=%T", stmt)
            continue
        }
        if returnStmt.TokenLiteral() != "return" {
            t.Errorf("returnStmt.TokenLiteral not 'return', got %q",
                returnStmt.TokenLiteral())
        }
    }
}
```

Of course these test cases will also have to be extended as soon as expression parsing is in place. But that's okay, tests are not immutable. But they are, in fact, failing:

```
$ go test ./parser
--- FAIL: TestReturnStatements (0.00s)
  parser_test.go:77: program.Statements does not contain 3 statements. got=0
FAIL
FAIL    monkey/parser   0.007s
```

So let's make them pass by changing our `ParseProgram` method to also take `token.RETURN` tokens into account:

```
// parser/parser.go

func (p *Parser) parseStatement() ast.Statement {
    switch p.curToken.Type {
    case token.LET:
        return p.parseLetStatement()
    case token.RETURN:
```

```
        return p.parseReturnStatement()
    default:
        return nil
    }
}
```

I could make a lot of fuzz about the `parseReturnStatement` method before showing it to you, but, well, I won't. Because it's tiny. There is nothing to fuzz about.

```
// parser/parser.go

func (p *Parser) parseReturnStatement() *ast.ReturnStatement {
    stmt := &ast.ReturnStatement{Token: p.curToken}

    p.nextToken()

    // TODO: We're skipping the expressions until we
    // encounter a semicolon
    for !p.curTokenIs(token.SEMICOLON) {
        p.nextToken()
    }

    return stmt
}
```

I told you: it's tiny. The only thing it does is construct a `ast.ReturnStatement`, with the current token it's sitting on as `Token`. It then brings the parser in place for the expression that comes next by calling `nextToken()` and finally, there's the cop-out. It skips over every expression until it encounters a semicolon. That's it. Our tests pass:

```
$ go test ./parser
ok      monkey/parser   0.009s
```

It's time to celebrate again! We can now parse all of the statements in the Monkey programming language! That's right: there are only two of them. Let statements and return statements. The rest of the language consists solely of expressions. And that's what we're going to parse next.

2.6 - PARSING EXPRESSIONS

Personally, I think that parsing expressions is the most interesting part of writing a parser. As we just saw, parsing statements is relatively straightforward. We process tokens from "left to right", expect or reject the next tokens and if everything fits we return an AST node.

Parsing expressions, on the other hand, contains a few more challenges. Operator precedence is probably the first one that comes to mind and is best illustrated with an example. Let's say we want to parse the following arithmetic expression:

```
5 * 5 + 10
```

What we want here is an AST that represents the expression like this:

```
((5 * 5) + 10)
```

That is to say, `5 * 5` needs to be "deeper" in the AST and evaluated earlier than the addition. In order to produce an AST that looks like this, the parser has to know about operator precedences where the precedence of `*` is higher than `+`. That's the most common example for operator precedence, but there are a lot more cases where it's important. Consider this expression:

```
5 * (5 + 10)
```

Here the parenthesis group together the `5 + 10` expression and give them a "precedence bump": the addition now has to be evaluated before the multiplication. That's because parentheses have a higher precedence than the `*` operator. As we will soon see, there are a few more cases where precedence is playing a crucial role.

The other big challenge is that in expressions tokens of the same type can appear in multiple positions. In contrast to this, the `let` token can only appear once at the beginning of a let statement, which makes it easy to determine what the rest of the statement is supposed to be. Now look at this expression:

```
-5 - 10
```

Here the `-` operator appears at the beginning of the expression, as a prefix operator, and then as an infix operator in the middle. A variation of the same challenge appears here:

```
5 * (add(2, 3) + 10)
```

Even though you might not recognize the parentheses as operators yet, they pose the same problem to us as the `-` in the previous example. The outer pair of parentheses in this example denotes a grouped expression. The inner pair denotes a "call expression". The validity of a token's position now depends on the context, the tokens that come before and after, and their precedence.

EXPRESSIONS IN MONKEY

In the Monkey programming language everything besides let and return statements is an expression. These expressions come in different varieties.

Monkey has expressions involving prefix operators:

```
-5
!true
!false
```

And of course it has infix operators (or "binary operators"):

```
5 + 5
5 - 5
5 / 5
5 * 5
```

Besides these basic arithmetic operators, there are also the following comparison operators:

```
foo == bar
foo != bar
foo < bar
foo > bar
```

And of course, as we previously saw, we can use parentheses to group expressions and influence the order of evaluation:

```
5 * (5 + 5)
((5 + 5) * 5) * 5
```

Then there are call expressions:

```
add(2, 3)
add(add(2, 3), add(5, 10))
max(5, add(5, (5 * 5)))
```

Identifiers are expressions too:

```
foo * bar / foobar
add(foo, bar)
```

Functions in Monkey are first-class citizens and, yes, function literals are expressions too. We can use a let statement to bind a function to a name. The function literal is just the expression in the statement:

```
let add = fn(x, y) { return x + y };
```

And here we use a function literal in place of an identifier:

```
fn(x, y) { return x + y }(5, 5)
(fn(x) { return x }(5) + 10 ) * 10
```

In contrast to a lot of widely used programming languages we also have "if expressions" in Monkey:

```
let result = if (10 > 5) { true } else { false };
result // => true
```

Looking at all these different forms of expressions it becomes clear that we need a really good approach to parse them correctly and in an understandable and extendable way. Our old approach of deciding what to do based on the current token won't get us very far - at least not without wanting to tear our hair out. And that is where Vaughan Pratt comes in.

TOP DOWN OPERATOR PRECEDENCE (OR: PRATT PARSING)

In his paper "Top Down Operator Precedence" Vaughan Pratt presents an approach to parsing expressions that, in his own words:

> [...] is very simple to understand, trivial to implement, easy to use, extremely efficient in practice if not in theory, yet flexible enough to meet most reasonable syntactic needs of users [...]

The paper was published in 1973 but in the many years since then the ideas presented by Pratt didn't gain a huge following. Only in recent years, other programmers rediscovered Pratt's paper, wrote about it and caused Pratt's approach to parsing to rise in popularity. There's Douglas Crockford's (of "JavaScript: The Good Parts" fame) article called "Top Down Operator Precedence"[3] that shows how to translate Pratt's ideas to JavaScript (which Crockford did when building JSLint). And then there's the highly recommended article by Bob Nystrom[4], author of the excellent "Game Programming Patterns" book, that makes Pratt's approach really easy to understand and to follow by providing clean example code in Java.

The parsing approach described by all three, which is called Top Down Operator Precedence Parsing, or Pratt parsing, was invented as an alternative to parsers based on context-free grammars and the Backus-Naur-Form.

And that is also the main difference: instead of associating parsing functions (think of our `parseLetStatement` method here) with grammar rules (defined in BNF or EBNF), Pratt associates these functions (which he calls "semantic code") with single token types. A crucial part of this idea is that each token type can have two parsing functions associated with it, depending on the token's position - infix or prefix.

I guess that doesn't make a lot of sense yet. We never saw how to associate parsing functions with grammar rules, so the idea of using token types instead of these rules doesn't register as anything really novel or revelatory. To be completely honest: I was facing a chicken-and-egg problem when writing this section. Is it

[3] http://javascript.crockford.com/tdop/tdop.html

[4] http://journal.stuffwithstuff.com/2011/03/19/pratt-parsers-expression-parsing-made-easy/

better to explain this algorithm in abstract terms and then show the implementation, possibly causing you to jump back and forth between pages, or to show the implementation with the explanation following, causing you to probably skip over the implementation and not getting a lot out of the explanation?

The answer, I decided, is neither of these two options. What we're going to do instead is start implementing the expression parsing part of our parser. Then we're going to take a closer look at it and its algorithm. Afterwards we will extend and complete it so it's able to parse all possible expressions in Monkey.

And before we start writing any code, let's just be clear on the terminology.

TERMINOLOGY

A **prefix operator** is an operator "in front of" its operand. Example:

```
--5
```

Here the operator is `--` (decrement), the operand is the integer literal `5` and the operator is in the prefix position.

A **postfix operator** is an operator "after" its operand. Example:

```
foobar++
```

Here the operator is `++` (increment), the operand is the identifier `foobar` and the operator is in the postfix position. The Monkey interpreter we'll build won't have postfix operators. Not because of some technical limitations, but purely in order to keep the scope of the book limited.

Now, **infix operators** are something we've all seen before. An infix operator sits between its operands, like this:

```
5 * 8
```

The `*` operator sits in the infix position between the two integer literals `5` and `8`. Infix operators appear in **binary expressions** - where the operator has two operands.

The other term we already stumbled upon and will find again later is **operator precedence**. And alternative term for this is **order of operations**, which should make clearer what operator precedence describes: which priority do different operators have. The canonical example is this one, which we saw earlier:

```
5 + 5 * 10
```

The result of this expression is `55` and not `100`. And that's because the `*` operator has a higher precedence, a "higher rank". It's "more important" than the `+`

operator. It gets evaluated before the other operator. I sometimes think of operator precedence as "operator stickiness": how much do the operands next to the operator "stick" to it.

These are all basic terms: prefix, postfix, infix operator and precedence. But it's important that we keep these simple definitions in mind later on, where we'll use these terms in other places.

But for now: let's get typing and write some code!

PREPARING THE AST

The first thing we need to do for expression parsing is to prepare our AST. As we saw before, a program in Monkey is a series of statements. Some are let statements, others return statements. We need to add a third type of statement to our AST: expression statements.

This may sound confusing, after I told you that let and return statements are the only type of statements in Monkey. But an expression statement is not really a distinct statement; it's a statement that consists solely of one expression. It's only a wrapper. We need it because it's totally legal in Monkey to write the following code:

```
let x = 5;
x + 10;
```

The first line is a let statement, the second line is an expression statement. Other languages don't have these expression statements, but most scripting languages do. They make it possible to have one line consisting only of an expression. So let's add this node type to our AST:

```
// ast/ast.go

type ExpressionStatement struct {
    Token      token.Token // the first token of the expression
    Expression Expression
}

func (es *ExpressionStatement) statementNode()       {}
func (es *ExpressionStatement) TokenLiteral() string { return es.Token.Literal }
```

The `ast.ExpressionStatement` type has two fields: the `Token` field, which every node has, and the `Expression` field, which holds the expression. `ast.ExpressionStatement` fulfills the `ast.Statement` interface, which means we can add it to the `Statements` slice of `ast.Program`. And that's the whole reason why we're adding `ast.ExpressionStatement`.

With `ast.ExpressionStatement` defined we could resume work on the parser. But instead, let's make our lives much easier by adding a `String()` method to our AST nodes. This will allow us to print AST nodes for debugging and to compare them with other AST nodes. This is going to be really handy in tests!

We're going to make this `String()` method part of the `ast.Node` interface:

```
// ast/ast.go

type Node interface {
    TokenLiteral() string
    String() string
}
```

Now every node type in our `ast` package has to implement this method. With that change made, our code won't compile because the compiler complains about our AST nodes not fully implementing the updated `Node` interface. Let's start with `*ast.Program` and add its `String()` method first:

```
// ast/ast.go

import (
// [...]
    "bytes"
)

func (p *Program) String() string {
    var out bytes.Buffer

    for _, s := range p.Statements {
        out.WriteString(s.String())
    }

    return out.String()
}
```

This method doesn't do much. It only creates a buffer and writes the return value of each statements `String()` method to it. And then it returns the buffer as a string. It delegates most of its work to the `Statements` of `*ast.Program`.

The "real work" happens in the `String()` methods of our three statement types `ast.LetStatement`, `ast.ReturnStatement` and `ast.ExpressionStatement`:

```
// ast/ast.go

func (ls *LetStatement) String() string {
    var out bytes.Buffer

    out.WriteString(ls.TokenLiteral() + " ")
```

```go
    out.WriteString(ls.Name.String())
    out.WriteString(" = ")

    if ls.Value != nil {
        out.WriteString(ls.Value.String())
    }

    out.WriteString(";")

    return out.String()
}

func (rs *ReturnStatement) String() string {
    var out bytes.Buffer

    out.WriteString(rs.TokenLiteral() + " ")

    if rs.ReturnValue != nil {
        out.WriteString(rs.ReturnValue.String())
    }

    out.WriteString(";")

    return out.String()
}

func (es *ExpressionStatement) String() string {
    if es.Expression != nil {
        return es.Expression.String()
    }
    return ""
}
```

The nil-checks will be taken out, later on, when we can fully build expressions.

Now we only need to add a last `String()` method to `ast.Identifier`:

```go
// ast/ast.go

func (i *Identifier) String() string { return i.Value }
```

With these methods in place, we can now just call `String()` on `*ast.Program` and get our whole program back as a string. That makes the structure of `*ast.Program` easily testable. Let's use the following line of Monkey source code as an example:

```
let myVar = anotherVar;
```

If we construct an AST out of this, we can make an assertion about the return value of `String()` like this:

```go
// ast/ast_test.go

package ast

import (
	"monkey/token"
	"testing"
)

func TestString(t *testing.T) {
	program := &Program{
		Statements: []Statement{
			&LetStatement{
				Token: token.Token{Type: token.LET, Literal: "let"},
				Name: &Identifier{
					Token: token.Token{Type: token.IDENT, Literal: "myVar"},
					Value: "myVar",
				},
				Value: &Identifier{
					Token: token.Token{Type: token.IDENT, Literal: "anotherVar"},
					Value: "anotherVar",
				},
			},
		},
	}

	if program.String() != "let myVar = anotherVar;" {
		t.Errorf("program.String() wrong. got=%q", program.String())
	}
}
```

In this test we construct the AST by hand. When writing tests for the parser we don't, of course, but make assertions about the AST the parser produces. For demonstration purposes, this test shows us how we can add another easily readable layer of tests for our parser by just comparing the parser output with strings. That's going to be especially handy when parsing expressions.

So, good news: preparation is done! It's time to write a Pratt parser.

IMPLEMENTING THE PRATT PARSER

A Pratt parser's main idea is the association of parsing functions (which Pratt calls "semantic code") with token types. Whenever this token type is encountered, the parsing functions are called to parse the appropriate expression and return an AST node that represents it. Each token type can have up to two parsing functions associated with it, depending on whether the token is found in a prefix or an infix position.

The first thing we need to do is to setup these associations. We define two types of functions: a prefix parsing functions and an infix parsing function.

```
// parser/parser.go

type (
    prefixParseFn func() ast.Expression
    infixParseFn  func(ast.Expression) ast.Expression
)
```

Both function types return an `ast.Expression`, since that's what we're here to parse. But only the `infixParseFn` takes an argument: another `ast.Expression`. This argument is "left side" of the infix operator that's being parsed. A prefix operator doesn't have a "left side", per definition. I know that this doesn't make a lot of sense yet, but bear with me here, you'll see how this works. For now, just remember that `prefixParseFns` gets called when we encounter the associated token type in prefix position and `infixParseFn` gets called when we encounter the token type in infix position.

In order for our parser to get the correct `prefixParseFn` or `infixParseFn` for the current token type, we add two maps to the `Parser` structure:

```
// parser/parser.go

type Parser struct {
    l      *lexer.Lexer
    errors []string

    curToken  token.Token
    peekToken token.Token

    prefixParseFns map[token.TokenType]prefixParseFn
    infixParseFns  map[token.TokenType]infixParseFn
}
```

With these maps in place, we can just check if the appropriate map (infix or prefix) has a parsing function associated with `curToken.Type`.

We also give the `Parser` two helper methods that add entries to these maps:

```
// parser/parser.go

func (p *Parser) registerPrefix(tokenType token.TokenType, fn prefixParseFn) {
    p.prefixParseFns[tokenType] = fn
}

func (p *Parser) registerInfix(tokenType token.TokenType, fn infixParseFn) {
```

```
    p.infixParseFns[tokenType] = fn
}
```

Now we are ready to get to the heart of the algorithm.

IDENTIFIERS

We're going to start with possibly the simplest expression type in the Monkey programming language: identifiers. Used in an expression statement an identifier looks like this:

```
foobar;
```

Of course, the `foobar` is arbitrary and identifiers are expressions in other contexts too, not just in an expression statements:

```
add(foobar, barfoo);
foobar + barfoo;
if (foobar) {
  // [...]
}
```

Here we have identifiers as arguments in a function call, as operands in an infix expression and as a standalone expression as part of a conditional. They can be used in all of these contexts, because identifiers are expressions just like `1 + 2`. And just like any other expression identifiers produce a value: they evaluate to the value they are bound to.

We start with a test:

```
// parser/parser_test.go

func TestIdentifierExpression(t *testing.T) {
    input := "foobar;"

    l := lexer.New(input)
    p := New(l)
    program := p.ParseProgram()
    checkParserErrors(t, p)

    if len(program.Statements) != 1 {
        t.Fatalf("program has not enough statements. got=%d",
            len(program.Statements))
    }
    stmt, ok := program.Statements[0].(*ast.ExpressionStatement)
    if !ok {
        t.Fatalf("program.Statements[0] is not ast.ExpressionStatement. got=%T",
            program.Statements[0])
```

```
    }

    ident, ok := stmt.Expression.(*ast.Identifier)
    if !ok {
        t.Fatalf("exp not *ast.Identifier. got=%T", stmt.Expression)
    }
    if ident.Value != "foobar" {
        t.Errorf("ident.Value not %s. got=%s", "foobar", ident.Value)
    }
    if ident.TokenLiteral() != "foobar" {
        t.Errorf("ident.TokenLiteral not %s. got=%s", "foobar",
            ident.TokenLiteral())
    }
}
```

That's a lot of lines, but it's mostly just grunt work. We parse our input `foobar;`, check the parser for errors, make an assertion about the number of statements in the `*ast.Program` node and then check that the only statement in `program.Statements` is an `*ast.ExpressionStatement`. Then we check that the `*ast.ExpressionStatement.Expression` is an `*ast.Identifier`. Finally we check that our identifier has the correct value of `"foobar"`.

Of course, the parser tests fail:

```
$ go test ./parser
--- FAIL: TestIdentifierExpression (0.00s)
  parser_test.go:110: program has not enough statements. got=0
FAIL
FAIL    monkey/parser   0.007s
```

The parser doesn't know anything about expressions yet. We need to write a `parseExpression` method.

The first thing we need to do is to extend the `parseStatement()` method of the parser, so that it parses expression statements. Since the only two real statement types in Monkey are let and return statements, we try to parse expression statements if we don't encounter one of the other two:

```
// parser/parser.go

func (p *Parser) parseStatement() ast.Statement {
    switch p.curToken.Type {
    case token.LET:
        return p.parseLetStatement()
    case token.RETURN:
        return p.parseReturnStatement()
    default:
        return p.parseExpressionStatement()
```

```go
    }
}
```

The parseExpressionStatement method looks like this:

```go
// parser/parser.go

func (p *Parser) parseExpressionStatement() *ast.ExpressionStatement {
    stmt := &ast.ExpressionStatement{Token: p.curToken}

    stmt.Expression = p.parseExpression(LOWEST)

    if p.peekTokenIs(token.SEMICOLON) {
        p.nextToken()
    }

    return stmt
}
```

We already know the drill: we build our AST node and then try to fill its field by calling other parsing functions. In this case there are a few differences though: we call `parseExpression()`, which doesn't exist yet, with the constant `LOWEST`, that doesn't exist yet, and then we check for an optional semicolon. Yes, it's optional. If the `peekToken` is a `token.SEMICOLON`, we advance so it's the `curToken`. If it's not there, that's okay too, we don't add an error to the parser if it's not there. That's because we want expression statements to have optional semicolons (which makes it easier to type something like `5 + 5` into the REPL later on).

If we now run the tests we can see that compilation fails, because `LOWEST` is undefined. That's alright, let's add it now, by defining the precedences of the Monkey programming language:

```go
// parser/parser.go

const (
    _ int = iota
    LOWEST
    EQUALS      // ==
    LESSGREATER // > or <
    SUM         // +
    PRODUCT     // *
    PREFIX      // -X or !X
    CALL        // myFunction(X)
)
```

Here we use `iota` to give the following constants incrementing numbers as values. The blank identifier _ takes the zero value and the following constants get assigned the values `1` to `7`. Which numbers we use doesn't matter, but the **order** and the relation to each other do. What we want out of these constants is to later be able to answer: "does the * operator have a higher precedence than the == operator? Does a prefix operator have a higher preference than a call expression?"

In `parseExpressionStatement` we pass the lowest possible precedence to `parseExpression`, since we didn't parse anything yet and we can't compare precedences. That's going to make more sense in a short while, I promise. Let's write `parseExpression`:

```
// parser/parser.go

func (p *Parser) parseExpression(precedence int) ast.Expression {
    prefix := p.prefixParseFns[p.curToken.Type]
    if prefix == nil {
        return nil
    }
    leftExp := prefix()

    return leftExp
}
```

That's the first version. All it does is checking whether we have a parsing function associated with `p.curToken.Type` in the prefix position. If we do, it calls this parsing function, if not, it returns nil. Which it does at the moment, since we haven't associated any tokens with any parsing functions yet. That's our next step:

```
// parser/parser.go

func New(l *lexer.Lexer) *Parser {
// [...]

    p.prefixParseFns = make(map[token.TokenType]prefixParseFn)
    p.registerPrefix(token.IDENT, p.parseIdentifier)

// [...]
}

func (p *Parser) parseIdentifier() ast.Expression {
    return &ast.Identifier{Token: p.curToken, Value: p.curToken.Literal}
}
```

We modified the `New()` function to initialize the `prefixParseFns` map on `Parser` and register a parsing function: if we encounter a token of type `token.IDENT` the parsing function to call is `parseIdentifier`, a method we defined on `*Parser`.

The `parseIdentifier` method doesn't do a lot. It only returns a `*ast.Identifier` with the current token in the `Token` field and the literal value of the token in

Value. It doesn't advance the tokens, it doesn't call nextToken. That's important. All of our parsing functions, prefixParseFn or infixParseFn, are going to follow this protocol: start with curToken being the type of token you're associated with and return with curToken being the last token that's part of your expression type. Never advance the tokens too far.

Believe it or not, our tests pass:

```
$ go test ./parser
ok      monkey/parser   0.007s
```

We successfully parsed an identifier expression! Alright! But, before we get off the computer, find someone and proudly tell them, let's keep our breath a little longer and write some more parsing functions.

INTEGER LITERALS

Nearly as easy to parse as identifiers are integer literals, which look like this:

```
5;
```

Yes, that's it. Integer literals are expressions. The value they produce is the integer itself. Again, imagine in which places integer literals can occur to understand why they are expressions:

```
let x = 5;
add(5, 10);
5 + 5 + 5;
```

We can use any other expression instead of integer literals here and it would still be valid: identifiers, call expressions, grouped expressions, function literals and so on. All the expression types are interchangeable and integer literals are one of them.

The test case for integer literals looks really similar to the one for identifiers:

```
// parser/parser_test.go

func TestIntegerLiteralExpression(t *testing.T) {
    input := "5;"

    l := lexer.New(input)
    p := New(l)
    program := p.ParseProgram()
    checkParserErrors(t, p)

    if len(program.Statements) != 1 {
        t.Fatalf("program has not enough statements. got=%d",
```

```go
            len(program.Statements))
    }
    stmt, ok := program.Statements[0].(*ast.ExpressionStatement)
    if !ok {
        t.Fatalf("program.Statements[0] is not ast.ExpressionStatement. got=%T",
            program.Statements[0])
    }

    literal, ok := stmt.Expression.(*ast.IntegerLiteral)
    if !ok {
        t.Fatalf("exp not *ast.IntegerLiteral. got=%T", stmt.Expression)
    }
    if literal.Value != 5 {
        t.Errorf("literal.Value not %d. got=%d", 5, literal.Value)
    }
    if literal.TokenLiteral() != "5" {
        t.Errorf("literal.TokenLiteral not %s. got=%s", "5",
            literal.TokenLiteral())
    }
}
```

And as in the test case for identifiers we use a simple input, feed it to the parser and then check that the parser didn't encounter any errors and produced the correct number of statements in `*ast.Program.Statements`. Then we add an assertion that the first statement is an `*ast.ExpressionStatement`. And finally we expect a well-formed `*ast.IntegerLiteral`.

The tests do not compile, since `*ast.IntegerLiteral` doesn't exist yet. Defining it is easy though:

```go
// ast/ast.go

type IntegerLiteral struct {
    Token token.Token
    Value int64
}

func (il *IntegerLiteral) expressionNode()      {}
func (il *IntegerLiteral) TokenLiteral() string { return il.Token.Literal }
func (il *IntegerLiteral) String() string       { return il.Token.Literal }
```

`*ast.IntegerLiteral` fulfills the `ast.Expression` interface, just like `*ast.Identifier` does, but there's a notable difference to `ast.Identifier` in the structure itself: `Value` is an `int64` and not a `string`. This is the field that's going to contain the actual value the integer literal represents in the source code. When we build an `*ast.IntegerLiteral` we have to convert the string in `*ast.IntegerLiteral.Token.Literal` (which is something like `"5"`) to an `int64`.

The best place to do this is in the parsing function associated with token.INT, called parseIntegerLiteral:

```
// parser/parser.go

import (
// [...]
	"strconv"
)

func (p *Parser) parseIntegerLiteral() ast.Expression {
	lit := &ast.IntegerLiteral{Token: p.curToken}

	value, err := strconv.ParseInt(p.curToken.Literal, 0, 64)
	if err != nil {
		msg := fmt.Sprintf("could not parse %q as integer", p.curToken.Literal)
		p.errors = append(p.errors, msg)
		return nil
	}

	lit.Value = value

	return lit
}
```

Like parseIdentifier the method is strikingly simple. The only thing that's really different is a call to strconv.ParseInt, which converts the string in p.curToken.Literal into an int64. The int64 then gets saved to the Value field and we return the newly constructed *ast.IntegerLiteral node. If that doesn't work, we add a new error to the parser's errors field.

But the tests don't pass yet:

```
$ go test ./parser
--- FAIL: TestIntegerLiteralExpression (0.00s)
  parser_test.go:162: exp not *ast.IntegerLiteral. got=<nil>
FAIL
FAIL	monkey/parser	0.008s
```

We have a nil instead of an *ast.IntegerLiteral in our AST. The reason is that parseExpression can't find a prefixParseFn for a token of type token.INT. All we have to do to make the tests pass is to register our parseIntegerLiteral method:

```
// parser/parser.go

func New(l *lexer.Lexer) *Parser {
// [...]
	p.prefixParseFns = make(map[token.TokenType]prefixParseFn)
	p.registerPrefix(token.IDENT, p.parseIdentifier)
```

```go
    p.registerPrefix(token.INT, p.parseIntegerLiteral)

// [...]
}
```

With `parseIntegerLiteral` registered, `parseExpression` now knows what to do with a `token.INT` token, calls `parseIntegerLiteral` and returns its return value, an `*ast.IntegerLiteral`. The tests pass:

```
$ go test ./parser
ok      monkey/parser   0.007s
```

I think it's time to say: we are on a roll here! Identifiers and integer literals are in the bag, let's step it up a notch and parse prefix operators.

PREFIX OPERATORS

There are two prefix operators in the Monkey programming language: `!` and `-`. Their usage is pretty much what you'd expect from other languages:

```
-5;
!foobar;
5 + -10;
```

The structure of their usage is the following:

```
<prefix operator><expression>;
```

Yes, that's right. Any expression can follow a prefix operator as operand. These are valid:

```
!isGreaterThanZero(2);
5 + -add(5, 5);
```

That means that an AST node for a prefix operator expression has to be flexible enough to point to any expression as its operand.

But first things first, here is the test case for prefix operators, or "prefix expressions":

```go
// parser/parser_test.go

func TestParsingPrefixExpressions(t *testing.T) {
    prefixTests := []struct {
        input        string
        operator     string
        integerValue int64
    }{
        {"!5;", "!", 5},
        {"-15;", "-", 15},
```

```
    }

    for _, tt := range prefixTests {
        l := lexer.New(tt.input)
        p := New(l)
        program := p.ParseProgram()
        checkParserErrors(t, p)

        if len(program.Statements) != 1 {
            t.Fatalf("program.Statements does not contain %d statements. got=%d\n",
                1, len(program.Statements))
        }

        stmt, ok := program.Statements[0].(*ast.ExpressionStatement)
        if !ok {
            t.Fatalf("program.Statements[0] is not ast.ExpressionStatement. got=%T",
                program.Statements[0])
        }

        exp, ok := stmt.Expression.(*ast.PrefixExpression)
        if !ok {
            t.Fatalf("stmt is not ast.PrefixExpression. got=%T", stmt.Expression)
        }
        if exp.Operator != tt.operator {
            t.Fatalf("exp.Operator is not '%s'. got=%s",
                tt.operator, exp.Operator)
        }
        if !testIntegerLiteral(t, exp.Right, tt.integerValue) {
            return
        }
    }
}
```

This test function, again, has a lot of lines. For two reasons: manually creating error messages with `t.Errorf` takes up some space and we're using a table-driven testing approach. The reason for this approach is that it saves us a lot of test code. Yes, it's only two test cases, but duplicating the complete test setup for each case would mean a lot more lines. And since the logic behind the test assertions is the same, we share the test setup. Both test cases (`!5` and `-15` as input) differ only in the expected operators and integer values (which we define here in `prefixTests`).

In the test function we iterate through our slice of test inputs and make assertions about the produced AST based on the values defined in the `prefixTests` slice of structs. As you can see, at the end we use a new helper function called `testIntegerLiteral` to test that the `Right` value of `*ast.PrefixExpression` is the correct integer literal. We introduce this helper function here, so the focus of the test case is on `*ast.PrefixExpression` and its fields and we will soon enough need it again.

It looks like this:

```go
// parser/parser_test.go

func testIntegerLiteral(t *testing.T, il ast.Expression, value int64) bool {
    integ, ok := il.(*ast.IntegerLiteral)
    if !ok {
        t.Errorf("il not *ast.IntegerLiteral. got=%T", il)
        return false
    }

    if integ.Value != value {
        t.Errorf("integ.Value not %d. got=%d", value, integ.Value)
        return false
    }

    if integ.TokenLiteral() != fmt.Sprintf("%d", value) {
        t.Errorf("integ.TokenLiteral not %d. got=%s", value,
            integ.TokenLiteral())
        return false
    }

    return true
}
```

There is nothing new here, we've seen this before in `TestIntegerLiteralExpression`. But now it's hidden behind a small helper function that makes these new tests more readable.

As expected the tests don't even compile:

```
$ go test ./parser
# monkey/parser
parser/parser_test.go:210: undefined: ast.PrefixExpression
FAIL    monkey/parser [build failed]
```

We need to define the `ast.PrefixExpression` node:

```go
// ast/ast.go

type PrefixExpression struct {
    Token    token.Token // The prefix token, e.g. !
    Operator string
    Right    Expression
}

func (pe *PrefixExpression) expressionNode()      {}
func (pe *PrefixExpression) TokenLiteral() string { return pe.Token.Literal }
func (pe *PrefixExpression) String() string {
    var out bytes.Buffer
```

```go
    out.WriteString("(")
    out.WriteString(pe.Operator)
    out.WriteString(pe.Right.String())
    out.WriteString(")")

    return out.String()
}
```

This doesn't contain any surprises. The `*ast.PrefixExpression` node has two noteworthy fields: `Operator` and `Right`. `Operator` is a string that's going to contain either `"-"` or `"!"`. The `Right` field contains the expression to the right of the operator.

In the `String()` method we deliberately add parentheses around the operator and its operand, the expression in `Right`. That allows us to see which operands belong to which operator.

With `*ast.PrefixExpression` defined, the tests now fail with a strange error message:

```
$ go test ./parser
--- FAIL: TestParsingPrefixExpressions (0.00s)
  parser_test.go:198: program.Statements does not contain 1 statements. got=2
FAIL
FAIL    monkey/parser   0.007s
```

Why does `program.Statements` contain one statement instead of the expected two? The reason is that `parseExpression` doesn't recognize our prefix operators yet and simply returns `nil`. `program.Statements` does not contain one statement but simply one `nil`.

We can do better than this, we can extend our parser and the `parseExpression` method to give us better error messages when this happens:

```go
// parser/parser.go

func (p *Parser) noPrefixParseFnError(t token.TokenType) {
    msg := fmt.Sprintf("no prefix parse function for %s found", t)
    p.errors = append(p.errors, msg)
}

func (p *Parser) parseExpression(precedence int) ast.Expression {
    prefix := p.prefixParseFns[p.curToken.Type]
    if prefix == nil {
        p.noPrefixParseFnError(p.curToken.Type)
        return nil
    }
    leftExp := prefix()
```

```
    return leftExp
}
```

The small helper method `noPrefixParseFnError` just adds a formatted error message to our parser's `errors` field. But that's enough to get better error messages in our failing test:

```
$ go test ./parser
--- FAIL: TestParsingPrefixExpressions (0.00s)
  parser_test.go:227: parser has 1 errors
  parser_test.go:229: parser error: "no prefix parse function for ! found"
FAIL
FAIL    monkey/parser   0.010s
```

Now it's clear what we have to do: write a parsing function for prefix expressions and register it in our parser.

```
// parser/parser.go

func New(l *lexer.Lexer) *Parser {
// [...]
    p.registerPrefix(token.BANG, p.parsePrefixExpression)
    p.registerPrefix(token.MINUS, p.parsePrefixExpression)
// [...]
}

func (p *Parser) parsePrefixExpression() ast.Expression {
    expression := &ast.PrefixExpression{
        Token:    p.curToken,
        Operator: p.curToken.Literal,
    }

    p.nextToken()

    expression.Right = p.parseExpression(PREFIX)

    return expression
}
```

For `token.BANG` and `token.MINUS` we register the same method as `prefixParseFn`: the newly created `parsePrefixExpression`. This method builds an AST node, in this case `*ast.PrefixExpression`, just like the parsing functions we saw before. But then it does something different: it actually advances our tokens by calling `p.nextToken()`!

When `parsePrefixExpression` is called, `p.curToken` is either of type `token.BANG` or `token.MINUS`, because otherwise it wouldn't have been called. But in order to correctly parse a prefix expression like `-5` more than one token has to be "consumed".

So after using p.curToken to build a *ast.PrefixExpression node, the method advances the tokens and calls parseExpression again. This time with the precedence of prefix operators as argument. It's still unused, but we'll shortly see what it's good for and how to make use of it.

Now, when parseExpression is called by parsePrefixExpression the tokens have been advanced and the current token is the one after the prefix operator. In the case of -5, when parseExpression is called the p.curToken.Type is token.INT. parseExpression then checks the registered prefix parsing functions and finds parseIntegerLiteral, which builds an *ast.IntegerLiteral node and returns it. parseExpression returns this newly constructed node and parsePrefixExpression uses it to fill the Right field of *ast.PrefixExpression.

Yes, this works, our tests pass:

```
$ go test ./parser
ok      monkey/parser   0.007s
```

Note how the "protocol" for our parsing functions plays out here: parsePrefixExpression starts with p.curToken being the token of the prefix operator and it returns with p.curToken being the operand of the prefix expression, which is the last token of the expression. The tokens get advanced just enough, which works beautifully. The neat thing is how few lines of code are needed for this. The power lies in the recursive approach.

Granted, the precedence argument in parseExpression is confusing, since it's unused. But we've already seen something important about its usage: the value changes depending on the caller's knowledge and its context. parseExpressionStatement (the top-level method that kicks off expression parsing here) knows nothing about a precedence level and just uses LOWEST. But parsePrefixExpression passes the PREFIX precedence to parseExpression, since it's parsing a prefix expression.

And now we'll see how precedence in parseExpression is used. Because now we're going to parse infix expressions.

INFIX OPERATORS

Next up we're going to parse these eight infix operators:

```
5 + 5;
5 - 5;
5 * 5;
5 / 5;
5 > 5;
5 < 5;
```

```
5 == 5;
5 != 5;
```

Don't be bothered by the `5` here. As with prefix operator expressions, we can use any expressions to the left and right of the operator.

```
<expression> <infix operator> <expression>
```

Because of the two operands (left and right) these expressions are sometimes called "binary expressions" (whereas our prefix expressions would be called "unary expressions"). Even though we can use any expressions on either side of the operator, we're going to start by writing a test that only uses integer literals as operands. As soon as we can get the test to pass, we'll extend it to incorporate more operand types. Here it is:

```
// parser/parser_test.go

func TestParsingInfixExpressions(t *testing.T) {
    infixTests := []struct {
        input      string
        leftValue  int64
        operator   string
        rightValue int64
    }{
        {"5 + 5;", 5, "+", 5},
        {"5 - 5;", 5, "-", 5},
        {"5 * 5;", 5, "*", 5},
        {"5 / 5;", 5, "/", 5},
        {"5 > 5;", 5, ">", 5},
        {"5 < 5;", 5, "<", 5},
        {"5 == 5;", 5, "==", 5},
        {"5 != 5;", 5, "!=", 5},
    }

    for _, tt := range infixTests {
        l := lexer.New(tt.input)
        p := New(l)
        program := p.ParseProgram()
        checkParserErrors(t, p)

        if len(program.Statements) != 1 {
            t.Fatalf("program.Statements does not contain %d statements. got=%d\n",
                1, len(program.Statements))
        }

        stmt, ok := program.Statements[0].(*ast.ExpressionStatement)
        if !ok {
            t.Fatalf("program.Statements[0] is not ast.ExpressionStatement. got=%T",
```

```
                program.Statements[0])
        }

        exp, ok := stmt.Expression.(*ast.InfixExpression)
        if !ok {
            t.Fatalf("exp is not ast.InfixExpression. got=%T", stmt.Expression)
        }

        if !testIntegerLiteral(t, exp.Left, tt.leftValue) {
            return
        }

        if exp.Operator != tt.operator {
            t.Fatalf("exp.Operator is not '%s'. got=%s",
                tt.operator, exp.Operator)
        }

        if !testIntegerLiteral(t, exp.Right, tt.rightValue) {
            return
        }
    }
}
```

This test is nearly a straight copy of `TestParsingPrefixExpressions`, except that we now make assertions about the `Right` *and* `Left` fields of the resulting AST node. Here the table-driven approach gives us great leverage that we'll soon use when we extend the test to also include identifiers.

The tests fail, of course, because they can't find a definition of `*ast.InfixExpression`. And in order to get real failing tests, we define `ast.InfixExpression`:

```
// ast/ast.go

type InfixExpression struct {
    Token    token.Token // The operator token, e.g. +
    Left     Expression
    Operator string
    Right    Expression
}

func (oe *InfixExpression) expressionNode()      {}
func (oe *InfixExpression) TokenLiteral() string { return oe.Token.Literal }
func (oe *InfixExpression) String() string {
    var out bytes.Buffer

    out.WriteString("(")
    out.WriteString(oe.Left.String())
    out.WriteString(" " + oe.Operator + " ")
```

```go
    out.WriteString(oe.Right.String())
    out.WriteString(")")

    return out.String()
}
```

Just like with `ast.PrefixExpression`, we define `ast.InfixExpression` to fulfill the `ast.Expression` and `ast.Node` interfaces, by defining the `expressionNode()`, `TokenLiteral()` and `String()` methods. The only difference to `ast.PrefixExpression` is the new field called `Left`, which can hold any expression.

With that out of the way, we can build and run our tests. And the tests even return one of our own new error messages:

```
$ go test ./parser
--- FAIL: TestParsingInfixExpressions (0.00s)
  parser_test.go:246: parser has 1 errors
  parser_test.go:248: parser error: "no prefix parse function for + found"
FAIL
FAIL    monkey/parser   0.007s
```

But that error message is deceiving. It says "no prefix parse function for + found". The problem is that we do not want our parser to find a prefix parse function for `+`. We want it to find an infix parse function.

This is the point where we're going from "I guess it's neat" to "Wow, this is beautiful", because we now need to complete our `parseExpression` method. And to do that, we first need a precedence table and a few helper methods:

```go
// parser/parser.go

var precedences = map[token.TokenType]int{
    token.EQ:       EQUALS,
    token.NOT_EQ:   EQUALS,
    token.LT:       LESSGREATER,
    token.GT:       LESSGREATER,
    token.PLUS:     SUM,
    token.MINUS:    SUM,
    token.SLASH:    PRODUCT,
    token.ASTERISK: PRODUCT,
}

// [...]

func (p *Parser) peekPrecedence() int {
    if p, ok := precedences[p.peekToken.Type]; ok {
        return p
    }
```

```
    return LOWEST
}

func (p *Parser) curPrecedence() int {
    if p, ok := precedences[p.curToken.Type]; ok {
        return p
    }

    return LOWEST
}
```

`precedences` is our precedence table: it associates token types with their precedence. The precedence values themselves are the constants we defined earlier, the integers with increasing value. This table can now tell us that `+` (`token.PLUS`) and `-` (`token.MINUS`) have the same precedence, which is lower than the precedence of `*` (`token.ASTERISK`) and `/` (`token.SLASH`), for example.

The `peekPrecedence` method returns the precedence associated with the token type of `p.peekToken`. If it doesn't find a precedence for `p.peekToken` it defaults to `LOWEST`, the lowest possible precedence any operator can have. The `curPrecedence` method does the same thing, but for `p.curToken`.

The next step is to register one infix parse function for all of our infix operators:

```
// parser/parser.go

func New(l *lexer.Lexer) *Parser {
// [...]
    p.infixParseFns = make(map[token.TokenType]infixParseFn)
    p.registerInfix(token.PLUS, p.parseInfixExpression)
    p.registerInfix(token.MINUS, p.parseInfixExpression)
    p.registerInfix(token.SLASH, p.parseInfixExpression)
    p.registerInfix(token.ASTERISK, p.parseInfixExpression)
    p.registerInfix(token.EQ, p.parseInfixExpression)
    p.registerInfix(token.NOT_EQ, p.parseInfixExpression)
    p.registerInfix(token.LT, p.parseInfixExpression)
    p.registerInfix(token.GT, p.parseInfixExpression)
// [...]
}
```

We already have the `registerInfix` method in our repertoire and now we finally use it. Every infix operator gets associated with the same parsing function called `parseInfixExpression`, which looks like this:

```
// parser/parser.go

func (p *Parser) parseInfixExpression(left ast.Expression) ast.Expression {
    expression := &ast.InfixExpression{
        Token:    p.curToken,
```

```go
        Operator: p.curToken.Literal,
        Left:     left,
    }

    precedence := p.curPrecedence()
    p.nextToken()
    expression.Right = p.parseExpression(precedence)

    return expression
}
```

The notable difference here is that, in contrast to `parsePrefixExpression`, this new method takes an argument, an `ast.Expression` called `left`. It uses this argument to construct an `*ast.InfixExpression` node, with `left` being in the `Left` field. Then it assigns the precedence of the current token (which is the operator of the infix expression) to the local variable `precedence`, before advancing the tokens by calling `nextToken` and filling the `Right` field of the node with another call to `parseExpression` - this time passing in the precedence of the operator token.

It's time to lift the curtain. Here is the heart of our Pratt parser, here is the final version of `parseExpression`:

```go
// parser/parser.go

func (p *Parser) parseExpression(precedence int) ast.Expression {
    prefix := p.prefixParseFns[p.curToken.Type]
    if prefix == nil {
        p.noPrefixParseFnError(p.curToken.Type)
        return nil
    }
    leftExp := prefix()

    for !p.peekTokenIs(token.SEMICOLON) && precedence < p.peekPrecedence() {
        infix := p.infixParseFns[p.peekToken.Type]
        if infix == nil {
            return leftExp
        }

        p.nextToken()

        leftExp = infix(leftExp)
    }

    return leftExp
}
```

And, boom! Our tests pass! It's all green, baby:

```
$ go test ./parser
```

```
ok      monkey/parser   0.006s
```

We are now officially able to parse infix operator expressions correctly! *Wait, what? What the hell did just happen? How does this work?*

Obviously `parseExpression` now does a few more things. We already know how it finds an associated `prefixParseFn` with the current token and calls it. We've seen this work with prefix operators, identifiers and integer literals.

What's new is the loop right in the middle of `parseExpression`. In the loop's body the method tries to find `infixParseFns` for the next token. If it finds such a function, it calls it, passing in the expression returned by a `prefixParseFn` as an argument. And it does all this again and again until it encounters a token that has a higher precedence.

This works beautifully. Look at these tests that use multiple operators with different precedences and how the AST in string form correctly represents this:

```go
// parser/parser_test.go

func TestOperatorPrecedenceParsing(t *testing.T) {
    tests := []struct {
        input    string
        expected string
    }{
        {
            "-a * b",
            "((-a) * b)",
        },
        {
            "!-a",
            "(!(-a))",
        },
        {
            "a + b + c",
            "((a + b) + c)",
        },
        {
            "a + b - c",
            "((a + b) - c)",
        },
        {
            "a * b * c",
            "((a * b) * c)",
        },
        {
            "a * b / c",
            "((a * b) / c)",
```

```go
        },
        {
            "a + b / c",
            "(a + (b / c))",
        },
        {
            "a + b * c + d / e - f",
            "(((a + (b * c)) + (d / e)) - f)",
        },
        {
            "3 + 4; -5 * 5",
            "(3 + 4)((-5) * 5)",
        },
        {
            "5 > 4 == 3 < 4",
            "((5 > 4) == (3 < 4))",
        },
        {
            "5 < 4 != 3 > 4",
            "((5 < 4) != (3 > 4))",
        },
        {
            "3 + 4 * 5 == 3 * 1 + 4 * 5",
            "((3 + (4 * 5)) == ((3 * 1) + (4 * 5)))",
        },
    }

    for _, tt := range tests {
        l := lexer.New(tt.input)
        p := New(l)
        program := p.ParseProgram()
        checkParserErrors(t, p)

        actual := program.String()
        if actual != tt.expected {
            t.Errorf("expected=%q, got=%q", tt.expected, actual)
        }
    }
}
```

They're all passing! That's pretty amazing, isn't it?

The different `*ast.InfixExpressions` are nested correctly, which we can observe thanks to our usage of parentheses in the `String()` methods of the AST nodes.

If you're scratching your head and wondering how all of this works, don't worry. We're now going to take a really close look at our `parseExpression` method.

2.7 - How Pratt Parsing Works

The algorithm behind the `parseExpression` method and its combination of parsing functions and precedences is fully described by Vaughan Pratt in his "Top Down Operator Precedence" paper. But there are differences between his and our implementation.

Pratt doesn't use a `Parser` structure and doesn't pass around methods defined on `*Parser`. He also doesn't use maps and, of course, he didn't use Go. His paper predates the release of Go by 36 years. And then there are naming differences: what we call `prefixParseFns` are "nuds" (for "null denotations") for Pratt. `infixParseFns` are "leds" (for "left denotations").

Formulated in pseudocode though, our `parseExpression` method looks strikingly similar to the code presented in Pratt's paper. It uses the same algorithm with barely any changes.

We're going to skip the theory that answers *why* it works and just follow *how* it works and how all the pieces (`parseExpression`, parsing functions and precedences) fit together by looking at an example. Suppose we're parsing the following expression statement:

```
1 + 2 + 3;
```

The big challenge here is not to represent every operator and operand in the resulting AST, but to nest the nodes of the AST correctly. What we want is an AST that (serialized as a string) looks like this:

```
((1 + 2) + 3)
```

The AST needs to have two `*ast.InfixExpression` nodes. The `*ast.InfixExpression` higher in the tree should have the integer literal `3` as its `Right` child node and its `Left` child node needs to be the other `*ast.InfixExpression`. This second `*ast.InfixExpression` then needs to have the integer literals `1` and `2` as its `Left` and `Right` child nodes, respectively. Like this:

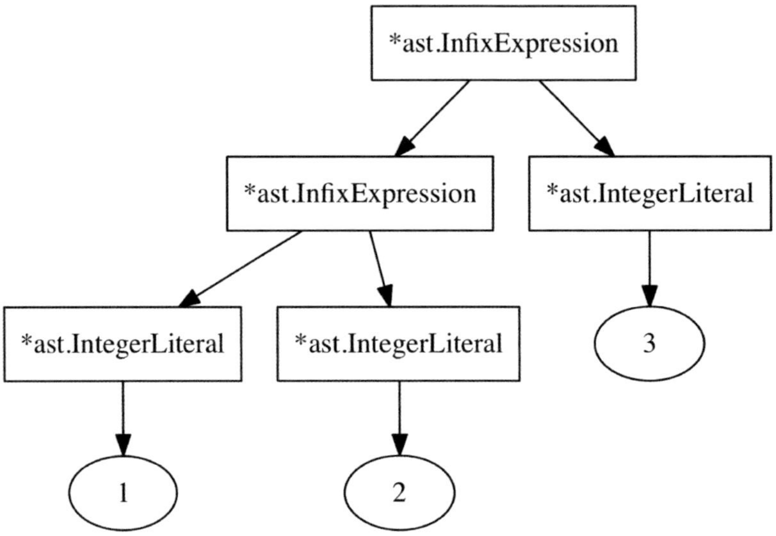

And this is exactly what our parser outputs when it parses `1 + 2 + 3;`. But how? We'll answer that question in the following paragraphs. We're going take a close look at what the parser does as soon as `parseExpressionStatement` is called for the first time. It's not a mistake to have the code open while reading the following paragraphs.

So here we go. Here is what happens when we parse `1 + 2 + 3;`:

`parseExpressionStatement` calls `parseExpression(LOWEST)`. The `p.curToken` and `p.peekToken` are the `1` and the first `+`:

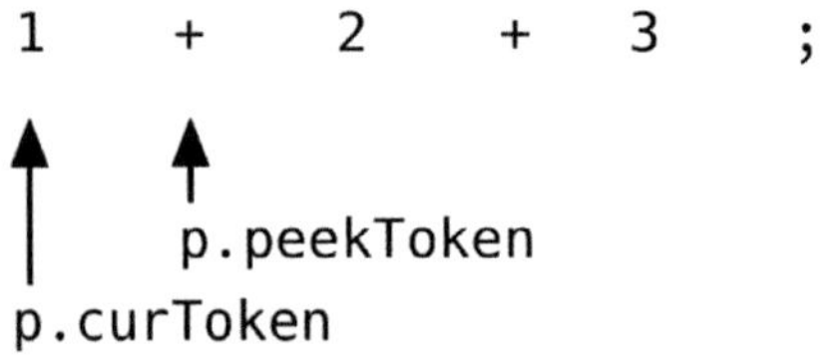

The first thing `parseExpression` then does is to check whether there is a `prefixParseFn` associated with the current `p.curToken.Type`, which is a `token.INT`. And, yes, there is: `parseIntegerLiteral`. So it calls `parseIntegerLiteral`, which returns an `*ast.IntegerLiteral`. `parseExpression` assigns this to `leftExp`.

Then comes the new for-loop in `parseExpression`. Its condition evaluates to true:

```
for !p.peekTokenIs(token.SEMICOLON) && precedence < p.peekPrecedence() {
// [...]
}
```

`p.peekToken` is not a `token.SEMICOLON` and `peekPrecedence` (which returns the precedence of the `+` token) is higher than the argument passed to `parseExpression`, which is `LOWEST`. Here are our defined precedences again to refresh our memory:

```
// parser/parser.go

const (
	_ int = iota
	LOWEST
	EQUALS      // ==
	LESSGREATER // > or <
	SUM         // +
	PRODUCT     // *
	PREFIX      // -X or !X
	CALL        // myFunction(X)
)
```

So the condition evaluates to true and `parseExpression` executes the body of the loop, which looks like this:

```
infix := p.infixParseFns[p.peekToken.Type]
if infix == nil {
  return leftExp
}

p.nextToken()

leftExp = infix(leftExp)
```

Now it fetches the `infixParseFn` for `p.peekToken.Type`, which is `parseInfixExpression` defined on `*Parser`. Before calling it and assigning its return value to `leftExp` (reusing the `leftExp` variable!) it advances the tokens so they now look like this:

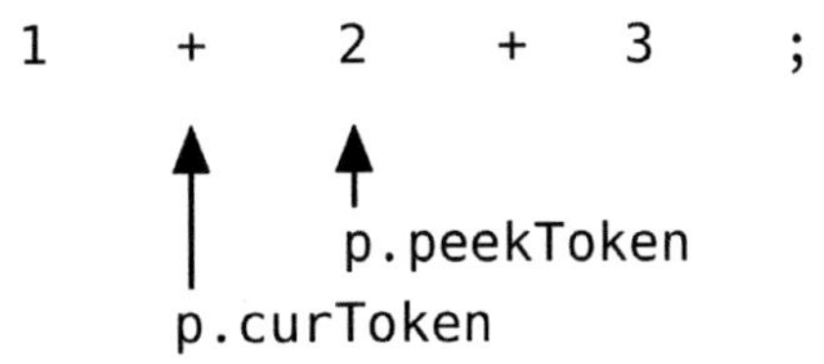

With the tokens in this state, it calls `parseInfixExpression` and passes in the already parsed `*ast.IntegerLiteral` (assigned to `leftExp` outside the for-loop). What happens next in `parseInfixExpression` is where things get interesting. Here is the method again:

```go
// parser/parser.go

func (p *Parser) parseInfixExpression(left ast.Expression) ast.Expression {
    expression := &ast.InfixExpression{
        Token:    p.curToken,
        Operator: p.curToken.Literal,
        Left:     left,
    }

    precedence := p.curPrecedence()
    p.nextToken()
    expression.Right = p.parseExpression(precedence)

    return expression
}
```

It's important to note that `left` is our already parsed `*ast.IntegerLiteral` that represents the `1`.

`parseInfixExpression` saves the precedence of `p.curToken` (the first `+` token!), advances the tokens and calls `parseExpression` - passing in the just saved precedence. So now `parseExpression` is called the second time, with the tokens looking like this:

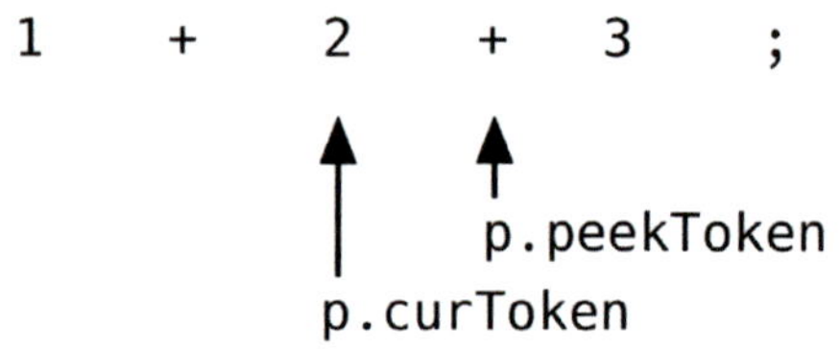

The first thing `parseExpression` does again is to look for a `prefixParseFn` for `p.curToken`. And again it's `parseIntegerLiteral`. But now the condition of the for-loop doesn't evaluate to true: `precedence` (the argument passed to `parseExpression`) is the precedence of the *first* `+` operator in `1 + 2 + 3`, which is *not* smaller than the precedence of `p.peekToken`, the second `+` operator. They are equal. The body of the for-loop is not executed and the `*ast.IntegerLiteral` representing the `2` is returned.

Now back in `parseInfixExpression` the return-value of `parseExpression` is assigned to the Right field of the newly constructed *ast.InfixExpression. So now we have this:

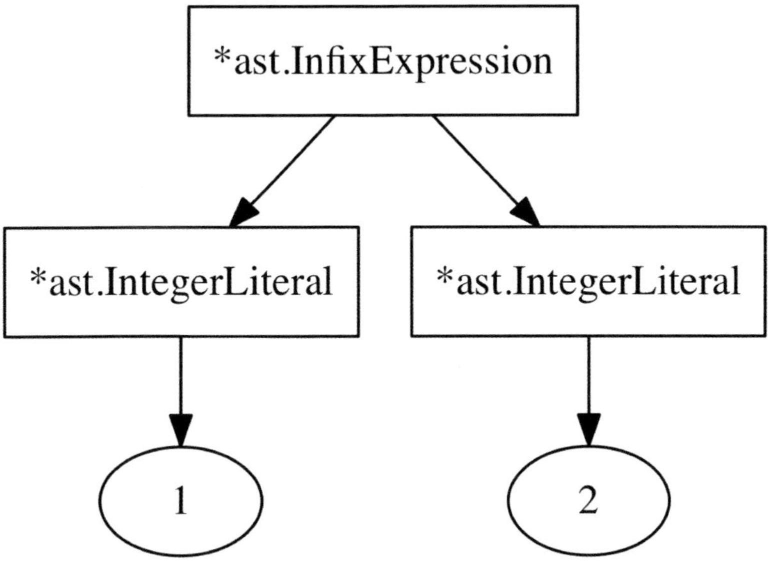

This *ast.InfixExpressions gets returned by parseInfixExpression and now we're back in the outer-most call to parseExpression, where precedence is still LOWEST. We are back where we started and the condition of the for-loop is evaluated again.

```
for !p.peekTokenIs(token.SEMICOLON) && precedence < p.peekPrecedence() {
// [...]
}
```

This still evaluates to true, since precedence is LOWEST and peekPrecedence now returns the precedence of the second + in our expression, which is higher. parseExpression executes the body of the for-loop a second time. The difference is that now leftExp is not an *ast.IntegerLiteral representing the 1, but the *ast.InfixExpression returned by parseInfixExpression, representing 1 + 2.

In the body of the loop parseExpression fetches parseInfixExpression as the infixParseFn for p.peekToken.Type (which is the second +), advances the tokens and calls parseInfixExpression with leftExp as the argument. parseInfixExpression in turn calls parseExpression again, which returns the last *ast.IntegerLiteral (that represents the 3 in our expression).

After all this, at the end of the loop-body, leftExp looks like this:

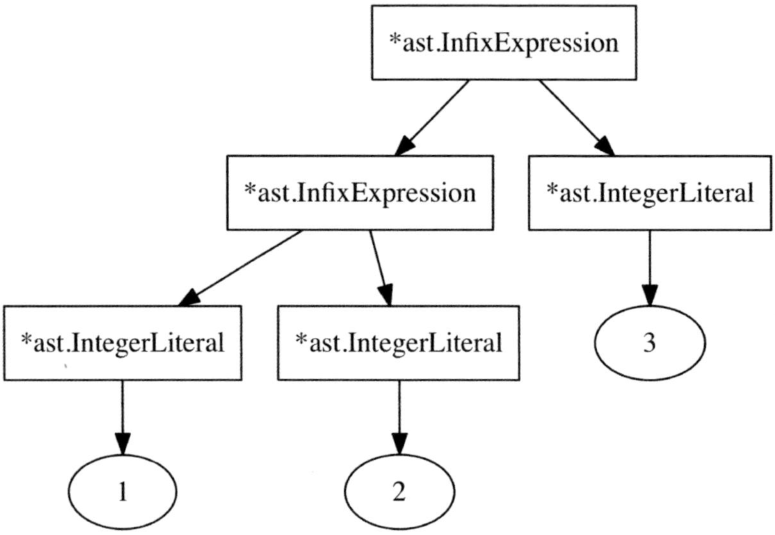

That's exactly what we wanted! The operators and operands are nested correctly! And our tokens look like this:

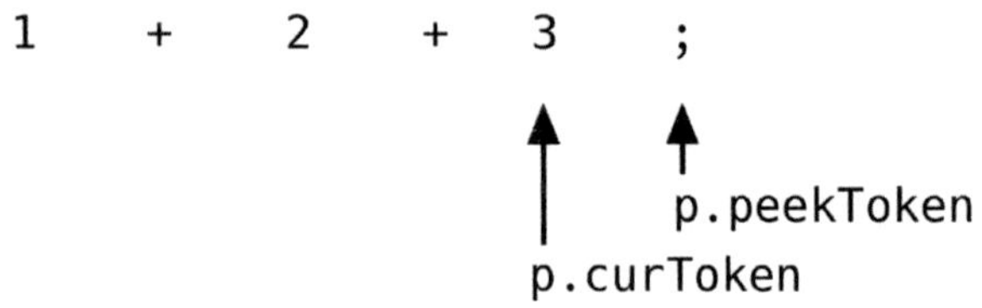

The condition of the for-loop evaluates to false:

```
for !p.peekTokenIs(token.SEMICOLON) && precedence < p.peekPrecedence() {
// [...]
}
```

Now `p.peekTokenIs(token.SEMICOLON)` evaluates to true, which stops the body of the loop from being executed again.

(The call to `p.peekTokenIs(token.SEMICOLON)` is not strictly necessary. Our `peekPrecedence` method returns `LOWEST` as the default value if no precedence for `p.peekToken.Type` can be found - which is the case for `token.SEMICOLON` tokens. But I think it makes the behaviour of semicolons as expression-ending-delimiters more explicit and easier to understand.)

And that's it! The for-loop is done and `leftExp` is returned. We're back in `parseExpressionStatement` and have the final and correct `*ast.InfixExpression` at hand. And that's used as the `Expression` in `*ast.ExpressionStatement`.

Now we know how our parser manages to parse `1 + 2 + 3` correctly. It's pretty fascinating, isn't it? I think the usage of `precedence` and `peekPrecedence` is particularly interesting.

But what about "real precedence issues"? In our example every operator (the `+`) had the same precedence. What do the different precedence levels for operators accomplish? Couldn't we just use `LOWEST` per default and something called `HIGHEST` for all operators?

No, because that would give us a wrong AST. The goal is to have expressions involving operators with a higher precedence to be deeper in the tree than expressions with lower precedence operators. This is accomplished by the `precedence` value (the argument) in `parseExpression`.

When `parseExpression` is called the value of `precedence` stands for the current "right-binding power" of the current `parseExpression` invocation. What does "right-binding power" mean? Well, the higher it is, the more tokens/operators/operands to the right of the current expressions (the future peek tokens) can we "bind" to it, or as I like to think, "suck in".

In case our current right-binding power is of the highest possible value, what we parsed so far (assigned to `leftExp`) is *never* passed to an `infixParseFn` associated with the next operator (or token). It will never end up as a "left" child node. Because the condition of the for-loop never evaluates to true.

A counterpart to right-binding power exists and it's called (you guessed it!) "left-binding power". But which value signifies this left-binding power? Since the `precedence` argument in `parseExpression` stands for the current right-binding power, where does the left-binding power of the next operator come from? Simply put: from our call to `peekPrecedence`. The value this call returns stands for the left-binding power of the next operator, of `p.peekToken`.

It all comes down to the `precedence < p.peekPrecedence()` condition of our for-loop. This condition checks if the left-binding power of the next operator/token is higher than our current right-binding power. If it is, what we parsed so far gets "sucked in" by the next operator, from left to right, and ends up being passed to the `infixParseFn` of the next operator.

An example: let's say we're parsing the expression statement `-1 + 2;`. What we want the AST to represent is `(-1) + 2` and not `-(1 + 2)`. The first method we end up in (after `parseExpressionStatement` and `parseExpression`) is the `prefixParseFn` we associated with `token.MINUS`: `parsePrefixExpression`. To refresh our memory of parsePrefixExpression here it is in its entirety:

```
// parser/parser.go

func (p *Parser) parsePrefixExpression() ast.Expression {
  expression := &ast.PrefixExpression{
    Token:    p.curToken,
    Operator: p.curToken.Literal,
  }
  p.nextToken()
  expression.Right = p.parseExpression(PREFIX)
  return expression
}
```

This passes `PREFIX` to `parseExpression` as `precedence`, turning `PREFIX` into the right-binding power of that `parseExpression` invocation. `PREFIX` is a really high precedence, as per our definition. The result of this is that `parseExpression(PREFIX)` is *never* going to parse the `1` in `-1` and pass it to another `infixParseFn`. The `precedence < p.peekPrecedence()` will never be true in this case, meaning that no other `infixParseFn` is going to get our `1` as the left arm. Instead the `1` is returned as the "right" arm of our prefix expression. Just the `1`, not some other expression that comes after and needs to be parsed.

Back in the outer call to `parseExpression` (in which we called `parsePrefixExpression` as a `prefixParseFn`), right after the first `leftExp := prefix()`, the value of `precedence` is still `LOWEST`. Since that was the value we used in the outer-most call. Our right-binding power is still `LOWEST`. The `p.peekToken` is now the `+` in `-1 + 2`.

We're now sitting on the condition of the for-loop and evaluate it to determine whether we should execute the body of the loop. And it turns out that the precedence of the `+` operator (returned by `p.peekPrecedence()`) is higher than our current right-binding power. What we parsed so far (the `-1` prefix expression) is now passed to the `infixParseFn` associated with `+`. The left-binding power of the `+` "sucks in" what we parsed so far and uses it as the "left arm" of the AST node it is constructing.

The `infixParseFn` for `+` is `parseInfixExpression`, which now uses the precedence of `+` as the right-binding power in its call to `parseExpression`. It doesn't use `LOWEST`, because that would result in another `+` having a higher left-binding power and "sucking" away our "right arm". If it did, then an expression like `a + b + c` would result in `(a + (b + c))`, which is not what we want. We want `((a + b) + c)`.

The high precedence of prefix operators worked. And it even works great for infix operators. In the classic example for operator precedences `1 + 2 * 3`, the left-binding power of `*` would be higher than the right-binding power of `+`. Parsing this would result in the `2` being passed to the `infixParseFn` associated with the `*` token.

Notable is that in our parser, every token has the same right- and left-binding power. We simply use one value (in our `precedences` table) as both. What this value means changes depending on the context.

If an operator should be right-associative instead of left-associative (in the case of `+` that would result in `(a + (b + c))` instead of `((a + b) + c)`, then we must use a smaller "right-binding power" when parsing the "right arm" of the operator expression. If you think about the `++` and `--` operators in other languages, where they can be used in a pre- and a postfix position, you can see why it's sometimes useful to have differing left- and right-binding powers for operators.

Since we did not define separate right- and left-binding powers for operators, but only use one value, we can't just change a definition to achieve this. But, as an example, to make `+` right-associate we can decrement its precedence when calling `parseExpression`:

```
// parser/parser.go

func (p *Parser) parseInfixExpression(left ast.Expression) ast.Expression {
    expression := &ast.InfixExpression{
        Token:    p.curToken,
        Operator: p.curToken.Literal,
        Left:     left,
    }

    precedence := p.curPrecedence()
    p.nextToken()
    expression.Right = p.parseExpression(precedence)
    //                                   ^^^ decrement here for right-associativity

    return expression
}
```

For demonstration purposes, let's change this method for a minute and see what happens:

```
// parser/parser.go

func (p *Parser) parseInfixExpression(left ast.Expression) ast.Expression {
    expression := &ast.InfixExpression{
        Token:    p.curToken,
        Operator: p.curToken.Literal,
        Left:     left,
    }

    precedence := p.curPrecedence()
```

```
    p.nextToken()

    if expression.Operator == "+" {
        expression.Right = p.parseExpression(precedence - 1)
    } else {
        expression.Right = p.parseExpression(precedence)
    }

    return expression
}
```

With this change made, our tests tell us that + is officially right-associative:

```
$ go test -run TestOperatorPrecedenceParsing ./parser
--- FAIL: TestOperatorPrecedenceParsing (0.00s)
  parser_test.go:359: expected="((a + b) + c)", got="(a + (b + c))"
  parser_test.go:359: expected="((a + b) - c)", got="(a + (b - c))"
  parser_test.go:359: expected="(((a + (b * c)) + (d / e)) - f)",\
    got="(a + ((b * c) + ((d / e) - f)))"
FAIL
```

And that marks the end of our deep dive into the bowels of `parseExpression`. If you're still unsure and can't grasp how it works, don't worry, I felt the same. What really helped though was putting tracing statements in the methods of `Parser` to see what was happening when parsing certain expressions. In the folder of code accompanying this chapter I've included a file called `./parser/parser_tracing.go`, which we haven't looked at before. The file includes two function definitions that are really helpful when trying to understand what the parser does: `trace` and `untrace`. Use them like this:

```
// parser/parser.go

func (p *Parser) parseExpressionStatement() *ast.ExpressionStatement {
    defer untrace(trace("parseExpressionStatement"))
// [...]
}

func (p *Parser) parseExpression(precedence int) ast.Expression {
    defer untrace(trace("parseExpression"))
// [...]
}

func (p *Parser) parseIntegerLiteral() ast.Expression {
    defer untrace(trace("parseIntegerLiteral"))
// [...]
}

func (p *Parser) parsePrefixExpression() ast.Expression {
```

```
    defer untrace(trace("parsePrefixExpression"))
// [...]
}

func (p *Parser) parseInfixExpression(left ast.Expression) ast.Expression {
    defer untrace(trace("parseInfixExpression"))
// [...]
}
```

With these tracing statements included we can now use our parser and see what it does. Here is the output when parsing the expression statement `-1 * 2 + 3` in the test suite:

```
$ go test -v -run TestOperatorPrecedenceParsing ./parser
=== RUN   TestOperatorPrecedenceParsing
BEGIN parseExpressionStatement
        BEGIN parseExpression
                BEGIN parsePrefixExpression
                        BEGIN parseExpression
                                BEGIN parseIntegerLiteral
                                END parseIntegerLiteral
                        END parseExpression
                END parsePrefixExpression
                BEGIN parseInfixExpression
                        BEGIN parseExpression
                                BEGIN parseIntegerLiteral
                                END parseIntegerLiteral
                        END parseExpression
                END parseInfixExpression
                BEGIN parseInfixExpression
                        BEGIN parseExpression
                                BEGIN parseIntegerLiteral
                                END parseIntegerLiteral
                        END parseExpression
                END parseInfixExpression
        END parseExpression
END parseExpressionStatement
--- PASS: TestOperatorPrecedenceParsing (0.00s)
PASS
ok      monkey/parser   0.008s
```

2.8 - EXTENDING THE PARSER

Before we move on and extend our parser, we first need to clean up and extend our existing test suite. I won't bore you by listing the complete changes, but I will show you a few small helper functions that make the tests easier to understand.

We already have a `testIntegerLiteral` test helper. A second function called `testIdentifier` can clean up a lot of other tests:

```
// parser/parser_test.go

func testIdentifier(t *testing.T, exp ast.Expression, value string) bool {
    ident, ok := exp.(*ast.Identifier)
    if !ok {
        t.Errorf("exp not *ast.Identifier. got=%T", exp)
        return false
    }

    if ident.Value != value {
        t.Errorf("ident.Value not %s. got=%s", value, ident.Value)
        return false
    }

    if ident.TokenLiteral() != value {
        t.Errorf("ident.TokenLiteral not %s. got=%s", value,
            ident.TokenLiteral())
        return false
    }

    return true
}
```

The fun part is now using `testIntegerLiteral` and `testIdentifier` to build more generic helper functions:

```
// parser/parser_test.go

func testLiteralExpression(
    t *testing.T,
    exp ast.Expression,
    expected interface{},
) bool {
    switch v := expected.(type) {
    case int:
        return testIntegerLiteral(t, exp, int64(v))
    case int64:
        return testIntegerLiteral(t, exp, v)
    case string:
        return testIdentifier(t, exp, v)
    }
    t.Errorf("type of exp not handled. got=%T", exp)
    return false
}

func testInfixExpression(t *testing.T, exp ast.Expression, left interface{},
```

```
    operator string, right interface{}) bool {

    opExp, ok := exp.(*ast.InfixExpression)
    if !ok {
        t.Errorf("exp is not ast.OperatorExpression. got=%T(%s)", exp, exp)
        return false
    }

    if !testLiteralExpression(t, opExp.Left, left) {
        return false
    }

    if opExp.Operator != operator {
        t.Errorf("exp.Operator is not '%s'. got=%q", operator, opExp.Operator)
        return false
    }

    if !testLiteralExpression(t, opExp.Right, right) {
        return false
    }

    return true
}
```

With these in place it's possible to write test code like this:

```
testInfixExpression(t, stmt.Expression, 5, "+", 10)
testInfixExpression(t, stmt.Expression, "alice", "*", "bob")
```

That makes it a lot easier to test properties of the ASTs produced by our parser. See `parser/parser_test.go` for the cleaned up and extended test suite.

BOOLEAN LITERALS

There are a few things in the Monkey programming language that we still need to implement in our parser and AST. Easiest are boolean literals. In Monkey we can use booleans in place of any other expression:

```
true;
false;
let foobar = true;
let barfoo = false;
```

Like identifiers and integer literals their AST representation is simple and small:

```
// ast/ast.go

type Boolean struct {
```

```go
	Token token.Token
	Value bool
}

func (b *Boolean) expressionNode()      {}
func (b *Boolean) TokenLiteral() string { return b.Token.Literal }
func (b *Boolean) String() string       { return b.Token.Literal }
```

The `Value` field can hold values of the type `bool`, which means that we're going to save either `true` or `false` in there (the Go `bool` values, not the Monkey literals).

With the AST node defined we can now add our tests. The single `TestBooleanExpression` test function is so similar to `TestIdentifierExpression` and `TestIntegerLiteralExpression` that I won't show it here. It's enough to show the error message which points us in the right direction as to how to implement boolean literal parsing:

```
$ go test ./parser
--- FAIL: TestBooleanExpression (0.00s)
  parser_test.go:470: parser has 1 errors
  parser_test.go:472: parser error: "no prefix parse function for true found"
FAIL
FAIL    monkey/parser   0.008s
```

Of course, yes. We need to register a `prefixParseFn` for `token.TRUE` and `token.FALSE` tokens.

```go
// parser/parser.go

func New(l *lexer.Lexer) *Parser {
// [...]
	p.registerPrefix(token.TRUE, p.parseBoolean)
	p.registerPrefix(token.FALSE, p.parseBoolean)
// [...]
}
```

And the `parseBoolean` method is exactly what you imagine it to be:

```go
// parser/parser.go

func (p *Parser) parseBoolean() ast.Expression {
	return &ast.Boolean{Token: p.curToken, Value: p.curTokenIs(token.TRUE)}
}
```

The only mildly interesting part about this method is the inlining of the `p.curTokenIs(token.TRUE)` call, which is not really interesting. Other than that it's straightforward, maybe even boring. Or in other words: the structure of our parser serves us well! That actually is one of the beauties of Pratt's approach: it's so easy to extend.

And boom! The tests are green:

```
$ go test ./parser
ok      monkey/parser   0.006s
```

But what's interesting is that we can now extend several tests to incorporate the newly implemented boolean literals. The first candidate is `TestOperatorPrecedenceParsing`, with its string comparison mechanism:

```go
// parser/parser_test.go

func TestOperatorPrecedenceParsing(t *testing.T) {
    tests := []struct {
        input    string
        expected string
    }{
// [...]
        {
            "true",
            "true",
        },
        {
            "false",
            "false",
        },
        {
            "3 > 5 == false",
            "((3 > 5) == false)",
        },
        {
            "3 < 5 == true",
            "((3 < 5) == true)",
        },
// [...]
}
```

We can test for boolean literals in even more tests by extending our `testLiteralExpression` helper and providing a new `testBooleanLiteral` function:

```go
// parser_test.go

func testLiteralExpression(
    t *testing.T,
    exp ast.Expression,
    expected interface{},
) bool {
    switch v := expected.(type) {
// [...]
    case bool:
```

```go
        return testBooleanLiteral(t, exp, v)
    }
// [...]
}

func testBooleanLiteral(t *testing.T, exp ast.Expression, value bool) bool {
    bo, ok := exp.(*ast.Boolean)
    if !ok {
        t.Errorf("exp not *ast.Boolean. got=%T", exp)
        return false
    }

    if bo.Value != value {
        t.Errorf("bo.Value not %t. got=%t", value, bo.Value)
        return false
    }

    if bo.TokenLiteral() != fmt.Sprintf("%t", value) {
        t.Errorf("bo.TokenLiteral not %t. got=%s",
            value, bo.TokenLiteral())
        return false
    }

    return true
}
```

Nothing surprising here, just another case in a switch statement and a new helper function. But with this in place, it's easy to extend `TestParsingInfixExpressions`:

```go
// parser/parser_test.go

func TestParsingInfixExpressions(t *testing.T) {
    infixTests := []struct {
        input      string
        leftValue  interface{}
        operator   string
        rightValue interface{}
    }{
// [...]
        {"true == true", true, "==", true},
        {"true != false", true, "!=", false},
        {"false == false", false, "==", false},
    }
// [...]

    if !testLiteralExpression(t, exp.Left, tt.leftValue) {
      return
    }
```

```go
        if !testLiteralExpression(t, exp.Right, tt.rightValue) {
            return
        }

    // [...]
}
```

And also TestParsingPrefixExpressions is easy to extend by just adding new entries to the test table:

```go
// parser/parser_test.go

func TestParsingPrefixExpressions(t *testing.T) {
    prefixTests := []struct {
        input    string
        operator string
        value    interface{}
    }{
// [...]
        {"!true;", "!", true},
        {"!false;", "!", false},
    }
// [...]
}
```

It's time to pat ourselves on the back! We implemented the parsing of booleans and extended our tests in a way that gives us more test coverage now and better tools later on. Good job!

GROUPED EXPRESSIONS

What we're about to see next is sometimes called "the greatest trick Vaughan Pratt ever pulled". Actually, no, I just lied there, nobody says that. But they should! I'm talking about parsing grouped expressions, of course. In Monkey we can group expression with parantheses to influence their precedence and thus the order in which they are evaluated in their context. We've seen the canonical example for this before:

```
(5 + 5) * 2;
```

The parentheses group the `5 + 5` expression in order to give them a higher precedence and position them deeper in the AST, resulting in the correct evaluation order for this mathematical expression.

Now you might be thinking *"Oh come on, not with the precedence stuff again! My head still hurts! This guy..."* and you contemplate whether to skip to the end of this chapter. Don't! You have to see this!

We're not going to write a unit test for grouped expressions, since they are not represented by a separate AST node type. Yes, that's right. We do not need to change our AST in order to parse grouped expressions correctly! What we're going to do instead is to extend our `TestOperatorPrecedenceParsing` test function to make sure that parentheses actually group expressions and have an effect on the resulting AST.

```go
// parser/parser_test.go

func TestOperatorPrecedenceParsing(t *testing.T) {
    tests := []struct {
        input    string
        expected string
    }{
// [...]
        {
            "1 + (2 + 3) + 4",
            "((1 + (2 + 3)) + 4)",
        },
        {
            "(5 + 5) * 2",
            "((5 + 5) * 2)",
        },
        {
            "2 / (5 + 5)",
            "(2 / (5 + 5))",
        },
        {
            "-(5 + 5)",
            "(-(5 + 5))",
        },
        {
            "!(true == true)",
            "(!(true == true))",
        },
    }

// [...]
}
```

They fail, as expected:

```
$ go test ./parser
--- FAIL: TestOperatorPrecedenceParsing (0.00s)
  parser_test.go:531: parser has 3 errors
  parser_test.go:533: parser error: "no prefix parse function for ( found"
  parser_test.go:533: parser error: "no prefix parse function for ) found"
```

```
  parser_test.go:533: parser error: "no prefix parse function for + found"
FAIL
FAIL    monkey/parser   0.007s
```

Here comes the mind-blowing part. In order to get these tests to pass, all we need to do is add this:

```go
// parser/parser.go

func New(l *lexer.Lexer) *Parser {
// [...]
    p.registerPrefix(token.LPAREN, p.parseGroupedExpression)
// [...]
}

func (p *Parser) parseGroupedExpression() ast.Expression {
    p.nextToken()

    exp := p.parseExpression(LOWEST)

    if !p.expectPeek(token.RPAREN) {
        return nil
    }

    return exp
}
```

And that's it! Yes, it really is. The tests pass and the parentheses work as expected by boosting the precedence of the enclosed expressions. The concept of associating token types with functions really shines here. That's all there is to it. There is nothing happening here that we haven't seen before.

I told you, didn't I? It's a great trick. With that said, let's keep some of the magic and move on.

IF EXPRESSIONS

In Monkey we can use `if` and `else` just like we did hundreds of times in other programming languages:

```
if (x > y) {
  return x;
} else {
  return y;
}
```

The `else` is optional and can be left out:

```
if (x > y) {
  return x;
}
```

That's all very familiar. In Monkey though, if-else-conditionals are expressions. That means that they produce a value and in the case of if expressions that's the last evaluated line. We don't need the return statements here:

```
let foobar = if (x > y) { x } else { y };
```

Explaining the structure of if-else-conditionals is probably not necessary, but just so we're clear on the naming, here it is:

```
if (<condition>) <consequence> else <alternative>
```

The braces are part of `consequence` and `alternative`, because both are block statements. Block statements are a series of statements (just like programs in Monkey) enclosed by an opening `{` and a closing `}`.

So far our recipe for success has been to "define AST nodes, write tests, make tests pass by writing parsing code, celebrate, pat ourselves on the back, congratulate each other, tell everyone" and, well, there's no reason to change it now.

Here is the definition of the `ast.IfExpression` AST node:

```
// ast/ast.go

type IfExpression struct {
	Token       token.Token // The 'if' token
	Condition   Expression
	Consequence *BlockStatement
	Alternative *BlockStatement
}

func (ie *IfExpression) expressionNode()      {}
func (ie *IfExpression) TokenLiteral() string { return ie.Token.Literal }
func (ie *IfExpression) String() string {
	var out bytes.Buffer

	out.WriteString("if")
	out.WriteString(ie.Condition.String())
	out.WriteString(" ")
	out.WriteString(ie.Consequence.String())

	if ie.Alternative != nil {
		out.WriteString("else ")
		out.WriteString(ie.Alternative.String())
	}
```

```go
    return out.String()
}
```

No surprises here. `ast.IfExpression` fulfills the `ast.Expression` interface and has three fields that can represent an if-else-conditional. `Condition` holds the condition, which can be any expression, and `Consequence` and `Alternative` point to the consequence and alternative of the conditional respectively. But they reference a new type, `ast.BlockStatement`. As we saw before, the consequence/alternative of an if-else-condition is just a series of statements. That's exactly what `ast.BlockStatement` represents:

```go
// ast/ast.go

type BlockStatement struct {
    Token      token.Token // the { token
    Statements []Statement
}

func (bs *BlockStatement) statementNode()       {}
func (bs *BlockStatement) TokenLiteral() string { return bs.Token.Literal }
func (bs *BlockStatement) String() string {
    var out bytes.Buffer

    for _, s := range bs.Statements {
        out.WriteString(s.String())
    }

    return out.String()
}
```

The next step in our recipe for success is to add a test. By now, we know the drill and the test looks familiar:

```go
// parser/parser_test.go

func TestIfExpression(t *testing.T) {
    input := `if (x < y) { x }`

    l := lexer.New(input)
    p := New(l)
    program := p.ParseProgram()
    checkParserErrors(t, p)

    if len(program.Statements) != 1 {
        t.Fatalf("program.Body does not contain %d statements. got=%d\n",
            1, len(program.Statements))
    }
```

```
    stmt, ok := program.Statements[0].(*ast.ExpressionStatement)
    if !ok {
        t.Fatalf("program.Statements[0] is not ast.ExpressionStatement. got=%T",
            program.Statements[0])
    }

    exp, ok := stmt.Expression.(*ast.IfExpression)
    if !ok {
        t.Fatalf("stmt.Expression is not ast.IfExpression. got=%T",
            stmt.Expression)
    }

    if !testInfixExpression(t, exp.Condition, "x", "<", "y") {
        return
    }

    if len(exp.Consequence.Statements) != 1 {
        t.Errorf("consequence is not 1 statements. got=%d\n",
            len(exp.Consequence.Statements))
    }

    consequence, ok := exp.Consequence.Statements[0].(*ast.ExpressionStatement)
    if !ok {
        t.Fatalf("Statements[0] is not ast.ExpressionStatement. got=%T",
            exp.Consequence.Statements[0])
    }

    if !testIdentifier(t, consequence.Expression, "x") {
        return
    }

    if exp.Alternative != nil {
        t.Errorf("exp.Alternative.Statements was not nil. got=%+v", exp.Alternative)
    }
}
```

I also added a `TestIfElseExpression` test function that uses the following test input:

```
if (x < y) { x } else { y }
```

In `TestIfElseExpression` there are additional assertions on the `Alternative` field of `*ast.IfExpression`. Both tests make assertions about the structure of the resulting `*ast.IfExpression` node and use the helper functions `testInfixExpression` and `testIdentifier` to keep the focus on the conditional itself but also make sure that the rest of our parser is correctly integrated.

Both tests fail with a lot of error messages. But we are familiar with all of them by now:

```
$ go test ./parser
--- FAIL: TestIfExpression (0.00s)
  parser_test.go:659: parser has 3 errors
  parser_test.go:661: parser error: "no prefix parse function for IF found"
  parser_test.go:661: parser error: "no prefix parse function for { found"
  parser_test.go:661: parser error: "no prefix parse function for } found"
--- FAIL: TestIfElseExpression (0.00s)
  parser_test.go:659: parser has 6 errors
  parser_test.go:661: parser error: "no prefix parse function for IF found"
  parser_test.go:661: parser error: "no prefix parse function for { found"
  parser_test.go:661: parser error: "no prefix parse function for } found"
  parser_test.go:661: parser error: "no prefix parse function for ELSE found"
  parser_test.go:661: parser error: "no prefix parse function for { found"
  parser_test.go:661: parser error: "no prefix parse function for } found"
FAIL
FAIL    monkey/parser   0.007s
```

We're going to start with the first failing test: `TestIfExpression`. Clearly, we need to register a `prefixParseFn` for `token.IF` tokens.

```go
// parser/parser.go

func New(l *lexer.Lexer) *Parser {
// [...]
    p.registerPrefix(token.IF, p.parseIfExpression)
// [...]
}

func (p *Parser) parseIfExpression() ast.Expression {
    expression := &ast.IfExpression{Token: p.curToken}

    if !p.expectPeek(token.LPAREN) {
        return nil
    }

    p.nextToken()
    expression.Condition = p.parseExpression(LOWEST)

    if !p.expectPeek(token.RPAREN) {
        return nil
    }

    if !p.expectPeek(token.LBRACE) {
        return nil
    }

    expression.Consequence = p.parseBlockStatement()
```

```
    return expression
}
```

In no other parsing function did we use `expectPeek` so extensively. There just wasn't a need. Here it makes sense. `expectPeek` adds an error to the parser if `p.peekToken` is not of the expected type, but if it is, then it advances the tokens by calling the `nextToken` method. That's exactly what we need here. We need there to be a `(` right after the `if` and if it's there we need to jump over it. The same goes for the `)` after the expression and the `{` that marks the beginning of a block statement.

This method also follows our parsing function protocol: the tokens get advanced just enough so that `parseBlockStatement` sits on the `{` with `p.curToken` being of type `token.LBRACE`. Here is `parseBlockStatement`:

```go
// parser/parser.go

func (p *Parser) parseBlockStatement() *ast.BlockStatement {
    block := &ast.BlockStatement{Token: p.curToken}
    block.Statements = []ast.Statement{}

    p.nextToken()

    for !p.curTokenIs(token.RBRACE) && !p.curTokenIs(token.EOF) {
        stmt := p.parseStatement()
        if stmt != nil {
            block.Statements = append(block.Statements, stmt)
        }
        p.nextToken()
    }

    return block
}
```

`parseBlockStatement` calls `parseStatement` until it encounters either a `}`, which signifies the end of the block statement, or a `token.EOF`, which tells us that there's no more tokens left to parse. In that case, we can't successfully parse the block statement and there's no need to keep on calling `parseStatement` in an endless loop.

This looks really similar to our top-level `ParseProgram` method, where we also call `parseStatement` repeatedly until we encounter an "end token", which in the case of `ParseProgram` is just the `token.EOF` token. The duplication of the loop doesn't hurt though, so we leave these two methods be and instead take care of our tests:

```
$ go test ./parser
--- FAIL: TestIfElseExpression (0.00s)
  parser_test.go:659: parser has 3 errors
```

```
    parser_test.go:661: parser error: "no prefix parse function for ELSE found"
    parser_test.go:661: parser error: "no prefix parse function for { found"
    parser_test.go:661: parser error: "no prefix parse function for } found"
FAIL
FAIL    monkey/parser   0.007s
```

`TestIfExpression` passes and `TestIfElseExpression` does not, exactly as expected. Now, in order to support the `else` part of an if-else-condition, we need to check if it even exists and if so we need to parse the block statement that comes directly after the `else`:

```go
// parser/parser.go

func (p *Parser) parseIfExpression() ast.Expression {
// [...]
    expression.Consequence = p.parseBlockStatement()

    if p.peekTokenIs(token.ELSE) {
        p.nextToken()

        if !p.expectPeek(token.LBRACE) {
            return nil
        }

        expression.Alternative = p.parseBlockStatement()
    }

    return expression
}
```

That's all there is to it. The whole part of this method is constructed in a way that allows an optional `else` but doesn't add a parser error if there is none. After we parse the consequence-block-statement we check if the next token is a `token.ELSE` token. Remember, at the end of `parseBlockStatement` we're sitting on the `}`. If we have a `token.ELSE`, we advance the tokens two times. The first time with a call to `nextToken`, since we already know that the `p.peekToken` is the `else`. Then with a call to `expectPeek` since now the next token has to be the opening brace of a block statement, otherwise the program is invalid.

Yes, parsing is prone to off-by-one errors. It's easy to forget advancing the tokens or make a wrong call to `nextToken`. Having a strict protocol that dictates how every parsing function has to advance tokens helps a lot. Luckily we also have a great test suite that lets us know everything works:

```
$ go test ./parser
ok      monkey/parser   0.007s
```

I don't think I have to tell you anymore: good job all around! We did it - again.

FUNCTION LITERALS

You may have noticed that the `parseIfExpression` method we just added has a lot more meat to it than any of the `prefixParseFns` or `infixParseFns` we wrote before. The main reason is that we had to work with many different token and expression types and even optional parts. What we're going to do next is similar in its difficulty and variety of involved token types. We're going to parse function literals.

In Monkey a function literal is how we define functions: which parameters they have and what the function does. Function literals look like this:

```
fn(x, y) {
  return x + y;
}
```

It starts with the keyword `fn`, followed by a list of parameters, followed by a block statement, which is the function's body, that gets executed when the function is called. The abstract structure of a function literal is this:

```
fn <parameters> <block statement>
```

We already know what block statements are and how to parse them. The parameters are new though, but not much more difficult to parse. They are just a list of identifiers that are comma-separated and surrounded by parentheses:

```
(<parameter one>, <parameter two>, <parameter three>, ...)
```

This list can also be empty:

```
fn() {
  return foobar + barfoo;
}
```

That's the structure of function literals. But what type of AST node are they? Expressions, of course! We can use function literals in every place where any other expression is valid. For example, here is a function literal as the expression in a let statement:

```
let myFunction = fn(x, y) { return x + y; }
```

And here is a function literal as the expression in a return statement inside another function literal:

```
fn() {
  return fn(x, y) { return x > y; };
}
```

Using a function literal as an argument when calling another function is also possible:

```
myFunc(x, y, fn(x, y) { return x > y; });
```

That does sound complicated, but it's not. One of the great things about our parser is that once we define function literals as expressions and provide a function to correctly parse them the rest works. Sounds amazing? I agree.

We just saw that the two main parts of a function literal are the list of parameters and the block statement that is the function's body. That's all we need to keep in mind when defining the AST node:

```
// ast/ast.go

type FunctionLiteral struct {
    Token      token.Token // The 'fn' token
    Parameters []*Identifier
    Body       *BlockStatement
}

func (fl *FunctionLiteral) expressionNode()      {}
func (fl *FunctionLiteral) TokenLiteral() string { return fl.Token.Literal }
func (fl *FunctionLiteral) String() string {
    var out bytes.Buffer

    params := []string{}
    for _, p := range fl.Parameters {
        params = append(params, p.String())
    }

    out.WriteString(fl.TokenLiteral())
    out.WriteString("(")
    out.WriteString(strings.Join(params, ", "))
    out.WriteString(") ")
    out.WriteString(fl.Body.String())

    return out.String()
}
```

The `Parameters` field is a slice of `*ast.Identifiers`, because that's all there is to it, and `Body` is an `*ast.BlockStatement`, which we saw and used before.

Here is the test, in which we can use our helper functions `testLiteralExpression` and `testInfixExpression` again:

```
// parser/parser_test.go

func TestFunctionLiteralParsing(t *testing.T) {
    input := `fn(x, y) { x + y; }`

    l := lexer.New(input)
```

```
    p := New(l)
    program := p.ParseProgram()
    checkParserErrors(t, p)

    if len(program.Statements) != 1 {
        t.Fatalf("program.Body does not contain %d statements. got=%d\n",
            1, len(program.Statements))
    }

    stmt, ok := program.Statements[0].(*ast.ExpressionStatement)
    if !ok {
        t.Fatalf("program.Statements[0] is not ast.ExpressionStatement. got=%T",
            program.Statements[0])
    }

    function, ok := stmt.Expression.(*ast.FunctionLiteral)
    if !ok {
        t.Fatalf("stmt.Expression is not ast.FunctionLiteral. got=%T",
            stmt.Expression)
    }

    if len(function.Parameters) != 2 {
        t.Fatalf("function literal parameters wrong. want 2, got=%d\n",
            len(function.Parameters))
    }

    testLiteralExpression(t, function.Parameters[0], "x")
    testLiteralExpression(t, function.Parameters[1], "y")

    if len(function.Body.Statements) != 1 {
        t.Fatalf("function.Body.Statements has not 1 statements. got=%d\n",
            len(function.Body.Statements))
    }

    bodyStmt, ok := function.Body.Statements[0].(*ast.ExpressionStatement)
    if !ok {
        t.Fatalf("function body stmt is not ast.ExpressionStatement. got=%T",
            function.Body.Statements[0])
    }

    testInfixExpression(t, bodyStmt.Expression, "x", "+", "y")
}
```

So, the test has three main parts: check that the `*ast.FunctionLiteral` is there, check that the parameter list is correct and make sure that the function body contains the correct statements. The last part is not strictly necessary, since we already tested parsing block statements before in our tests for `IfExpressions`. But I'm okay with duplicating some test assertions here that possibly alarm us when hooking up the parsing of block statements failed.

With only `ast.FunctionLiteral` defined and nothing changed in the parser, the tests fail:

```
$ go test ./parser
--- FAIL: TestFunctionLiteralParsing (0.00s)
  parser_test.go:755: parser has 6 errors
  parser_test.go:757: parser error: "no prefix parse function for FUNCTION found"
  parser_test.go:757: parser error: "expected next token to be ), got , instead"
  parser_test.go:757: parser error: "no prefix parse function for , found"
  parser_test.go:757: parser error: "no prefix parse function for ) found"
  parser_test.go:757: parser error: "no prefix parse function for { found"
  parser_test.go:757: parser error: "no prefix parse function for } found"
FAIL
FAIL    monkey/parser   0.007s
```

It's clear that we need to register a new `prefixParseFn` for `token.FUNCTION` tokens.

```go
// parser/parser.go

func New(l *lexer.Lexer) *Parser {
// [...]
    p.registerPrefix(token.FUNCTION, p.parseFunctionLiteral)
// [...]
}

func (p *Parser) parseFunctionLiteral() ast.Expression {
    lit := &ast.FunctionLiteral{Token: p.curToken}

    if !p.expectPeek(token.LPAREN) {
        return nil
    }

    lit.Parameters = p.parseFunctionParameters()

    if !p.expectPeek(token.LBRACE) {
        return nil
    }

    lit.Body = p.parseBlockStatement()

    return lit
}
```

The `parseFunctionParameters` method we use here to parse the literal's parameters looks like this:

```go
// parser/parser.go
```

```
func (p *Parser) parseFunctionParameters() []*ast.Identifier {
    identifiers := []*ast.Identifier{}

    if p.peekTokenIs(token.RPAREN) {
        p.nextToken()
        return identifiers
    }

    p.nextToken()

    ident := &ast.Identifier{Token: p.curToken, Value: p.curToken.Literal}
    identifiers = append(identifiers, ident)

    for p.peekTokenIs(token.COMMA) {
        p.nextToken()
        p.nextToken()
        ident := &ast.Identifier{Token: p.curToken, Value: p.curToken.Literal}
        identifiers = append(identifiers, ident)
    }

    if !p.expectPeek(token.RPAREN) {
        return nil
    }

    return identifiers
}
```

There's the heart of the matter. `parseFunctionParameters` constructs the slice of parameters by repeatedly building identifiers from the comma separated list. It also makes an early exit if the list is empty and it carefully handles lists of varying sizes.

For a method like this it really pays off to have another set of tests that check the edge cases: an empty parameter list, a list with one parameter and a list with multiple parameters.

```
// parser/parser_test.go

func TestFunctionParameterParsing(t *testing.T) {
    tests := []struct {
        input          string
        expectedParams []string
    }{
        {input: "fn() {};", expectedParams: []string{}},
        {input: "fn(x) {};", expectedParams: []string{"x"}},
        {input: "fn(x, y, z) {};", expectedParams: []string{"x", "y", "z"}},
    }
```

```go
    for _, tt := range tests {
        l := lexer.New(tt.input)
        p := New(l)
        program := p.ParseProgram()
        checkParserErrors(t, p)

        stmt := program.Statements[0].(*ast.ExpressionStatement)
        function := stmt.Expression.(*ast.FunctionLiteral)

        if len(function.Parameters) != len(tt.expectedParams) {
            t.Errorf("length parameters wrong. want %d, got=%d\n",
                len(tt.expectedParams), len(function.Parameters))
        }

        for i, ident := range tt.expectedParams {
            testLiteralExpression(t, function.Parameters[i], ident)
        }
    }
}
```

Both of these test functions now pass:

```
$ go test ./parser
ok      monkey/parser   0.007s
```

Function literals are in the bag! Sweet! There is only one last thing to do now before we can leave the parser and start talking about the evaluation of our AST.

Call Expressions

Now that we know how to parse function literals the next step is to parse the calling of a function: call expressions. Here is their structure:

```
<expression>(<comma separated expressions>)
```

What? Yup, that's it, but granted, a few examples are needed. Here is the normal call expression we all know:

```
add(2, 3)
```

Now think about this: the `add` is an identifier. And identifiers are expressions. The arguments `2` and `3` are expressions too - integer literals. But they don't have to be, the arguments are just a list of expressions:

```
add(2 + 2, 3 * 3 * 3)
```

That's valid, too. The first argument is the infix expression `2 + 2` and the second one is `3 * 3 * 3`. So far, so good. Now, let's look at the function that's being called here. In this case the function is bound to the identifier `add`. The identifier add returns this function when it's evaluated. That means, we could go straight to the source, skip the identifier and replace add with a function literal:

```
fn(x, y) { x + y; }(2, 3)
```

Yes, that's valid. We can also use function literals as arguments:

```
callsFunction(2, 3, fn(x, y) { x + y; });
```

Let's look at the structure again:

```
<expression>(<comma separated expressions>)
```

Call expressions consist of an expression that results in a function when evaluated and a list of expressions that are the arguments to this function call. As an AST node they look like this:

```
// ast/ast.go

type CallExpression struct {
    Token     token.Token // The '(' token
    Function  Expression  // Identifier or FunctionLiteral
    Arguments []Expression
}

func (ce *CallExpression) expressionNode()      {}
func (ce *CallExpression) TokenLiteral() string { return ce.Token.Literal }
func (ce *CallExpression) String() string {
    var out bytes.Buffer

    args := []string{}
    for _, a := range ce.Arguments {
        args = append(args, a.String())
    }

    out.WriteString(ce.Function.String())
    out.WriteString("(")
    out.WriteString(strings.Join(args, ", "))
    out.WriteString(")")

    return out.String()
}
```

The test case for call expressions is just like the rest of our test suite and makes assertions about the *ast.CallExpression structure:

```
// parser/parser_test.go

func TestCallExpressionParsing(t *testing.T) {
    input := "add(1, 2 * 3, 4 + 5);"
```

```go
    l := lexer.New(input)
    p := New(l)
    program := p.ParseProgram()
    checkParserErrors(t, p)

    if len(program.Statements) != 1 {
        t.Fatalf("program.Statements does not contain %d statements. got=%d\n",
            1, len(program.Statements))
    }

    stmt, ok := program.Statements[0].(*ast.ExpressionStatement)
    if !ok {
        t.Fatalf("stmt is not ast.ExpressionStatement. got=%T",
            program.Statements[0])
    }

    exp, ok := stmt.Expression.(*ast.CallExpression)
    if !ok {
        t.Fatalf("stmt.Expression is not ast.CallExpression. got=%T",
            stmt.Expression)
    }

    if !testIdentifier(t, exp.Function, "add") {
        return
    }

    if len(exp.Arguments) != 3 {
        t.Fatalf("wrong length of arguments. got=%d", len(exp.Arguments))
    }

    testLiteralExpression(t, exp.Arguments[0], 1)
    testInfixExpression(t, exp.Arguments[1], 2, "*", 3)
    testInfixExpression(t, exp.Arguments[2], 4, "+", 5)
}
```

As with function literals and parameter parsing it's also a good idea to add a separate test for the argument parsing. Just to make sure that every corner case works and is covered by a test. I added a `TestCallExpressionParameterParsing` test function that does exactly this. You can see it in the code for this chapter.

So far, so familiar. But now comes the twist. If we run the tests we get this error message:

```
$ go test ./parser
--- FAIL: TestCallExpressionParsing (0.00s)
  parser_test.go:853: parser has 4 errors
  parser_test.go:855: parser error: "expected next token to be ), got , instead"
  parser_test.go:855: parser error: "no prefix parse function for , found"
```

```
  parser_test.go:855: parser error: "no prefix parse function for , found"
  parser_test.go:855: parser error: "no prefix parse function for ) found"
FAIL
FAIL    monkey/parser   0.007s
```

Huh, that doesn't make a lot of sense. Why is there no error message telling us to register a `prefixParseFn` for call expressions? Because there *are no new token types* in call expressions. So what do we do instead of registering a `prefixParseFn`? Take at look at this:

```
add(2, 3);
```

The `add` is an identifier that's parsed by a `prefixParseFn`. And after the identifier comes a `token.LPAREN`, right between the identifier and the list of arguments, just in the middle, in infix position... Yes, we need to register an `infixParseFn` for `token.LPAREN`. This way we parse the expression that is the function (either an identifier, or a function literal), then check for an `infixParseFn` associated with `token.LPAREN` and call it with the already parsed expression as argument. And in this `infixParseFn` we can then parse the argument list. Perfect!

```
// parser/parser.go

func New(l *lexer.Lexer) *Parser {
// [...]
    p.registerInfix(token.LPAREN, p.parseCallExpression)
// [...]
}

func (p *Parser) parseCallExpression(function ast.Expression) ast.Expression {
    exp := &ast.CallExpression{Token: p.curToken, Function: function}
    exp.Arguments = p.parseCallArguments()
    return exp
}

func (p *Parser) parseCallArguments() []ast.Expression {
    args := []ast.Expression{}

    if p.peekTokenIs(token.RPAREN) {
        p.nextToken()
        return args
    }

    p.nextToken()
    args = append(args, p.parseExpression(LOWEST))

    for p.peekTokenIs(token.COMMA) {
        p.nextToken()
        p.nextToken()
```

```
        args = append(args, p.parseExpression(LOWEST))
    }

    if !p.expectPeek(token.RPAREN) {
        return nil
    }

    return args
}
```

parseCallExpression receives the already parsed function as argument and uses it to construct an *ast.CallExpression node. To parse the argument list we call parseCallArguments, which looks strikingly similar to parseFunctionParameters, except that it's more generic and returns a slice of ast.Expression and not *ast.Identifier.

There is nothing here we haven't seen before. All we did was register a new infixParseFn. The tests still fail though:

```
$ go test ./parser
--- FAIL: TestCallExpressionParsing (0.00s)
  parser_test.go:853: parser has 4 errors
  parser_test.go:855: parser error: "expected next token to be ), got , instead"
  parser_test.go:855: parser error: "no prefix parse function for , found"
  parser_test.go:855: parser error: "no prefix parse function for , found"
  parser_test.go:855: parser error: "no prefix parse function for ) found"
FAIL
FAIL    monkey/parser   0.007s
```

The reason that it still doesn't work is that the (in add(1, 2) acts like an infix operator now, but we haven't assigned a precedence to it. It doesn't have the right "stickiness" yet, so parseExpression doesn't return what we want. But call expressions have the highest precedence of all, so it's important that we fix our precedences table:

```
// parser/parser.go

var precedences = map[token.TokenType]int{
// [...]
    token.LPAREN:   CALL,
}
```

To make sure that call expressions really have the highest precedence we can just extend our TestOperatorPrecedenceParsing test function:

```
// parser/parser_test.go

func TestOperatorPrecedenceParsing(t *testing.T) {
    tests := []struct {
```

```
        input    string
        expected string
    }{
// [...]
        {
            "a + add(b * c) + d",
            "((a + add((b * c))) + d)",
        },
        {
            "add(a, b, 1, 2 * 3, 4 + 5, add(6, 7 * 8))",
            "add(a, b, 1, (2 * 3), (4 + 5), add(6, (7 * 8)))",
        },
        {
            "add(a + b + c * d / f + g)",
            "add((((a + b) + ((c * d) / f)) + g))",
        },
    }

// [...]
}
```

If we now run the tests again, we can see that all of them pass:

```
$ go test ./parser
ok      monkey/parser   0.008s
```

Yes, all of them: the unit test, the test for argument parsing and the precedence tests - wow! They all pass! And if that wasn't enough, here's some more good news: we are done. Yes, the parser is finished. Granted, we'll come back to it later, at the end of the book, to extend it once more. But for now: that's it! The AST is fully defined and the parser works - it's time to move on to the topic of evaluation.

Before we do that though, let's remove the TODOs we left in the code and extend our REPL to integrate the parser.

REMOVING TODOS

When we wrote the code that parses let and return statements we took a shortcut by skipping over the expressions:

```
// parser/parser.go

func (p *Parser) parseLetStatement() *ast.LetStatement {
    stmt := &ast.LetStatement{Token: p.curToken}

    if !p.expectPeek(token.IDENT) {
```

```go
        return nil
    }

    stmt.Name = &ast.Identifier{Token: p.curToken, Value: p.curToken.Literal}

    if !p.expectPeek(token.ASSIGN) {
        return nil
    }

    // TODO: We're skipping the expressions until we
    // encounter a semicolon
    for !p.curTokenIs(token.SEMICOLON) {
        p.nextToken()
    }

    return stmt
}
```

The same TODO sits in parseReturnStatement. It's time to get rid of them. No shortcuts. First of all, we need to extend our existing tests to make sure that the expressions, that are parsed as part of a let or return statement, are actually there. We do this by using our helper functions (that don't distract from the focus of the test) and different expression types, so we know that parseExpression is correctly integrated.

Here is what the TestLetStatement function looks like:

```go
// parser/parser_test.go

func TestLetStatements(t *testing.T) {
    tests := []struct {
        input              string
        expectedIdentifier string
        expectedValue      interface{}
    }{
        {"let x = 5;", "x", 5},
        {"let y = true;", "y", true},
        {"let foobar = y;", "foobar", "y"},
    }

    for _, tt := range tests {
        l := lexer.New(tt.input)
        p := New(l)
        program := p.ParseProgram()
        checkParserErrors(t, p)

        if len(program.Statements) != 1 {
            t.Fatalf("program.Statements does not contain 1 statements. got=%d",
```

```
                len(program.Statements))
        }

        stmt := program.Statements[0]
        if !testLetStatement(t, stmt, tt.expectedIdentifier) {
            return
        }

        val := stmt.(*ast.LetStatement).Value
        if !testLiteralExpression(t, val, tt.expectedValue) {
            return
        }
    }
}
```

The same needs to be done for `TestReturnStatements`. And the fix is trivial, since we did such great work before. We merely need to hook up `parseExpression` in `parseReturnStatement` and `parseLetStatement`. And we also need to take care of optional semicolons, which we already know how to do from `parseExpressionStatement`. The updated, fully-working versions of `parseReturnStatement` and `parseLetStatement` look like this:

```
// parser/parser.go

func (p *Parser) parseReturnStatement() *ast.ReturnStatement {
    stmt := &ast.ReturnStatement{Token: p.curToken}

    p.nextToken()

    stmt.ReturnValue = p.parseExpression(LOWEST)

    if p.peekTokenIs(token.SEMICOLON) {
        p.nextToken()
    }

    return stmt
}

func (p *Parser) parseLetStatement() *ast.LetStatement {
    stmt := &ast.LetStatement{Token: p.curToken}

    if !p.expectPeek(token.IDENT) {
        return nil
    }

    stmt.Name = &ast.Identifier{Token: p.curToken, Value: p.curToken.Literal}

    if !p.expectPeek(token.ASSIGN) {
```

```
        return nil
    }

    p.nextToken()

    stmt.Value = p.parseExpression(LOWEST)

    if p.peekTokenIs(token.SEMICOLON) {
        p.nextToken()
    }

    return stmt
}
```

Ah! All TODOs removed from the code. Let's take this parser for a test drive.

2.9 - Read-Parse-Print-Loop

Up until now our REPL was more of a RLPL, a read-lex-print-loop. We don't know how to evaluate code yet, so replacing the "lex" with "evaluate" is still out of the question. But what we most certainly know by now is parsing. It's time to replace the "lex" with "parse" and build a RPPL.

```
// repl/repl.go

func Start(in io.Reader, out io.Writer) {
    scanner := bufio.NewScanner(in)

    for {
        fmt.Printf(PROMPT)
        scanned := scanner.Scan()
        if !scanned {
            return
        }

        line := scanner.Text()
        l := lexer.New(line)
        p := parser.New(l)

        program := p.ParseProgram()
        if len(p.Errors()) != 0 {
            printParserErrors(out, p.Errors())
            continue
        }

        io.WriteString(out, program.String())
```

```
        io.WriteString(out, "\n")
    }
}

func printParserErrors(out io.Writer, errors []string) {
    for _, msg := range errors {
        io.WriteString(out, "\t"+msg+"\n")
    }
}
```

Here we extend our loop to parse the line we just entered in the REPL. The output of the parser, an `*ast.Program`, is then printed by calling its `String` method, which recursively calls the `String` method of all statements belonging to that program. Now we can take the parser for a spin - interactively on the command line:

```
$ go run main.go
Hello mrnugget! This is the Monkey programming language!
Feel free to type in commands
>> let x = 1 * 2 * 3 * 4 * 5
let x = ((((1 * 2) * 3) * 4) * 5);
>> x * y / 2 + 3 * 8 - 123
((((x * y) / 2) + (3 * 8)) - 123)
>> true == false
(true == false)
>>
```

Sweet! Now instead of calling `String` we could use any string-based representation of the AST to output here. We could add a `PrettyPrint` method that prints the type of the AST node and intends its child nodes correctly, or we could use ASCII color codes, or we could print an ASCII graph, or... The point is: the sky is the limit.

But our RPPL still has a huge drawback. Here is what happens when the parser runs into an error:

```
$ go run main.go
Hello mrnugget! This is the Monkey programming language!
Feel free to type in commands
>> let x 12 * 3;
        expected next token to be =, got INT instead
>>
```

That's not a very nice error message. I mean, it does the job, yes, but it's not very nice, is it? The Monkey programming language deserves better. Here is a more user-friendly `printParseError` function that enhances the user-experience:

```
// repl/repl.go

const MONKEY_FACE = `            __,__
```

```
   .--.  .-"     "-.  .--.
  / .. \/  .-. .-.  \/ .. \
 | |  '|  /   Y   \  |'  | |
 | \   \  \ 0 | 0 /  /   / |
  \ '- ,\.-"""""""-./, -' /
   ''-' /_   ^ ^   _\ '-''
       |  \._   _./  |
       \   \ '~' /   /
        '._ '-=-' _.'
           '-----'
`

func printParserErrors(out io.Writer, errors []string) {
    io.WriteString(out, MONKEY_FACE)
    io.WriteString(out, "Woops! We ran into some monkey business here!\n")
    io.WriteString(out, " parser errors:\n")
    for _, msg := range errors {
        io.WriteString(out, "\t"+msg+"\n")
    }
}
```

That's better! If we now run into any parser errors, we get to see a monkey, which, really, is more than anyone could ask for:

```
$ go run main.go
Hello mrnugget! This is the Monkey programming language!
Feel free to type in commands
>> let x 12 * 3
            __,__
   .--.  .-"     "-.  .--.
  / .. \/  .-. .-.  \/ .. \
 | |  '|  /   Y   \  |'  | |
 | \   \  \ 0 | 0 /  /   / |
  \ '- ,\.-"""""""-./, -' /
   ''-' /_   ^ ^   _\ '-''
       |  \._   _./  |
       \   \ '~' /   /
        '._ '-=-' _.'
           '-----'
Woops! We ran into some monkey business here!
 parser errors:
	expected next token to be =, got INT instead
>>
```

On second thought... Anyway, it's time to start evaluating our AST.

CHAPTER 3

EVALUATION

3.1 - GIVING MEANING TO SYMBOLS

We are finally here. Evaluation. The E in REPL and the last thing an interpreter has to do when processing source code. This is where code becomes meaningful. Without evaluation an expression like `1 + 2` is just a series of characters, tokens, or a tree structure that represents this expression. It doesn't mean anything. Evaluated, of course, `1 + 2` becomes `3`. `5 > 1` becomes `true`, `5 < 1` becomes `false` and `puts("Hello World!")` becomes the friendly message we all know.

The evaluation process of an interpreter defines how the programming language being interpreted works.

```
let num = 5;
if (num) {
  return a;
} else {
  return b;
}
```

Whether this returns `a` or `b` depends on the decision of the interpreter's evaluation process whether the integer `5` is truthy or not. In some languages it's truthy, in others we'd need to use an expression that produces a boolean like `5 != 0`.

Consider this:

```
let one = fn() {
  printLine("one");
  return 1;
};

let two = fn() {
```

```
    printLine("two");
    return 2;
};

add(one(), two());
```

Does this first output `one` and then `two` or the other way around? It depends on the specification of the language and ultimately on the implementation of its interpreter and in which order it evaluates the arguments in a call expression.

In this chapter there will be many more small choices like these, where we get to decide how Monkey is going to work and how our interpreter evaluates Monkey source code.

Maybe you're skeptical, after I told you that writing a parser was fun, but trust me: this is the best part. This is where the Monkey programming language comes to life, where source code quickens and starts to breathe.

3.2 - Strategies of Evaluation

Evaluation is also where interpreter implementations (regardless of which language they're interpreting) diverge the most. There are a lot of different strategies to choose from when evaluating source code. I've already hinted at this in the introduction of this book, where we took a brief look at different interpreter architectures. Now that we're here, AST in hand, the question of what to do with it and how to evaluate this shiny tree of ours is more relevant than ever, so looking at different options again is worthwhile.

Before we start, though, it's also worth noting again that the line between interpreters and compilers is a blurry one. The notion of an interpreter as something that doesn't leave executable artifacts behind (in contrast to a compiler, which does just that) gets fuzzy real fast when looking at the implementations of real-world and highly-optimized programming languages.

With that said, the most obvious and classical choice of what to do with the AST is to just interpret it. Traverse the AST, visit each node and do what the node signifies: print a string, add two numbers, execute a function's body - all on the fly. Interpreters working this way are called "tree-walking interpreters" and are the archetype of interpreters. Sometimes their evaluation step is preceded by small optimizations that rewrite the AST (e.g. remove unused variable bindings) or convert it into another intermediate representation (IR) that's more suitable for recursive and repeated evaluation.

Other interpreters also traverse the AST, but instead of interpreting the AST itself they first convert it to bytecode. Bytecode is another IR of the AST and a really dense one at that. The exact format and of which opcodes (the instructions that make up the bytecode) it's composed of varies and depends on the guest and host programming languages. In general though, the opcodes are pretty similar to the mnemonics of most assembly languages; it's a safe bet to say that most bytecode definitions contain opcodes for `push` and `pop` to do stack operations. But bytecode is not native machine code, nor is it assembly language. It can't and won't be executed by the operating system and the CPU of the machine the interpreter is running on. Instead it's interpreted by a virtual machine, that's part of the interpreter. Just like VMWare and VirtualBox emulate real machines and CPUs, these virtual machines emulate a machine that understands this particular bytecode format. This approach can yield great performance benefits.

A variation of this strategy doesn't involve an AST at all. Instead of building an AST the parser emits bytecode directly. Now, are we still talking about interpreters or compilers? Isn't emitting bytecode that gets then interpreted (or should we say "executed"?) a form of compilation? I told you: the line becomes blurry. And to make it even more fuzzy, consider this: some implementations of programming languages parse the source code, build an AST and convert this AST to bytecode. But instead of executing the operations specified by the bytecode directly in a virtual machine, the virtual machine then compiles the bytecode to native machine code, right before its executed - just in time. That's called a JIT (for "just in time") interpreter/compiler.

Others skip the compilation to bytecode. They recursively traverse the AST but before executing a particular branch of it the node is compiled to native machine code. And then executed. Again, "just in time".

A slight variation of this is a mixed mode of interpretation where the interpreter recursively evaluates the AST and only after evaluating a particular branch of the AST multiple times does it compile the branch to machine code.

Amazing, isn't it? So many different ways to go about this task of evaluation, so many twists and variations.

The choice of which strategy to choose largely depends on performance and portability needs, the programming language that's being interpreted and how far you're willing to go. A tree-walking interpreter that recursively evaluates an AST is probably the slowest of all approaches, but easy to build, extend, reason about and as portable as the language it's implemented in.

An interpreter that compiles to bytecode and uses a virtual machine to evaluate said bytecode is going to be a lot faster. But more complicated and harder to build, too. Throw JIT compilation to machine code into the mix and now you also need to support multiple machine architectures if you want the interpreter to work on both ARM and x86 CPUs.

All of these approaches can be found in real-world programming languages. And most of the time the chosen approach changed with the lifetime of the language. Ruby is a great example here. Up to and including version 1.8 the interpreter was a tree-walking interpreter, executing the AST while traversing it. But with version 1.9 came the switch to a virtual machine architecture. Now the Ruby interpreter parses source code, builds an AST and then compiles this AST into bytecode, which gets then executed in a virtual machine. The increase in performance was huge.

The WebKit JavaScript engine JavaScriptCore and its interpreter named "Squirrelfish" also used AST walking and direct execution as its approach. Then in 2008 came the switch to a virtual machine and bytecode interpretation. Nowadays the engine has four (!) different stages of JIT compilation, which kick in at different times in the lifetime of the interpreted program – depending on which part of the program needs the best performance.

Another example is Lua. The main implementation of the Lua programming language started out as an interpreter that compiles to bytecode and executes the bytecode in a register-based virtual machine. 12 years after its first release another implementation of the language was born: LuaJIT. The clear goal of Mike Pall, the creator of LuaJIT, was to create the fastest Lua implementation possible. And he did. By JIT compiling a dense bytecode format to highly-optimized machine code for different architectures the LuaJIT implementation beats the original Lua in every benchmark. And not just by a tiny bit, no; it's sometimes 50 times faster.

So, a lot of interpreters started out small with room for improvement. That's exactly what we're going to do. There are a lot of ways to build a faster interpreter, but not necessarily one that's easier to understand. We are here to learn, to understand and to be able to build upon our work.

3.3 - A Tree-Walking Interpreter

What we're going to build is a tree-walking interpreter. We're going to take the AST our parser builds for us and interpret it "on the fly", without any preprocessing or compilation step.

Our interpreter will be a lot like a classic Lisp interpreter. The design we're going to use is heavily inspired by the interpreter presented in "The Structure and Interpretation of Computer Programs" (SICP), especially its usage of environments. That doesn't mean that we're copying one particular interpreter, no, we're rather using a blueprint that you can see in lot of other interpreters too, if you squint hard enough. There are really good reasons for the prevalence of this particular design: it's the easiest way to get started, it's easy to understand and to extend later on.

We only need two things really: a tree-walking evaluator and a way to represent Monkey values in our host language Go. Evaluator sounds mighty and grand, but it will be just one function called "eval". Its job is to evaluate the AST. Here is a pseudocode version that illustrates what "evaluating on the fly" and "tree-walking" mean in the context of interpretation:

```
function eval(astNode) {
  if (astNode is integerliteral) {
    return astNode.integerValue

  } else if (astNode is booleanLiteral) {
    return astNode.booleanValue

  } else if (astNode is infixExpression) {

    leftEvaluated = eval(astNode.Left)
    rightEvaluated = eval(astNode.Right)

    if astNode.Operator == "+" {
      return leftEvaluated + rightEvaluated
    } else if ast.Operator == "-" {
      return leftEvaluated - rightEvaluated
    }
  }
}
```

As you can see, `eval` is recursive. When `astNode is infixExpression` is true, `eval` calls itself again two times to evaluate the left and the right operands of the infix expression. This in turn may lead to the evaluation of another infix expression or an integer literal or a boolean literal or an identifier... We've already seen recursion at work when building and testing the AST. The same concepts apply here, except that we're evaluating the tree and not building it.

Looking at this snippet of pseudocode you can probably imagine how easy it is to extend this function. That comes to our advantage. We're going to build up our own `Eval` function piece by piece and add new branches and capabilities as we go along and extend our interpreter.

But the most interesting lines of this snippet are the return statements. What do they return? Here are two lines that bind the return value of a call to `eval` to names:

```
leftEvaluated = eval(astNode.Left)
```

```
rightEvaluated = eval(astNode.Right)
```

What does `eval` return here? Of which type are the return values? The answer to these questions is the same as the one for "what kind of internal object system will our interpreter have?"

3.4 - REPRESENTING OBJECTS

Wait, what? You never said Monkey was object oriented! Yes, I never did and it's not. *Why do we need "a object system" then?* Call it a "value system" or "object representation" then. The point is, we need to define what our "eval" function returns. We need a system that can represent the values our AST represents or values that we generate when evaluating the AST in memory.

Let's say we're evaluating the following Monkey code:

```
let a = 5;
// [...]
a + a;
```

As you can see, we're binding the integer literal `5` to the name `a`. Then things happen. It doesn't matter what. What matters is that when we come across the `a + a` expression later we need to access the value `a` is bound to. In order to evaluate `a + a` we need to get to the `5`. In the AST it's represented as an `*ast.IntegerLiteral`, but how are we going to keep track of and represent the `5` while we're evaluating the rest of the AST?

There are a lot of different choices when building an internal representation of values in an interpreted language. And there is a lot of wisdom about this topic spread throughout the codebases of the world's interpreters and compilers. Each interpreter has its own way to represent values, always slightly differing from the solution that came before, adjusted for the requirements of the interpreted language.

Some use native types (integers, booleans, etc.) of the host language to represent values in the interpreted language, not wrapped in anything. In other languages values/objects are represented only as pointers, whereas in some programming languages native types and pointers are mixed.

Why the variety? For one, the host languages differ. How you represent a string of your interpreted language depends on how a string can be represented in the language the interpreter is implemented in. An interpreter written in Ruby can't represent values the same way an interpreter written in C can.

And not only do the host languages differ, but the languages being interpreted do too. Some interpreted languages may only need representations of primitive data types, like integers, characters or bytes. But in others you'll have lists, dictionaries, functions or compound data types. These differences lead to highly different requirements in regards to value representation.

Besides the host language and the interpreted language, the biggest influence on the design and implementation of value representations are the resulting execution speed and the memory consumption while evaluating programs. If you want to build a fast interpreter you can't get away with a slow and bloated object system. And if you're going to write your own garbage collector, you need to think about how it'll keep track of the values in the system. But, on the other hand, if you don't care about performance, then it does make sense to keep things simple and easy to understand until further requirements arise.

The point is this: there are a lot of different ways to represent values of the interpreted languages in the host language. The best (and maybe the only) way to learn about these different representations is to actually read through the source code of some popular interpreters. I heartily recommended the Wren source code[1], which includes two types of value representation, enabled/disabled by using a compiler flag.

Besides the representation of values inside the host language there is also the matter of how to expose these values and their representation to the user of the interpreted language. What does the "public API" of these values look like?

Java, for example, offers both "primitive data types" (int, byte, short, long, float, double, boolean, char) and reference types to the user. The primitive data types do not have a huge representation inside the Java implementation, they closely map to their native counterparts. Reference types on the other hand are references to compound data structures defined in the host language.

In Ruby the user doesn't have access to "primitive data types", nothing like a native value type exists because everything is an object and thus wrapped inside an internal representation. Internally Ruby doesn't distinguish between a byte and an instance of the class `Pizza`: both are the same value type, wrapping different values.

There are a myriad ways to expose data to users of programming languages. Which one to choose depends on the language design and also, again, on performance requirements. If you don't care about performance everything goes. But if you do, you need to make some smart decisions to achieve your goals.

---

[1] https://github.com/munificent/wren

FOUNDATION OF OUR OBJECT SYSTEM

Carefree as we still are about the performance of our Monkey interpreter, we choose the easy way: we're going to represent every value we encounter when evaluating Monkey source code as an `Object`, an interface of our design. Every value will be wrapped inside a struct, which fulfills this `Object` interface.

In a new `object` package we define the `Object` interface and the `ObjectType` type:

```
// object/object.go

package object

type ObjectType string

type Object interface {
    Type() ObjectType
    Inspect() string
}
```

That's pretty simple and looks a lot like what we did in the `token` package with the `Token` and `TokenType` types. Except that instead of being a struct like `Token` the `Object` type is an interface. The reason is that every value needs a different internal representation and it's easier to define two different struct types than trying to fit booleans and integers into the same struct field.

At the moment we only have three data types in our Monkey interpreter: null, booleans and integers. Let's start with implementing the integer representation and build up our object system.

INTEGERS

The `object.Integer` type is as small as you'd expect it to be:

```
// object/object.go

import (
    "fmt"
)

type Integer struct {
    Value int64
}

func (i *Integer) Inspect() string { return fmt.Sprintf("%d", i.Value) }
```

Whenever we encounter an integer literal in the source code we first turn it into an `ast.IntegerLiteral` and then, when evaluating that AST node, we turn it into an `object.Integer`, saving the value inside our struct and passing around a reference to this struct.

In order for `object.Integer` to fulfill the `object.Object` interface, it still needs a `Type()` method that returns its `ObjectType`. Just like we did with `token.TokenType` we define constants for each `ObjectType`:

```
// object/object.go

import "fmt"

type ObjectType string

const (
    INTEGER_OBJ = "INTEGER"
)
```

As I said, this is pretty much what we did in the `token` package. And with that in place we can add the `Type()` method to `*object.Integer`:

```
// object/object.go

func (i *Integer) Type() ObjectType { return INTEGER_OBJ }
```

And we're done with `Integer`! Onto another data type: booleans.

BOOLEANS

If you were expecting big things of this section, I'm sorry to disappoint. `object.Boolean` is as tiny as it gets:

```
// object/object.go

const (
// [...]
    BOOLEAN_OBJ = "BOOLEAN"
)

type Boolean struct {
    Value bool
}

func (b *Boolean) Type() ObjectType { return BOOLEAN_OBJ }
func (b *Boolean) Inspect() string  { return fmt.Sprintf("%t", b.Value) }
```

Just a struct that wraps a single value, a `bool`.

We're close to finishing the foundation of our object system. The last thing we need to do now, before we can start with our `Eval` function, is to represent a value that isn't there.

NULL

Tony Hoare introduced null references to the ALGOL W language in 1965 and called this his "billion-dollar mistake"[2]. Since their introduction countless systems have crashed because of references to "null", a value that represents the absence of a value. Null (or "nil" as in some languages) doesn't have the best reputation, to say the least.

I debated with myself whether Monkey should have null. On one hand, yes, the language would be safer to use if it doesn't allow null or null references. But on the other, we're not trying to reinvent the wheel, but to learn something. And I found that having null at my disposal lead me to think twice whenever there was a chance to use it. Kinda like having something explosive in your car leads you to driving slower and more carefully. It really made me appreciate the choices that go into the design of a programming language. That's something I consider worthwhile. So let's implement the `Null` type and keep a close look and steady hand when using it later on.

```
// object/object.go

const (
// [...]
	NULL_OBJ  = "NULL"
)

type Null struct{}

func (n *Null) Type() ObjectType { return NULL_OBJ }
func (n *Null) Inspect() string  { return "null" }
```

`object.Null` is a struct just like `object.Boolean` and `object.Integer`, except that it doesn't wrap any value. It represents the absence of any value.

With `object.Null` added, our object system is now capable of representing boolean, integer and null values. That's more than enough to get started with `Eval`.

[2]https://www.infoq.com/presentations/Null-References-The-Billion-Dollar-Mistake-Tony-Hoare

3.5 - Evaluating Expressions

Alright, here we go. Let's start writing `Eval`! We have our AST and we have a new object system, that allows us to keep track of values we encounter when executing Monkey source code. It's time to finally evaluate the AST.

Here is what the signature of `Eval` will look like in its first version:

```
func Eval(node ast.Node) object.Object
```

`Eval` will take an `ast.Node` as input and return an `object.Object`. Remember that every node we defined in the `ast` package fulfills the `ast.Node` interface and can thus be passed to `Eval`. This allows us to use `Eval` recursively and call itself while evaluating a part of the AST. Each AST node needs a different form of evaluation and `Eval` is the place where we decide what these forms look like. As an example, let's say that we pass an `*ast.Program` node to `Eval`. What `Eval` should do then is to evaluate each of `*ast.Program.Statements` by calling itself with a single statement. The return value of the outer call to `Eval` is the return value of the last call.

We're going to start by implementing self-evaluating expressions. That's what we call literals in the land of `Eval`. Specifically, boolean and integer literals. They are the constructs in Monkey that are easiest to evaluate, because they evaluate to themselves. If I type `5` into my REPL then `5` is also what should come out. And if I type in `true` then `true` is what I want.

Sounds easy enough? It is! So, let's turn "type in 5, get back 5" into reality.

Integer Literals

Before writing any code though, what does this mean exactly? We're given a single expression statement as input, which only contains an integer literal, and want to evaluate it so that the integer itself is returned.

Translated into the language of our system, it means that, given an `*ast.IntegerLiteral`, our `Eval` function should return an `*object.Integer` whose `Value` field contains the same integer as `*ast.IntegerLiteral.Value`.

We can easily write a test for this in our new `evaluator` package:

```
// evaluator/evaluator_test.go

package evaluator

import (
    "monkey/lexer"
    "monkey/object"
```

```go
    "monkey/parser"
    "testing"
)

func TestEvalIntegerExpression(t *testing.T) {
    tests := []struct {
        input    string
        expected int64
    }{
        {"5", 5},
        {"10", 10},
    }

    for _, tt := range tests {
        evaluated := testEval(tt.input)
        testIntegerObject(t, evaluated, tt.expected)
    }
}

func testEval(input string) object.Object {
    l := lexer.New(input)
    p := parser.New(l)
    program := p.ParseProgram()

    return Eval(program)
}

func testIntegerObject(t *testing.T, obj object.Object, expected int64) bool {
    result, ok := obj.(*object.Integer)
    if !ok {
        t.Errorf("object is not Integer. got=%T (%+v)", obj, obj)
        return false
    }
    if result.Value != expected {
        t.Errorf("object has wrong value. got=%d, want=%d",
            result.Value, expected)
        return false
    }

    return true
}
```

That's a lot of code for such a small test, isn't it? As with our parser tests, we're building up our testing infrastructure here. The `TestEvalIntegerExpression` test will need to grow and its current structure makes this really easy. The `testEval` and `testIntegerObject` will also find a lot of use.

The heart of the test is the call to `Eval` inside `testEval`. We take our input, pass it to the lexer, pass the lexer to the parser and get back an AST. And then, this is new, we pass the AST to `Eval`. The return value of `Eval` is what we make assertions about. In this case, we want the return value to be an `*object.Integer` with the correct `.Value`. In other words: we want `5` to evaluate to `5`.

Of course, the test fails because we haven't defined `Eval` yet. But we already know that `Eval` should take an `ast.Node` as argument and return an `object.Object`. And whenever it encounters an `*ast.IntegerLiteral` it should return an `*object.Integer` with the correct `.Value`. Turning this into code and defining our new `Eval` with this behaviour in the `evaluator` package, we get this:

```go
// evaluator/evaluator.go

package evaluator

import (
    "monkey/ast"
    "monkey/object"
)

func Eval(node ast.Node) object.Object {
    switch node := node.(type) {
    case *ast.IntegerLiteral:
        return &object.Integer{Value: node.Value}
    }

    return nil
}
```

Nothing surprising here, it does just what we said it should. Except that it doesn't work. The test still fails because `Eval` returns `nil` instead of an `*object.Integer`.

```
$ go test ./evaluator
--- FAIL: TestEvalIntegerExpression (0.00s)
  evaluator_test.go:36: object is not Integer. got=<nil> (<nil>)
  evaluator_test.go:36: object is not Integer. got=<nil> (<nil>)
FAIL
FAIL    monkey/evaluator        0.006s
```

The reason for this failure is that we never encounter an `*ast.IntegerLiteral` in `Eval`. We don't traverse the AST. We should always start at the top of the tree, receiving an `*ast.Program`, and then traverse every node in it. And that's exactly what we're not doing here. We're just waiting for an `*ast.IntegerLiteral`. The fix is to actually traverse the tree and evaluate every statement of the `*ast.Program`:

```go
// evaluator/evaluator.go

func Eval(node ast.Node) object.Object {
```

```
    switch node := node.(type) {

    // Statements
    case *ast.Program:
        return evalStatements(node.Statements)

    case *ast.ExpressionStatement:
        return Eval(node.Expression)

    // Expressions
    case *ast.IntegerLiteral:
        return &object.Integer{Value: node.Value}
    }

    return nil
}

func evalStatements(stmts []ast.Statement) object.Object {
    var result object.Object

    for _, statement := range stmts {
        result = Eval(statement)
    }

    return result
}
```

With this changes we evaluate every statement in a Monkey program. And if the statement is an `*ast.ExpressionStatement` we evaluate its expression. That mirrors the AST structure we get from a one line input like `5`: a program that consists of one statement, an expression statement (not a return statement and not a let statement) with an integer literal as its expression.

```
$ go test ./evaluator
ok      monkey/evaluator        0.006s
```

Alright, the tests pass! We can evaluate integer literals! *Hey everyone, if we type in a number, a number comes out and it only took us a couple thousand lines of code and tests to do so!* Okay, granted, it doesn't look like much. But it's a start. We're beginning to see how evaluation works and how we can extend our evaluator. The structure of `Eval` won't change, we'll only add to and extend it.

Next up on our list of self-evaluating expressions are boolean literals. But before we do that, we should celebrate our first evaluation success and treat ourselves. Let's put the E in REPL!

COMPLETING THE REPL

Up until now the E in in our REPL was missing and we had nothing but a RPPL - a Read-Parse-Print-Loop. Now that we have `Eval` we can build a real Read-Evaluate-Print-Loop!

Using the evaluator in the `repl` package is as easy as you'd think it is:

```
// repl/repl.go

import (
// [...]
    "monkey/evaluator"
)

// [...]

func Start(in io.Reader, out io.Writer) {
    scanner := bufio.NewScanner(in)

    for {
        fmt.Printf(PROMPT)
        scanned := scanner.Scan()
        if !scanned {
            return
        }

        line := scanner.Text()
        l := lexer.New(line)
        p := parser.New(l)

        program := p.ParseProgram()
        if len(p.Errors()) != 0 {
            printParserErrors(out, p.Errors())
            continue
        }

        evaluated := evaluator.Eval(program)
        if evaluated != nil {
            io.WriteString(out, evaluated.Inspect())
            io.WriteString(out, "\n")
        }
    }
}
```

Instead of printing `program` (the AST returned by the parser) we pass `program` to `Eval`. If `Eval` returns a non-nil value, an `object.Object`, we print the output of its `Inspect()` method. In the case of an `*object.Integer` that would be the string representation of the integer it's wrapping.

And with that we now have a working REPL:

```
$ go run main.go
Hello mrnugget! This is the Monkey programming language!
Feel free to type in commands
>> 5
5
>> 10
10
>> 999
999
>>
```

Feels good, doesn't it? Lexing, parsing, evaluating - it's all in there. We've come a long way.

BOOLEAN LITERALS

Boolean literals, just like their integer counterparts, evaluate to themselves. `true` evaluates to `true` and `false` to `false`. Implementing this in `Eval` is as easy as adding support for integer literals was. The tests are equally boring:

```go
// evaluator/evaluator_test.go

func TestEvalBooleanExpression(t *testing.T) {
    tests := []struct {
        input    string
        expected bool
    }{
        {"true", true},
        {"false", false},
    }

    for _, tt := range tests {
        evaluated := testEval(tt.input)
        testBooleanObject(t, evaluated, tt.expected)
    }
}

func testBooleanObject(t *testing.T, obj object.Object, expected bool) bool {
    result, ok := obj.(*object.Boolean)
    if !ok {
        t.Errorf("object is not Boolean. got=%T (%+v)", obj, obj)
        return false
    }
    if result.Value != expected {
```

```
        t.Errorf("object has wrong value. got=%t, want=%t",
            result.Value, expected)
        return false
    }
    return true
}
```

We'll extend the `tests` slice as soon as we support more expressions that result in booleans. For now, we only make sure that we get the correct output when we enter `true` or `false`. The tests fail:

```
$ go test ./evaluator
--- FAIL: TestEvalBooleanExpression (0.00s)
  evaluator_test.go:42: Eval didn't return BooleanObject. got=<nil> (<nil>)
  evaluator_test.go:42: Eval didn't return BooleanObject. got=<nil> (<nil>)
FAIL
FAIL    monkey/evaluator        0.006s
```

Making this green is as easy as copying the `case` branch from `*ast.IntegerLiteral` and changing two identifiers:

```
// evaluator/evaluator.go

func Eval(node ast.Node) object.Object {
// [...]
    case *ast.Boolean:
        return &object.Boolean{Value: node.Value}
// [...]
}
```

That's it! Let's give it a spin in the REPL:

```
$ go run main.go
Hello mrnugget! This is the Monkey programming language!
Feel free to type in commands
>> true
true
>> false
false
>>
```

Pretty! But, let me ask you this: the fact that we're creating a new `object.Boolean` every time we encounter a `true` or `false` is absurd, isn't it? There is no difference between two `true`s. The same goes for `false`. Why use new instances every time? There are only two possible values, so let's reference them instead of creating new ones.

```
// evaluator/evaluator.go

var (
```

```
    TRUE  = &object.Boolean{Value: true}
    FALSE = &object.Boolean{Value: false}
)

func Eval(node ast.Node) object.Object {
// [...]
    case *ast.Boolean:
        return nativeBoolToBooleanObject(node.Value)
// [...]
}

func nativeBoolToBooleanObject(input bool) *object.Boolean {
    if input {
        return TRUE
    }
    return FALSE
}
```

Now there are only two instances of `object.Boolean` in our package: `TRUE` and `FALSE` and we reference them instead of allocating new `object.Booleans`. That makes much more sense and is a small performance improvement we get without a lot of work. And while we're at it, let's take care of null, too.

NULL

Just as there is only one `true` and one `false`, there should only be one reference to a null value. There are no variations of null. No kinda-but-not-quite-null, no half-null and no basically-the-same-as-the-other-null. Either something is this one null, or it isn't. So let's create one `NULL` we can reference throughout our evaluator instead of creating new `object.Nulls`.

```
// evaluator/evaluator.go

var (
    NULL  = &object.Null{}
    TRUE  = &object.Boolean{Value: true}
    FALSE = &object.Boolean{Value: false}
)
```

And that's all there is to it. Now we have one `NULL` we can reference.

With integer literals and our trio of `NULL`, `TRUE` and `FALSE` in place we're ready to evaluate operator expressions.

PREFIX EXPRESSIONS

The simplest form of operator expressions Monkey supports is the prefix expression, or unary operator expression, where one operand follows the operator. In our parser we treated a lot of language constructs like prefix expressions, because that's the easiest way to parse them. But in this section prefix expressions are just operator expressions with one operator and one operand. Monkey supports two of these prefix operators: `!` and `-`.

Evaluating operator expression (especially with a prefix operator and one operand) isn't hard. We'll do it in small steps and build up the desired behaviour bit by bit. But we also need to pay close attention. What we're about to implement has far reaching consequences. Remember: in the evaluation process the input language receives meaning; we're defining the semantics of the Monkey programming language. A small change in the evaluation of operator expressions might cause something unintended in a part of the language that seems entirely unrelated. Tests help us to nail down the desired behaviour and also act as a specification for us.

We're going to start by implementing support for the `!` operator. The tests show that the operator should "convert" its operand to a boolean value and negate it:

```
// evaluator/evaluator_test.go

func TestBangOperator(t *testing.T) {
    tests := []struct {
        input    string
        expected bool
    }{
        {"!true", false},
        {"!false", true},
        {"!5", false},
        {"!!true", true},
        {"!!false", false},
        {"!!5", true},
    }

    for _, tt := range tests {
        evaluated := testEval(tt.input)
        testBooleanObject(t, evaluated, tt.expected)
    }
}
```

As I said, this is where we decide how the language works. The `!true` and `!false` expressions and their expected results seem like common sense, but the `!5` may be something where other language designers feel an error should be returned. But what we're saying here is that `5` acts as "truthy".

The tests don't pass, of course, because `Eval` returns `nil` instead of `TRUE` or `FALSE`. The first step to evaluating a prefix expression is to evaluate its operand and then use the result of this evaluation with the operator:

```
// evaluator/evaluator.go

func Eval(node ast.Node) object.Object {
// [...]
    case *ast.PrefixExpression:
        right := Eval(node.Right)
        return evalPrefixExpression(node.Operator, right)
// [...]
}
```

After the first call to `Eval` here, `right` may be an `*object.Integer` or an `*object.Boolean` or maybe even `NULL`. We then take this `right` operand and pass it to `evalPrefixExpression` which checks if the operator is supported:

```
// evaluator/evaluator.go

func evalPrefixExpression(operator string, right object.Object) object.Object {
    switch operator {
    case "!":
        return evalBangOperatorExpression(right)
    default:
        return NULL
    }
}
```

If the operator is not supported we return `NULL`. Is that the best choice? Maybe, maybe not. For now, it's definitely the easiest choice, since we don't have any error handling implemented yet.

The `evalBangOperatorExpression` function is where the behaviour of the `!` is specified:

```
// evaluator/evaluator.go

func evalBangOperatorExpression(right object.Object) object.Object {
    switch right {
    case TRUE:
        return FALSE
    case FALSE:
        return TRUE
    case NULL:
        return TRUE
    default:
        return FALSE
    }
```

```
}
```

And with that the tests pass!

```
$ go test ./evaluator
ok      monkey/evaluator        0.007s
```

Let's move on to the - prefix operator. We can extend our `TestEvalIntegerExpression` test function to incorporate it:

```
// evaluator/evaluator_test.go

func TestEvalIntegerExpression(t *testing.T) {
    tests := []struct {
        input    string
        expected int64
    }{
        {"5", 5},
        {"10", 10},
        {"-5", -5},
        {"-10", -10},
    }
// [...]
}
```

I choose to extend this test rather than writing a new test function solely for the - prefix operator for two reasons. First, integers are the only supported operands of the - operator in prefix position. And second, because this test function should grow to encompass all integer arithmetic in order to have one place that shows the desired behaviour in a clear and neat way.

We have to extend the `evalPrefixExpression` function we wrote earlier in order to make the test cases pass. A new branch in the switch statement is needed:

```
// evaluator/evaluator.go

func evalPrefixExpression(operator string, right object.Object) object.Object {
    switch operator {
    case "!":
        return evalBangOperatorExpression(right)
    case "-":
        return evalMinusPrefixOperatorExpression(right)
    default:
        return NULL
    }
}
```

The `evalMinusPrefixOperatorExpression` function looks like this:

```
// evaluator/evaluator.go
```

```go
func evalMinusPrefixOperatorExpression(right object.Object) object.Object {
    if right.Type() != object.INTEGER_OBJ {
        return NULL
    }

    value := right.(*object.Integer).Value
    return &object.Integer{Value: -value}
}
```

The first thing we do here is to check if the operand is an integer. If it isn't, we return `NULL`. But if it is, we extract the value of the `*object.Integer`. Then we allocate a new object to wrap a negated version of this value.

That wasn't a lot of code, was it? But still, it did the job:

```
$ go test ./evaluator
ok      monkey/evaluator        0.007s
```

Excellent! Now we can give our prefix expressions a spin in the REPL before moving on to their infix friends:

```
$ go run main.go
Hello mrnugget! This is the Monkey programming language!
Feel free to type in commands
>> -5
-5
>> !true
false
>> !-5
false
>> !!-5
true
>> !!!!-5
true
>> -true
null
```

Amazing!

INFIX EXPRESSIONS

As a refresher, here are the eight infix operators that Monkey supports:

```
5 + 5;
5 - 5;
5 * 5;
5 / 5;
```

```
5 > 5;
5 < 5;
5 == 5;
5 != 5;
```

These eight operators can be separated into two groups: one group of operators produces booleans as their result and one group doesn't. We'll start by implementing support for the second group: `+`, `-`, `*`, `/`. And first only in combination with integer operands. As soon as that works, we'll add support for booleans on either side of the operator.

The test infrastructure is already in place. We'll just extend our `TestEvalIntegerExpression` test function with test cases for these new operators:

```go
// evaluator/evaluator_test.go

func TestEvalIntegerExpression(t *testing.T) {
    tests := []struct {
        input    string
        expected int64
    }{
        {"5", 5},
        {"10", 10},
        {"-5", -5},
        {"-10", -10},
        {"5 + 5 + 5 + 5 - 10", 10},
        {"2 * 2 * 2 * 2 * 2", 32},
        {"-50 + 100 + -50", 0},
        {"5 * 2 + 10", 20},
        {"5 + 2 * 10", 25},
        {"20 + 2 * -10", 0},
        {"50 / 2 * 2 + 10", 60},
        {"2 * (5 + 10)", 30},
        {"3 * 3 * 3 + 10", 37},
        {"3 * (3 * 3) + 10", 37},
        {"(5 + 10 * 2 + 15 / 3) * 2 + -10", 50},
    }
// [...]
}
```

Yes, there are probably some test cases that can be removed because they duplicate another one and some add nothing new, but to be honest: I was really trigger happy with these tests once I realized that the implementation works and I just couldn't believe it. "It can't be that easy, can it?" Well, yes, it can.

To get these test cases to pass, the first thing we need to do is to extend our switch statement in `Eval`:

```go
// evaluator/evaluator.go
```

```go
func Eval(node ast.Node) object.Object {
// [...]
    case *ast.InfixExpression:
        left := Eval(node.Left)
        right := Eval(node.Right)
        return evalInfixExpression(node.Operator, left, right)
// [...]
}
```

Just as with `*ast.PrefixExpression` we evaluate the operands first. And now we have two: the left and the right arm of the AST node. We already know that these may be any other expression - a function call, an integer literal, an operator expression, etc. We don't care. We let `Eval` take care of it.

After evaluating the operands we take the returned values and the operator and pass them to `evalIntegerInfixExpressions`, which looks like this:

```go
// evaluator/evaluator.go

func evalInfixExpression(
    operator string,
    left, right object.Object,
) object.Object {
    switch {
    case left.Type() == object.INTEGER_OBJ && right.Type() == object.INTEGER_OBJ:
        return evalIntegerInfixExpression(operator, left, right)
    default:
        return NULL
    }
}
```

In case the operands aren't both integers we return `NULL`, just as I promised. Of course, we'll extend this function later on, but in order to get the tests to pass, this is enough. The heart of the matter lies in `evalIntegerInfixExpression`, where the values wrapped by `*object.Integers` are added, subtracted, multiplied and divided:

```go
// evaluator/evaluator.go

func evalIntegerInfixExpression(
    operator string,
    left, right object.Object,
) object.Object {
    leftVal := left.(*object.Integer).Value
    rightVal := right.(*object.Integer).Value

    switch operator {
```

```
    case "+":
        return &object.Integer{Value: leftVal + rightVal}
    case "-":
        return &object.Integer{Value: leftVal - rightVal}
    case "*":
        return &object.Integer{Value: leftVal * rightVal}
    case "/":
        return &object.Integer{Value: leftVal / rightVal}
    default:
        return NULL
    }
}
```

And now, believe it or not, the tests pass. Yes, really, they do:

```
$ go test ./evaluator
ok      monkey/evaluator        0.007s
```

Go on, add a few more. Knock yourself out. And then come back here so we can add support for the operators that result in booleans: `==`, `!=`, `<` and `>`.

We can extend our `TestEvalBooleanExpression` test function with test cases for these operators, since they all produce a boolean:

```
// evaluator/evaluator_test.go

func TestEvalBooleanExpression(t *testing.T) {
    tests := []struct {
        input    string
        expected bool
    }{
        {"true", true},
        {"false", false},
        {"1 < 2", true},
        {"1 > 2", false},
        {"1 < 1", false},
        {"1 > 1", false},
        {"1 == 1", true},
        {"1 != 1", false},
        {"1 == 2", false},
        {"1 != 2", true},
    }
// [...]
}
```

A few added lines in `evalIntegerInfixExpression` is all that's needed to get these tests to pass:

```
// evaluator/evaluator.go
```

```
func evalIntegerInfixExpression(
    operator string,
    left, right object.Object,
) object.Object {
    leftVal := left.(*object.Integer).Value
    rightVal := right.(*object.Integer).Value

    switch operator {
// [...]
    case "<":
        return nativeBoolToBooleanObject(leftVal < rightVal)
    case ">":
        return nativeBoolToBooleanObject(leftVal > rightVal)
    case "==":
        return nativeBoolToBooleanObject(leftVal == rightVal)
    case "!=":
        return nativeBoolToBooleanObject(leftVal != rightVal)
    default:
        return NULL
    }
}
```

The `nativeBoolToBooleanObject` function we already used for boolean literals now finds some reuse when we need to return either `TRUE` or `FALSE` based on the comparison between the unwrapped values.

And that's it! Well, at least for integers. We now fully support the eight infix operators when both operands are integers. What's left in this section is adding support for boolean operands.

Monkey only supports boolean operands for the equality operators `==` and `!=`. It doesn't support adding, subtracting, dividing and multiplying booleans. Checking whether `true` is greater than `false` with `<` or `>` is also unsupported. That reduces our task to just adding support for two operators.

The first thing we have to do, as you know, is to add tests. And, as before, we can extend an existing test function. In this case, we'll use `TestEvalBooleanExpression` and add test cases for the `==` and `!=` operators:

```
// evaluator/evaluator_test.go

func TestEvalBooleanExpression(t *testing.T) {
    tests := []struct {
        input    string
        expected bool
    }{
// [...]
        {"true == true", true},
```

```go
        {"false == false", true},
        {"true == false", false},
        {"true != false", true},
        {"false != true", true},
        {"(1 < 2) == true", true},
        {"(1 < 2) == false", false},
        {"(1 > 2) == true", false},
        {"(1 > 2) == false", true},
    }
// [...]
}
```

Strictly speaking, only the first five cases are necessary to test the new and desired behaviour. But let's throw in the other four too to check the comparison between generated booleans.

So far, so good. Nothing surprising here. Just another set of of failing tests:

```
$ go test ./evaluator
--- FAIL: TestEvalBooleanExpression (0.00s)
  evaluator_test.go:121: object is not Boolean. got=*object.Null (&{})
  evaluator_test.go:121: object is not Boolean. got=*object.Null (&{})
  evaluator_test.go:121: object is not Boolean. got=*object.Null (&{})
  evaluator_test.go:121: object is not Boolean. got=*object.Null (&{})
  evaluator_test.go:121: object is not Boolean. got=*object.Null (&{})
  evaluator_test.go:121: object is not Boolean. got=*object.Null (&{})
  evaluator_test.go:121: object is not Boolean. got=*object.Null (&{})
  evaluator_test.go:121: object is not Boolean. got=*object.Null (&{})
  evaluator_test.go:121: object is not Boolean. got=*object.Null (&{})
FAIL
FAIL    monkey/evaluator        0.007s
```

And here's something neat to make those tests pass:

```go
// evaluator/evaluator.go

func evalInfixExpression(
    operator string,
    left, right object.Object,
) object.Object {
    switch {
// [...]
    case operator == "==":
        return nativeBoolToBooleanObject(left == right)
    case operator == "!=":
        return nativeBoolToBooleanObject(left != right)
    default:
        return NULL
    }
```

```
}
```

Yes, that's right. We only add four lines to our existing `evalInfixExpression` and the tests pass. We're using pointer comparison here to check for equality between booleans. That works because we're always using pointers to our objects and in the case of booleans we only ever use two: `TRUE` and `FALSE`. So, if something has the same value as `TRUE` (the memory address that is) then it's true. This also works with `NULL`.

This doesn't work for integers or other data types we might add later on. In the case of `*object.Integer` we're always allocating new instances of `object.Integer` and thus use new pointers. We can't compare these pointers to different instances, otherwise `5 == 5` would be false, which is not what we want. In this case we want to explicitly compare the values and not the objects that wrap these values.

That's why the check for integer operands has to be higher up in the switch statement and match earlier than these newly added `case` branches. As long as we're taking care of other operand types before arriving at these pointer comparisons we're fine and it works.

In ten years, when Monkey is a famous programming language and the discussion about research-ignoring dilettantes designing programming languages is still ongoing and we're both rich and famous, someone will ask on StackOverflow why integer comparison in Monkey is slower than boolean comparison. The answer will be written by either you or me and one of us will say that Monkey's object system doesn't allow pointer comparison for integer objects. It has to unwrap the value before a comparison can be made. Thus the comparison between booleans is faster. We'll add a "Source: I wrote it." to the bottom of our answer and earn an unheard of amount of karma.

But I digress. To get back to topic, let me just say: Wow! We did it! I know, I'm pretty lavish with my praise and can spot a cause for celebration pretty easily, but if there ever was a time to pop the champagne, it's now. Yes, we did it. Just look at what our interpreter can do now:

```
$ go run main.go
Hello mrnugget! This is the Monkey programming language!
Feel free to type in commands
>> 5 * 5 + 10
35
>> 3 + 4 * 5 == 3 * 1 + 4 * 5
true
>> 5 * 10 > 40 + 5
true
>> (10 + 2) * 30 == 300 + 20 * 3
true
>> (5 > 5 == true) != false
```

```
false
>> 500 / 2 != 250
false
```

So, now we have a fully functional calculator that's ready to do more. Let's give him more. Let's make it look more like a programming language.

3.6 - Conditionals

You'll be amazed how easy it is to add support for conditionals in our evaluator. The only hard thing about their implementation is deciding when to evaluate what. Because that's the whole point of conditionals: only ever evaluate something based on a condition. Consider this:

```
if (x > 10) {
  puts("everything okay!");
} else {
  puts("x is too low!");
  shutdownSystem();
}
```

When evaluating this if-else-expression the important thing is to only evaluate the correct branch. If the condition is met, we must never evaluate the else-branch, only the if-branch. And if it isn't met we must only evaluate the else-branch.

In other words: we can only evaluate the else-branch of this conditional if the condition `x > 10` is not ... well, when it's not what exactly? Should we evaluate the consequence, the `"everything okay!"` branch, only when the condition expression generates a `true` or when it generates something "truthy", something that's not false or not null?

And *that's* the tough part about this, because that's a design decision, a language design decision to be exact, with wide ranging consequences.

In the case of Monkey, the consequence part of the conditional will be evaluated when the condition is "truthy". And "truthy" means: it's not null and it's not false. It doesn't necessarily need to be `true`.

```
let x = 10;
if (x) {
  puts("everything okay!");
} else {
  puts("x is too high!");
  shutdownSystem();
}
```

In this example "everything okay!" should be printed. Why? Because x is bound to 10, evaluates to 10 and 10 is not null and not false. That's how conditionals are supposed to work in Monkey.

Now that we've talked about this, we can turn this specification into a set of test cases:

```
// evaluator/evaluator_test.go

func TestIfElseExpressions(t *testing.T) {
    tests := []struct {
        input    string
        expected interface{}
    }{
        {"if (true) { 10 }", 10},
        {"if (false) { 10 }", nil},
        {"if (1) { 10 }", 10},
        {"if (1 < 2) { 10 }", 10},
        {"if (1 > 2) { 10 }", nil},
        {"if (1 > 2) { 10 } else { 20 }", 20},
        {"if (1 < 2) { 10 } else { 20 }", 10},
    }

    for _, tt := range tests {
        evaluated := testEval(tt.input)
        integer, ok := tt.expected.(int)
        if ok {
            testIntegerObject(t, evaluated, int64(integer))
        } else {
            testNullObject(t, evaluated)
        }
    }
}

func testNullObject(t *testing.T, obj object.Object) bool {
    if obj != NULL {
        t.Errorf("object is not NULL. got=%T (%+v)", obj, obj)
        return false
    }
    return true
}
```

This test function also specifies behaviour we haven't talked about yet. When a conditional doesn't evaluate to a value it's supposed to return NULL, e.g.:

```
if (false) { 10 }
```

The else is missing and thus the conditional should produce NULL.

We have to do a little type assertion and conversion dance to allow `nil` in our `expected` field, granted, but the tests are readable and clearly show the desired and hereby specified behaviour. They also fail, because we don't return any `*object.Integers` or `NULL`:

```
$ go test ./evaluator
--- FAIL: TestIfElseExpressions (0.00s)
  evaluator_test.go:125: object is not Integer. got=<nil> (<nil>)
  evaluator_test.go:153: object is not NULL. got=<nil> (<nil>)
  evaluator_test.go:125: object is not Integer. got=<nil> (<nil>)
  evaluator_test.go:125: object is not Integer. got=<nil> (<nil>)
  evaluator_test.go:153: object is not NULL. got=<nil> (<nil>)
  evaluator_test.go:125: object is not Integer. got=<nil> (<nil>)
  evaluator_test.go:125: object is not Integer. got=<nil> (<nil>)
FAIL
FAIL    monkey/evaluator        0.007s
```

Earlier I told you that you'll be amazed at how easy it is to implement support for conditionals. Didn't believe me? Well, look at this small amount of code necessary to make the tests pass:

```go
// evaluator/evaluator.go

func Eval(node ast.Node) object.Object {
// [...]
    case *ast.BlockStatement:
        return evalStatements(node.Statements)

    case *ast.IfExpression:
        return evalIfExpression(node)
// [...]
}

func evalIfExpression(ie *ast.IfExpression) object.Object {
    condition := Eval(ie.Condition)

    if isTruthy(condition) {
        return Eval(ie.Consequence)
    } else if ie.Alternative != nil {
        return Eval(ie.Alternative)
    } else {
        return NULL
    }
}

func isTruthy(obj object.Object) bool {
    switch obj {
    case NULL:
```

```
            return false
        case TRUE:
            return true
        case FALSE:
            return false
        default:
            return true
        }
    }
```

As I said: the only hard thing is deciding what to evaluate. And that decision is encapsulated in `evalIfExpression` where the logic of the behaviour is pretty clear. `isTruthy` is equally expressive. Besides these two functions we also added the `case` branch for `*ast.BlockStatement` to our `Eval` switch statement, because the `.Consequence` and `.Alternative` of `*ast.IfExpression` are both block statements.

We added two new and concise functions that show the semantics of the Monkey programming language in a clear way, reused another function we already had in place and with doing so added support for conditionals and made the tests pass. Our interpreter now supports if-else-expressions! We're now leaving calculator territory and heading straight towards programming language land:

```
$ go run main.go
Hello mrnugget! This is the Monkey programming language!
Feel free to type in commands
>> if (5 * 5 + 10 > 34) { 99 } else { 100 }
99
>> if ((1000 / 2) + 250 * 2 == 1000) { 9999 }
9999
>>
```

3.7 - Return Statements

Now here's something that you won't find on your standard calculator: return statements. Monkey has them, like a lot of other languages. They can be used in the bodies of functions but also as top-level statements in a Monkey program. But it doesn't really matter where they're used, because how they work doesn't change: return statements stop the evaluation of a series of statements and leave behind the value their expression has evaluated to.

Here is a top-level return statement in a Monkey program:

```
5 * 5 * 5;
return 10;
9 * 9 * 9;
```

When evaluated this program should return 10. If these statements were the body of a function, calling the function should evaluate to 10. The important thing is that the last line, the 9 * 9 * 9 expression, is never going to be evaluated.

There are a few different ways to implement return statements. In some host languages we could use gotos or exceptions. But in Go a "rescue" or "catch" are not easy to come by and we don't really have the option of using gotos in a clean way. That's why, in order to support return statements, we'll be passing a "return value" through our evaluator. Whenever we encounter a return we'll wrap the value it's supposed to return inside an object, so we can keep track of it. And we need to keep track of it so we can later decide whether to stop evaluation or not.

Here is the implementation of said object. Here is object.ReturnValue:

```
// object/object.go

const (
// [...]
    RETURN_VALUE_OBJ = "RETURN_VALUE"
)

type ReturnValue struct {
    Value Object
}

func (rv *ReturnValue) Type() ObjectType { return RETURN_VALUE_OBJ }
func (rv *ReturnValue) Inspect() string  { return rv.Value.Inspect() }
```

Since this is just a wrapper around another object nothing here is surprising. What's interesting about object.ReturnValue is when and how it's used.

Here are the tests that demonstrate what we expect of the return statement in the context of a Monkey program:

```
// evaluator/evaluator_test.go

func TestReturnStatements(t *testing.T) {
    tests := []struct {
        input    string
        expected int64
    }{
        {"return 10;", 10},
        {"return 10; 9;", 10},
        {"return 2 * 5; 9;", 10},
        {"9; return 2 * 5; 9;", 10},
    }

    for _, tt := range tests {
```

```
        evaluated := testEval(tt.input)
        testIntegerObject(t, evaluated, tt.expected)
    }
}
```

In order to get these tests to pass we have to change the `evalStatements` function we already have and add a `case` branch for `*ast.ReturnStatement` to `Eval`:

```
// evaluator/evaluator.go

func Eval(node ast.Node) object.Object {
// [...]
    case *ast.ReturnStatement:
        val := Eval(node.ReturnValue)
        return &object.ReturnValue{Value: val}
// [...]
}

func evalStatements(stmts []ast.Statement) object.Object {
    var result object.Object

    for _, statement := range stmts {
        result = Eval(statement)

        if returnValue, ok := result.(*object.ReturnValue); ok {
            return returnValue.Value
        }
    }

    return result
}
```

The first part of this change is the evaluation of `*ast.ReturnValue`, where we evaluate the expression associated with the return statement. We then wrap the result of this call to `Eval` in our new `object.ReturnValue` so we can keep track of it.

In `evalStatements`, which is used by `evalProgramStatements` and `evalBlockStatements` to evaluate a series of statements, we check if the last evaluation result is such an `object.ReturnValue` and if so, we stop the evaluation and return the unwrapped value. That's important. We don't return an `object.ReturnValue`, but only the value it's wrapping, which is what the user expects to be returned.

There's a problem, though. Sometimes we have to keep track of `object.ReturnValues` for longer and can't unwrap their values on the first encounter. That's the case with block statements. Take a look at this:

```
if (10 > 1) {
```

```
    if (10 > 1) {
      return 10;
    }

    return 1;
  }
```

This program should return `10`. But with our current implementation, it doesn't and returns `1`. A small test case confirms this:

```
// evaluator/evaluator_test.go

func TestReturnStatements(t *testing.T) {
    tests := []struct {
        input    string
        expected int64
    }{
// [...]
        {
            `
if (10 > 1) {
  if (10 > 1) {
    return 10;
  }

  return 1;
}
`,
            10,
        },
    }
// [...]
}
```

This test case fails with the expected message:

```
$ go test ./evaluator
--- FAIL: TestReturnStatements (0.00s)
  evaluator_test.go:159: object has wrong value. got=1, want=10
FAIL
FAIL    monkey/evaluator        0.007s
```

I bet that you've already figured out what the problem with our current implementation is. But if you want me to spell it out, here it comes: if we have nested block statements (which is totally legit in a Monkey program!) we can't unwrap the value of `object.ReturnValue` on first sight, because we need to further keep track of it so we can stop the execution in the outermost block statement.

Non-nested block statements work fine with our current implementation. But to get nested ones to work, the first thing we have to do is to accept that we can't reuse our `evalStatements` function for evaluating block statements. That's why we're going to rename it to `evalProgram` and make it less generic.

```go
// evaluator/evaluator.go

func Eval(node ast.Node) object.Object {
// [...]
    case *ast.Program:
        return evalProgram(node)
// [...]
}

func evalProgram(program *ast.Program) object.Object {
    var result object.Object

    for _, statement := range program.Statements {
        result = Eval(statement)

        if returnValue, ok := result.(*object.ReturnValue); ok {
            return returnValue.Value
        }
    }

    return result
}
```

For evaluating an `*ast.BlockStatement` we introduce a new function called `evalBlockStatement`:

```go
// evaluator/evaluator.go

func Eval(node ast.Node) object.Object {
// [...]
    case *ast.BlockStatement:
        return evalBlockStatement(node)
// [...]
}

func evalBlockStatement(block *ast.BlockStatement) object.Object {
    var result object.Object

    for _, statement := range block.Statements {
        result = Eval(statement)

        if result != nil && result.Type() == object.RETURN_VALUE_OBJ {
            return result
        }
    }
```

```
    return result
}
```

Here we explicitly don't unwrap the return value and only check the `Type()` of each evaluation result. If it's `object.RETURN_VALUE_OBJ` we simply return the `*object.ReturnValue`, without unwrapping its `.Value`, so it stops execution in a possible outer block statement and bubbles up to `evalProgram`, where it finally get's unwrapped. (That last part will change when we implement the evaluation of function calls.)

And with that the tests pass:

```
$ go test ./evaluator
ok      monkey/evaluator        0.007s
```

Return statements are implemented. Now we're definitely not building a calculator anymore. And since `evalProgram` and `evalBlockStatement` are still so fresh in our mind let's keep working on them.

3.8 - Abort! Abort! There's Been a Mistake!, or: Error Handling

Remember all the `NULL`s we were returning earlier and I said that you shouldn't worry and we'll come back to them? Here we are. It's time to implement some real error handling in Monkey before it's too late and we'd have to backpedal too much. Granted, we have to backpedal a little bit and correct previous code, but not much. We didn't implement error handling as the first thing in our interpreter, because, and to be completely honest, I thought implementing expressions first is a lot more fun than error handling. But we're now at a point where we need to add it, otherwise debugging and using our interpreter becomes too cumbersome in the near future.

First of all, let's define what I mean with "real error handling". It is *not* user-defined exceptions. It's internal error handling. Errors for wrong operators, unsupported operations, and other user or internal errors that may arise during execution.

As for the implementation of such errors: this will probably sound weird, but the error handling is implemented in nearly the same way as handling return statements is. The reason for this similarity is easy to find: errors and return statements both stop the evaluation of a series of statements.

The first thing we need is an error object:

```go
// object/object.go

const (
// [...]
    ERROR_OBJ = "ERROR"
)

type Error struct {
    Message string
}

func (e *Error) Type() ObjectType { return ERROR_OBJ }
func (e *Error) Inspect() string  { return "ERROR: " + e.Message }
```

As you can see, `object.Error` is really, really simple. It only wraps a string that serves as error message. In a production-ready interpreter we'd want to attach a stack trace to such error objects, add the line and column numbers of its origin and provide more than just a message. That's not so hard to do, provided that line and column numbers are attached to the tokens by the lexer. Since our lexer doesn't do that, to keep things simple, we only use an error message, which still serves us a great deal by giving us some feedback and stopping execution.

We will add support for errors in a few places now. Later, with increased capability of our interpreter, we'll add more where appropriate. For now, this test function shows what we expect the error handling to do:

```go
// evaluator/evaluator_test.go

func TestErrorHandling(t *testing.T) {
    tests := []struct {
        input           string
        expectedMessage string
    }{
        {
            "5 + true;",
            "type mismatch: INTEGER + BOOLEAN",
        },
        {
            "5 + true; 5;",
            "type mismatch: INTEGER + BOOLEAN",
        },
        {
            "-true",
            "unknown operator: -BOOLEAN",
        },
        {
            "true + false;",
            "unknown operator: BOOLEAN + BOOLEAN",
```

```
        },
        {
            "5; true + false; 5",
            "unknown operator: BOOLEAN + BOOLEAN",
        },
        {
            "if (10 > 1) { true + false; }",
            "unknown operator: BOOLEAN + BOOLEAN",
        },
        {
            `
if (10 > 1) {
  if (10 > 1) {
    return true + false;
  }

  return 1;
}
`,
            "unknown operator: BOOLEAN + BOOLEAN",
        },
    }

    for _, tt := range tests {
        evaluated := testEval(tt.input)

        errObj, ok := evaluated.(*object.Error)
        if !ok {
            t.Errorf("no error object returned. got=%T(%+v)",
                evaluated, evaluated)
            continue
        }

        if errObj.Message != tt.expectedMessage {
            t.Errorf("wrong error message. expected=%q, got=%q",
                tt.expectedMessage, errObj.Message)
        }
    }
}
```

When we run the tests we meet our old friend `NULL` again:

```
$ go test ./evaluator
--- FAIL: TestErrorHandling (0.00s)
  evaluator_test.go:193: no error object returned. got=*object.Null(&{})
  evaluator_test.go:193: no error object returned.\
    got=*object.Integer(&{Value:5})
  evaluator_test.go:193: no error object returned. got=*object.Null(&{})
```

```
    evaluator_test.go:193: no error object returned. got=*object.Null(&{})
    evaluator_test.go:193: no error object returned.\
      got=*object.Integer(&{Value:5})
    evaluator_test.go:193: no error object returned. got=*object.Null(&{})
    evaluator_test.go:193: no error object returned.\
      got=*object.Integer(&{Value:10})
FAIL
FAIL    monkey/evaluator        0.007s
```

But there are also unexpected `*object.Integers`. That's because these test cases actually assert two things: that errors are created for unsupported operations and that errors prevent any further evaluation. When the test fails because of an `*object.Integer` being returned, the evaluation didn't stop correctly.

Creating errors and passing them around in `Eval` is easy. We just need a helper function to help us create new `*object.Errors` and return them when we think we should:

```go
// evaluator/evaluator.go

func newError(format string, a ...interface{}) *object.Error {
    return &object.Error{Message: fmt.Sprintf(format, a...)}
}
```

This `newError` function finds its use in every place where we didn't know what to do before and returned `NULL` instead:

```go
// evaluator/evaluator.go

func evalPrefixExpression(operator string, right object.Object) object.Object {
    switch operator {
// [...]
    default:
        return newError("unknown operator: %s%s", operator, right.Type())
    }
}

func evalInfixExpression(
    operator string,
    left, right object.Object,
) object.Object {
    switch {
// [...]
    case left.Type() != right.Type():
        return newError("type mismatch: %s %s %s",
            left.Type(), operator, right.Type())
    default:
        return newError("unknown operator: %s %s %s",
            left.Type(), operator, right.Type())
```

```
    }
}

func evalMinusPrefixOperatorExpression(right object.Object) object.Object {
    if right.Type() != object.INTEGER_OBJ {
        return newError("unknown operator: -%s", right.Type())
    }
// [...]
}

func evalIntegerInfixExpression(
    operator string,
    left, right object.Object,
) object.Object {
// [...]
    switch operator {
// [...]
    default:
        return newError("unknown operator: %s %s %s",
            left.Type(), operator, right.Type())
    }
}
```

With these changes made the number of failing test cases has been reduced to just two:

```
$ go test ./evaluator
--- FAIL: TestErrorHandling (0.00s)
  evaluator_test.go:193: no error object returned.\
    got=*object.Integer(&{Value:5})
  evaluator_test.go:193: no error object returned.\
    got=*object.Integer(&{Value:5})
FAIL
FAIL    monkey/evaluator        0.007s
```

That output tells us that creating errors poses no problem but stopping the evaluation still does. We already know where to look though, don't we? Yes, that's right: `evalProgram` and `evalBlockStatement`. Here are both functions in their entirety, with newly added support for error handling:

```
// evaluator/evaluator.go

func evalProgram(program *ast.Program) object.Object {
    var result object.Object

    for _, statement := range program.Statements {
        result = Eval(statement)

        switch result := result.(type) {
```

```
        case *object.ReturnValue:
            return result.Value
        case *object.Error:
            return result
        }
    }

    return result
}

func evalBlockStatement(block *ast.BlockStatement) object.Object {
    var result object.Object

    for _, statement := range block.Statements {
        result = Eval(statement)

        if result != nil {
            rt := result.Type()
            if rt == object.RETURN_VALUE_OBJ || rt == object.ERROR_OBJ {
                return result
            }
        }
    }

    return result
}
```

That did it. Evaluation is stopped at the right places and the tests now pass:

```
$ go test ./evaluator
ok      monkey/evaluator        0.010s
```

There's still one last thing we need to do. We need to check for errors whenever we call `Eval` inside of `Eval`, in order to stop errors from being passed around and then bubbling up far away from their origin:

```
// evaluator/evaluator.go

func isError(obj object.Object) bool {
    if obj != nil {
        return obj.Type() == object.ERROR_OBJ
    }
    return false
}

func Eval(node ast.Node) object.Object {
    switch node := node.(type) {

// [...]
```

```go
    case *ast.ReturnStatement:
        val := Eval(node.ReturnValue)
        if isError(val) {
            return val
        }
        return &object.ReturnValue{Value: val}

// [...]
    case *ast.PrefixExpression:
        right := Eval(node.Right)
        if isError(right) {
            return right
        }
        return evalPrefixExpression(node.Operator, right)

    case *ast.InfixExpression:
        left := Eval(node.Left)
        if isError(left) {
            return left
        }

        right := Eval(node.Right)
        if isError(right) {
            return right
        }

        return evalInfixExpression(node.Operator, left, right)
// [...]
}

func evalIfExpression(ie *ast.IfExpression) object.Object {
    condition := Eval(ie.Condition)
    if isError(condition) {
        return condition
    }
// [...]
}
```

And that's it. Error handling is in place.

3.9 - BINDINGS & THE ENVIRONMENT

Up next we're going to add bindings to our interpreter by adding support for let statements. But not only do we need to support let statements, no, we need to support the evaluation of identifiers, too. Let's say we have evaluated the following piece of code:

```
let x = 5 * 5;
```

Only adding support for the evaluation of this statement is not enough. We also need to make sure that the `x` evaluates to `25` after interpreting the line above.

So, our task in this section is to evaluate let statements and identifiers. We evaluate let statements by evaluating their value-producing expression and keeping track of the produced value under the specified name. To evaluate identifiers we check if we already have a value bound to the name. If we do, the identifier evaluates to this value, and if we don't, we return an error.

Sounds like a good plan? Alright, so let's kick this off with a few tests:

```
// evaluator/evaluator_test.go

func TestLetStatements(t *testing.T) {
    tests := []struct {
        input    string
        expected int64
    }{
        {"let a = 5; a;", 5},
        {"let a = 5 * 5; a;", 25},
        {"let a = 5; let b = a; b;", 5},
        {"let a = 5; let b = a; let c = a + b + 5; c;", 15},
    }

    for _, tt := range tests {
        testIntegerObject(t, testEval(tt.input), tt.expected)
    }
}
```

The test cases assert that these two things should work: evaluating the value-producing expression in a let statement and evaluating an identifier that's bound to a name. But we also need tests to make sure that we get an error when we try to evaluate an unbound identifier. And for that we can simply extend our existing `TestErrorHandling` function:

```
// evaluator/evaluator_test.go

func TestErrorHandling(t *testing.T) {
    tests := []struct {
        input           string
        expectedMessage string
    }{
// [...]
        {
            "foobar",
            "identifier not found: foobar",
        },
```

```
    }
// [...]
}
```

How do we make these tests pass? Obviously the first thing we have to do is add a new `case` branch for `*ast.LetStatement` to `Eval`. And in this branch we need to `Eval` the expression of the let statement, correct? So let's start with that:

```
// evaluator/evaluator.go

func Eval(node ast.Node) object.Object {
// [...]
    case *ast.LetStatement:
        val := Eval(node.Value)
        if isError(val) {
            return val
        }

    // Huh? Now what?


// [...]
}
```

The comment is right: now what? How to we keep track of values? We have the value and we have the name we should bind it too, `node.Name.Value`. How do we associate one with the other?

This is where something called the environment comes into play. The environment is what we use to keep track of value by associating them with a name. The name "environment" is a classic one, used in a lot of other interpreters, especially Lispy ones. But even though the name may sound sophisticated, at its heart the environment is a hash map that associates strings with objects. And that's exactly what we're going to use for our implementation.

We'll add a new `Environment` struct to the `object` package. And yes, for now it really is just a thin wrapper around a `map`:

```
// object/environment.go

package object

func NewEnvironment() *Environment {
    s := make(map[string]Object)
    return &Environment{store: s}
}

type Environment struct {
```

```
    store map[string]Object
}

func (e *Environment) Get(name string) (Object, bool) {
    obj, ok := e.store[name]
    return obj, ok
}

func (e *Environment) Set(name string, val Object) Object {
    e.store[name] = val
    return val
}
```

Let me guess what you're thinking: *Why not use a map? Why the wrapper?* It'll all make sense as soon as we start implementing functions and function calls in the next section, I promise. This is the groundwork we'll build upon later.

As it is, the usage of `object.Environment` itself is self-explanatory. But how do we use it inside `Eval`? How and where do we keep track of the environment? We pass it around by making it a parameter of `Eval`:

```
// evaluator/evaluator.go

func Eval(node ast.Node, env *object.Environment) object.Object {
// [...]
}
```

With that change nothing compiles anymore, because we have to change every call to `Eval` make use of the environment. And not only the calls to `Eval` in `Eval` itself, but also the ones in functions such as `evalProgram`, `evalIfExpression` and so on. This requires more manual editor work than anything else, so I won't bore you by showing the list of changes here.

The calls to `Eval` in our REPL and in our test suite need to use an environment too, of course. In the REPL we use a single environment:

```
// repl/repl.go

func Start(in io.Reader, out io.Writer) {
    scanner := bufio.NewScanner(in)
    env := object.NewEnvironment()

    for {
// [...]
        evaluated := evaluator.Eval(program, env)
        if evaluated != nil {
            io.WriteString(out, evaluated.Inspect())
            io.WriteString(out, "\n")
        }
```

```
    }
}
```

The environment we use here, env, persists between calls to Eval. If it didn't, binding a value to a name in the REPL would be without any effect. As soon as the next line is evaluated, the association wouldn't be in the new environment.

That's exactly what we want in our test suite, though. We don't want to keep state around for each test function and each test case. Each call to testEval should have a fresh environment so we don't run into weird bugs involving global state caused by the order in which tests are run. Every call to Eval here gets a fresh environment:

```
// evaluator/evaluator_test.go

func testEval(input string) object.Object {
    l := lexer.New(input)
    p := parser.New(l)
    program := p.ParseProgram()
    env := object.NewEnvironment()

    return Eval(program, env)
}
```

With updated Eval calls the tests compile again and we can start making them pass, which is not too hard with *object.Environemnt available. In the case branch for *ast.LetStatement we can just use the name and value we already have and save them in the current environment:

```
// evaluator/evaluator.go

func Eval(node ast.Node, env *object.Environment) object.Object {
// [...]
    case *ast.LetStatement:
        val := Eval(node.Value, env)
        if isError(val) {
            return val
        }
        env.Set(node.Name.Value, val)
// [...]
}
```

Now we're adding associations to the environment when evaluating let statements. But we also need to get these values out when we're evaluating identifiers. Doing that is pretty easy, too:

```
// evaluator/evaluator.go

func Eval(node ast.Node, env *object.Environment) object.Object {
```

```go
// [...]
    case *ast.Identifier:
        return evalIdentifier(node, env)
// [...]
}

func evalIdentifier(
    node *ast.Identifier,
    env *object.Environment,
) object.Object {
    val, ok := env.Get(node.Value)
    if !ok {
        return newError("identifier not found: " + node.Value)
    }

    return val
}
```

`evalIdentifier` will be extended in the next section. For now it simply checks if a value has been associated with the given name in the current environment. If that's the case it returns the value, otherwise an error.

Look at this:

```
$ go test ./evaluator
ok      monkey/evaluator        0.007s
```

Yes, you're right, that's exactly what this means: we're now firmly standing in programming language land.

```
$ go run main.go
Hello mrnugget! This is the Monkey programming language!
Feel free to type in commands
>> let a = 5;
>> let b = a > 3;
>> let c = a * 99;
>> if (b) { 10 } else { 1 };
10
>> let d = if (c > a) { 99 } else { 100 };
>> d
99
>> d * c * a;
245025
```

3.10 - Functions & Function Calls

This is what we've been working towards. This is the third act. We're going to add support for functions and function calls to our interpreter. When we're done with this section, we'll be able to do this in our REPL:

```
>> let add = fn(a, b, c, d) { return a + b + c + d };
>> add(1, 2, 3, 4);
10
>> let addThree = fn(x) { return x + 3 };
>> addThree(3);
6
>> let max = fn(x, y) { if (x > y) { x } else { y } };
>> max(5, 10)
10
>> let factorial = fn(n) { if (n == 0) { 1 } else { n * factorial(n - 1) } };
>> factorial(5)
120
```

If that doesn't impress you then take a look at this. Passing around functions, higher-order functions and closures will also work:

```
>> let callTwoTimes = fn(x, func) { func(func(x)) };
>> callTwoTimes(3, addThree);
9
>> callTwoTimes(3, fn(x) { x + 1 });
5
>> let newAdder = fn(x) { fn(n) { x + n } };
>> let addTwo = newAdder(2);
>> addTwo(2);
4
```

Yes, that's right, we will be able to do all of *that*.

In order to get from where we currently are to *there* we need to do two things: define an internal representation of functions in our object system and add support for function calls to `Eval`.

But don't worry. It's easy. The work we did in the last sections now pays off. We can reuse and extend a lot of things we already built. You'll see that a lot of things just start to fit together at a certain point in this section.

Since "one step at a time" brought us here there's no reason to abandon this strategy now. The first step is to take care of the internal representation of functions.

The need to represent functions internally comes from the fact that functions in Monkey are treated like any other value: we can bind them to names, use them in expressions, pass them to other functions, return them from functions and so on.

And like other values, functions need a representation in our object system, so we can pass around, assign and return them.

But how do we represent a function internally, as an object? Our definition of `ast.FunctionLiteral` gives us a starting point:

```
// ast/ast.go

type FunctionLiteral struct {
    Token      token.Token // The 'fn' token
    Parameters []*Identifier
    Body       *BlockStatement
}
```

We don't need the `Token` field in a function object, but `Parameters` and `Body` make sense. We can't evaluate a function without its body and we can't evaluate the body if we don't know which parameters the function has. Besides `Parameters` and `Body` we also need a third field in our new function object:

```
// object/object.go

const (
// [...]
    FUNCTION_OBJ = "FUNCTION"
)

type Function struct {
    Parameters []*ast.Identifier
    Body       *ast.BlockStatement
    Env        *Environment
}

func (f *Function) Type() ObjectType { return FUNCTION_OBJ }
func (f *Function) Inspect() string {
    var out bytes.Buffer

    params := []string{}
    for _, p := range f.Parameters {
        params = append(params, p.String())
    }

    out.WriteString("fn")
    out.WriteString("(")
    out.WriteString(strings.Join(params, ", "))
    out.WriteString(") {\n")
    out.WriteString(f.Body.String())
    out.WriteString("\n}")

    return out.String()
```

```
}
```

This definition of `object.Function` has the `Parameters` and `Body` fields. But it also has `Env`, a field that holds a pointer to an `object.Environment`, because functions in Monkey carry their own environment with them. That allows for closures, which "close over" the environment they're defined in and can later access it. That will make more sense when we start using the `Env` field. You'll see.

With that definition done, we can now write a test to assert that our interpreter knows how to build functions:

```
// evaluator/evaluator_test.go

func TestFunctionObject(t *testing.T) {
    input := "fn(x) { x + 2; };"

    evaluated := testEval(input)
    fn, ok := evaluated.(*object.Function)
    if !ok {
        t.Fatalf("object is not Function. got=%T (%+v)", evaluated, evaluated)
    }

    if len(fn.Parameters) != 1 {
        t.Fatalf("function has wrong parameters. Parameters=%+v",
            fn.Parameters)
    }

    if fn.Parameters[0].String() != "x" {
        t.Fatalf("parameter is not 'x'. got=%q", fn.Parameters[0])
    }

    expectedBody := "(x + 2)"

    if fn.Body.String() != expectedBody {
        t.Fatalf("body is not %q. got=%q", expectedBody, fn.Body.String())
    }
}
```

This test function asserts that evaluating a function literal results in the correct `*object.Function` being returned, with correct parameters and the correct body. The function's environment will be tested later on in other tests, implicitly. Making this test pass takes just a few lines of code added to `Eval` in the form of a new `case` branch:

```
// evaluator/evaluator.go

func Eval(node ast.Node, env *object.Environment) object.Object {
// [...]
```

```go
    case *ast.FunctionLiteral:
        params := node.Parameters
        body := node.Body
        return &object.Function{Parameters: params, Env: env, Body: body}
// [...]
}
```

Easy, right? The test passes. We just reuse the `Parameters` and `Body` fields of the AST node. Notice how we use the current environment when building the function object.

With that relatively low-level test passing and thus having made sure that we build the internal representation of functions correctly, we can turn to the topic of function application. That means, extending our interpreter so that we can call functions. The tests for this are much more readable and easier to write:

```go
// evaluator/evaluator_test.go

func TestFunctionApplication(t *testing.T) {
    tests := []struct {
        input    string
        expected int64
    }{
        {"let identity = fn(x) { x; }; identity(5);", 5},
        {"let identity = fn(x) { return x; }; identity(5);", 5},
        {"let double = fn(x) { x * 2; }; double(5);", 10},
        {"let add = fn(x, y) { x + y; }; add(5, 5);", 10},
        {"let add = fn(x, y) { x + y; }; add(5 + 5, add(5, 5));", 20},
        {"fn(x) { x; }(5)", 5},
    }

    for _, tt := range tests {
        testIntegerObject(t, testEval(tt.input), tt.expected)
    }
}
```

Each test case here does the same thing: define a function, apply it to arguments and then make an assertion about the produced value. But with their slight differences they test multiple important things: returning values implicitly, returning values using `return` statements, using parameters in expressions, multiple parameters and evaluating arguments before passing them to the function.

We are also testing two possible forms of `*ast.CallExpression` here. One where the function is an identifier that evaluates to a function object, and the second one where the function is a function literal. The neat thing is that it doesn't really matter. We already know how to evaluate identifiers and function literals:

```go
// evaluator/evaluator.go
```

```go
func Eval(node ast.Node, env *object.Environment) object.Object {
// [...]
    case *ast.CallExpression:
        function := Eval(node.Function, env)
        if isError(function) {
            return function
        }
// [...]
}
```

Yes, we're just using `Eval` to get the function we want to call. Whether that's an `*ast.Identifier` or an `*ast.FunctionLiteral`: `Eval` returns an `*object.Function` (if there's no error, of course).

But how do we do call this `*object.Function`? The first step is to evaluate the arguments of a call expression. The reason is simple:

```
let add = fn(x, y) { x + y };
add(2 + 2, 5 + 5);
```

Here we want to pass `4` and `10` to the `add` function as arguments and not the expressions `2 + 2` and `5 + 5`.

Evaluating the arguments is nothing more than evaluating a list of expressions and keeping track of the produced values. But we also have to stop the evaluation process as soon as it encounters an error. That leads us to this code:

```go
// evaluator/evaluator.go

func Eval(node ast.Node, env *object.Environment) object.Object {
// [...]
    case *ast.CallExpression:
        function := Eval(node.Function, env)
        if isError(function) {
            return function
        }
        args := evalExpressions(node.Arguments, env)
        if len(args) == 1 && isError(args[0]) {
            return args[0]
        }
// [...]
}

func evalExpressions(
    exps []ast.Expression,
    env *object.Environment,
) []object.Object {
    var result []object.Object
```

```
    for _, e := range exps {
        evaluated := Eval(e, env)
        if isError(evaluated) {
            return []object.Object{evaluated}
        }
        result = append(result, evaluated)
    }

    return result
}
```

Nothing fancy going on here. We just iterate over a list of `ast.Expressions` and evaluate them in the context of the current environment. If we encounter an error, we stop the evaluation and return the error. This is also the part where we decided to evaluate the arguments from left-to-right. Hopefully we won't be writing code in Monkey that makes assertions about the order of argument evaluation, but if we do, we're on the conservative and safe side of programming language design.

So! Now that we have both the function and the list of evaluated arguments, how do we "call the function"? How do we apply the function to the arguments?

The obvious answer is that we have to evaluate the body of the function, which is just a block statement. We already know how to evaluate those, so why not just call `Eval` and pass it the body of the function? One word: arguments. The body of the function can contain references to the parameters of the function and just evaluating the body in the current environment would result in references to unknown names, which would lead to errors, which is not what we want. Evaluating the body as it is, in the current environment, does not work.

What we need to do instead is change the environment in which the function is evaluated, so that the references to parameters in the function's body resolve to the correct arguments. But we can't just add these arguments to the current environment. That could lead to previous bindings being overwritten, which is not what we want. We want this to work:

```
let i = 5;
let printNum = fn(i) {
  puts(i);
};

printNum(10);
puts(i);
```

With a `puts` function that prints lines, this should print two lines, containing `10` and `5` respectively. If we were to overwrite the current environment before evaluating the body of `printNum`, the last line would also result in `10` being printed.

So adding the arguments of the function call to the current environment in order to make them accessible in the function's body does not work. What we need to do instead is to preserve previous bindings while at the same time making new ones available - we'll call that "extending the environment".

Extending the environment means that we create a new instance of `object.Environment` with a pointer to the environment it should extend. By doing that we enclose a fresh and empty environment with an existing one.

When the new environment's `Get` method is called and it itself doesn't have a value associated with the given name, it calls the `Get` of the enclosing environment. That's the environment it's extending. And if that enclosing environment can't find the value, it calls its own enclosing environment and so on until there is no enclosing environment anymore and we can safely say that we have an "ERROR: unknown identifier: foobar".

```
// object/environment.go

package object

func NewEnclosedEnvironment(outer *Environment) *Environment {
    env := NewEnvironment()
    env.outer = outer
    return env
}

func NewEnvironment() *Environment {
    s := make(map[string]Object)
    return &Environment{store: s, outer: nil}
}

type Environment struct {
    store map[string]Object
    outer *Environment
}

func (e *Environment) Get(name string) (Object, bool) {
    obj, ok := e.store[name]
    if !ok && e.outer != nil {
        obj, ok = e.outer.Get(name)
    }
    return obj, ok
}

func (e *Environment) Set(name string, val Object) Object {
    e.store[name] = val
    return val
```

```
}
```

`object.Environment` now has a new field called `outer` that can contain a reference to another `object.Environment`, which is the enclosing environment, the one it's extending. The `NewEnclosedEnvironment` function makes creating such an enclosed environment easy. The `Get` method has also been changed. It now checks the enclosing environment for the given name, too.

This new behaviour mirrors how we think about variable scopes. There is an inner scope and an outer scope. If something is not found in the inner scope, it's looked up in the outer scope. The outer scope *encloses* the inner scope. And the inner scope *extends* the outer one.

With our updated `object.Environment` functionality we can correctly evaluate function bodies. Remember, the problem was this: possibly overwriting existing bindings in a environment when binding the arguments of a function call to the parameter names of the function. Now, instead of overwriting bindings, we create a new environment that's enclosed by the current environment and add our bindings to this fresh and empty environment.

But we won't use the current environment as the enclosing environment, no. Instead we'll use the environment our `*object.Function` carries around. Remember that one? That's the environment our function was defined in.

Here is the updated version of `Eval` that handles function calls completely and correctly:

```go
// evaluator/evaluator.go

func Eval(node ast.Node, env *object.Environment) object.Object {
// [...]
    case *ast.CallExpression:
        function := Eval(node.Function, env)
        if isError(function) {
            return function
        }
        args := evalExpressions(node.Arguments, env)
        if len(args) == 1 && isError(args[0]) {
            return args[0]
        }

        return applyFunction(function, args)
// [...]
}

func applyFunction(fn object.Object, args []object.Object) object.Object {
    function, ok := fn.(*object.Function)
    if !ok {
```

```go
        return newError("not a function: %s", fn.Type())
    }

    extendedEnv := extendFunctionEnv(function, args)
    evaluated := Eval(function.Body, extendedEnv)
    return unwrapReturnValue(evaluated)
}

func extendFunctionEnv(
    fn *object.Function,
    args []object.Object,
) *object.Environment {
    env := object.NewEnclosedEnvironment(fn.Env)

    for paramIdx, param := range fn.Parameters {
        env.Set(param.Value, args[paramIdx])
    }

    return env
}

func unwrapReturnValue(obj object.Object) object.Object {
    if returnValue, ok := obj.(*object.ReturnValue); ok {
        return returnValue.Value
    }

    return obj
}
```

In the new `applyFunction` function we not only check that we really have a `*object.Function` at hand but also convert the `fn` parameter to a `*object.Function` reference in order to get access to the function's `.Env` and `.Body` fields (which `object.Object` doesn't define).

The `extendFunctionEnv` function creates a new `*object.Environment` that's enclosed by the function's environment. In this new, enclosed environment it binds the arguments of the function call to the function's parameter names.

And this newly enclosed and updated environment is then the environment in which the function's body is evaluated. The result of this evaluation is unwrapped if it's an `*object.ReturnValue`. That's necessary, because otherwise a `return` statement would bubble up through several functions and stop the evaluation in all of them. But we only want to stop the evaluation of the last called function's body. That's why we need unwrap it, so that `evalBlockStatement` won't stop evaluating statements in "outer" functions. I also added a few test cases to our previous `TestReturnStatements` function to make sure that this works.

Those were the last missing pieces. *What? Really?* Yeah! Take a look a this:

```
$ go test ./evaluator
ok      monkey/evaluator        0.007s
$ go run main.go
Hello mrnugget! This is the Monkey programming language!
Feel free to type in commands
>> let addTwo = fn(x) { x + 2; };
>> addTwo(2)
4
>> let multiply = fn(x, y) { x * y };
>> multiply(50 / 2, 1 * 2)
50
>> fn(x) { x == 10 }(5)
false
>> fn(x) { x == 10 }(10)
true
```

Whaaat? Yes! It works! We can now finally define and call functions! There's a saying that goes "this is nothing to write home about". Well, this is! But before we put on our party hats, it's worth taking a closer look at the interaction between functions and their environment and what it means for function application. Because what we've seen is not all we can do, there is a lot more.

So, I bet that one question still bugs you: "Why extend the function's environment and not the current environment?" The short answer is this:

```
// evaluator/evaluator_test.go

func TestClosures(t *testing.T) {
    input := `
let newAdder = fn(x) {
  fn(y) { x + y };
};

let addTwo = newAdder(2);
addTwo(2);`

    testIntegerObject(t, testEval(input), 4)
}
```

This test passes. Yes, really:

```
$ go run main.go
Hello mrnugget! This is the Monkey programming language!
Feel free to type in commands
>> let newAdder = fn(x) { fn(y) { x + y } };
>> let addTwo = newAdder(2);
>> addTwo(3);
```

```
5
>> let addThree = newAdder(3);
>> addThree(10);
13
```

Monkey has closures and they already work in our interpreter. How cool is that? Exactly. Very cool. But the connection between closures and the original question might not be so clear yet. Closures are functions that "close over" the environment they were defined in. They carry their own environment around and whenever they're called they can access it.

The two important lines from the example above are these:

```
let newAdder = fn(x) { fn(y) { x + y } };
let addTwo = newAdder(2);
```

`newAdder` here is a higher-order function. Higher-order functions are functions that either return other functions or receive them as arguments. In this case `newAdder` returns another function. But not just any function: a closure. `addTwo` is bound to the closure that's returned when calling `newAdder` with `2` as the sole argument.

And what makes `addTwo` a closure? The bindings it has access to when called.

When `addTwo` is called it not only has access to the arguments of the call, the `y` parameter, but it can also reach the value `x` was bound to at the time of the `newAdder(2)` call, even though that binding is long out of scope and not existent in the current environment anymore:

```
>> let newAdder = fn(x) { fn(y) { x + y } };
>> let addTwo = newAdder(2);
>> x
ERROR: identifier not found: x
```

`x` is not bound to a value in our top-level environment. But `addTwo` still has access to it:

```
>> addTwo(3);
5
```

In other words: the closure `addTwo` still has access to the environment that was the current environment at the time of its definition. Which is when the last line of `newAdder`'s body was evaluated. This last line is a function literal. Remember: when function literals are evaluated we build an `object.Function` and keep a reference to the current environment in its `.Env` field.

When we later on evaluate the body of `addTwo`, we don't evaluate it in the current environment, but instead in the function's environment. And we do that by extending the function's environment and passing it to `Eval` instead of the current environment. Why? So it can still access it. Why? So we can use closures. Why? Because they're freaking amazing and I love them!

And since we're talking about amazing things, it's worth mentioning that we not only support returning functions from other functions but also accepting functions as arguments in a function call. Yes, functions are first-class citizens in Monkey and we can pass them around like any other value:

```
>> let add = fn(a, b) { a + b };
>> let sub = fn(a, b) { a - b };
>> let applyFunc = fn(a, b, func) { func(a, b) };
>> applyFunc(2, 2, add);
4
>> applyFunc(10, 2, sub);
8
```

Here we pass the `add` and `sub` functions as arguments to `applyFunc`. `applyFunc` then calls this function without any problems: the `func` parameter resolves to the function object which then gets called with two arguments. There is not much more to it, everything works already in our interpreter.

I know what you're thinking right now and here is a template for the message you want to send:

Dear NAME_OF_FRIEND, remember when I said that someday I'll be someone and do something great people will remember me for? Well, today's the day. My Monkey interpreter works and it supports functions, higher-order functions, closures and integers and arithmetic and long story short: I've never been happier in my life!

We did it. We built a fully working Monkey interpreter that supports functions and function calls, higher-order functions and closures. Go on, celebrate! I'll be waiting here.

3.11 - Who's Taking The Trash Out?

At the beginning of this book I promised you that we wouldn't take any shortcuts and build a fully functional interpreter with our own hands, from scratch and without any third party tools. And we did! But now I have a small confession to make.

Consider what happens when we run this snippet of Monkey code in our interpreter:

```
let counter = fn(x) {
  if (x > 100) {
```

```
    return true;
  } else {
    let foobar = 9999;
    counter(x + 1);
  }
};

counter(0);
```

Obviously, it would return 'true' after evaluating the body of `counter` 101 times. But a lot is happening until the last of these recursive calls to `counter` returns.

The first thing is the evaluation if-else-expression condition: `x > 100`. If the produced value is not truthy, the alternative of the if-else-expression gets evaluated. In the alternative the integer literal `9999` gets bound to the name `foobar`, which is never referenced again. Then `x + 1` is evaluated. The result of that call to `Eval` is then passed to another call to `counter`. And then it all starts again, until `x > 100` evaluates to `TRUE`.

The point is this: in each call to `counter` a lot of objects are allocated. Or to put it in terms of our `Eval` function and our object system: each evaluation of `counter`'s body results in a lot of `object.Integer` being allocated and instantiated. The unused `9999` integer literal and the result of `x + 1` are obvious. But even the literals `100` and `1` produce new `object.Integers` every time the body of `counter` is evaluated.

If we were to modify our `Eval` function to track every instance of `&object.Integer{}`, we'd see that running this small snippet of code results in around 400 allocated `object.Integers`.

What's the problem with that?

Our objects are stored in memory. The more objects we use the more memory we need. And even though the number of objects in the example is tiny compared to other programs memory is not infinite.

With each call to `counter` the memory usage of our interpreter process should rise until it eventually runs out of memory and the operating system kills it. But if we were to monitor memory usage while running the snippet above, we'd see that it doesn't steadily rise and never goes down. Instead it increases and decreases. Why?

The answer to that question is the heart of the confession I have to make: we're reusing Go's garbage collector as a garbage collector for our guest language. We do not need to write our own.

Go's garbage collector (GC) is the reason why we don't run out of memory. It manages memory for us. Even when we call the `counter` function from above many,

many times and thus add a lot more unused integer literals and object allocations, we won't run out of memory. Because the GC keeps track of which `object.Integer` are still reachable by us and which are not. When it notices that an object is not reachable anymore it makes the object's memory available again.

The example above generates a lot of integer objects that are unreachable after a call to `counter`: the literals `1` and `100` and the nonsense `9999` bound to `foobar`. There is no way to access these objects after `counter` returns. In the case of `1` and `100` it's clear that they're unreachable, since they're not bound to a name. But even the `9999` bound to `foobar` is unreachable since `foobar` is out of scope when the function returns. The environment that was constructed for the evaluation of `counter`'s body gets destroyed (also by Go's GC, mind you!) and with it the `foobar` binding.

These unreachable objects are useless and take up memory. That's why the GC collects them and frees up the memory they used.

And that's super handy for us! That saves us a lot of work! If we were to write our interpreter in a language like C, where we don't have a GC, we'd need to implement one ourselves to manage memory for users of the interpreter.

What would such a hypothetical GC need to do? In short: keep track of object allocations and references to objects, make enough memory available for future object allocations and give memory back when it's not needed anymore. This last point is what garbage collection is all about. Without it the programs would "leak" and finally run out of memory.

There are a myriad ways to accomplish all of the above, involving different algorithms and implementations. For example, there's the basic "mark and sweep" algorithm. In order to implement it one has to decide whether the GC will be a generational GC or not, or whether it's a stop-the-world GC or a concurrent GC, or how it's organizing memory and handling memory fragmentation. Having decided all of that an efficient implementation is still a lot of hard work.

But maybe you're asking yourself: *Okay, so we have the GC of Go available. But can't we just write our own GC for the guest language and use that one instead?*

Unfortunately, no. We'd have to disable Go's GC and find a way to take over all of its duties. That's easier said than done. It's a huge undertaking since we would also have to take care of allocating and freeing memory ourselves - in a language that per default prohibits exactly that.

That's why I decided to not add a "Let's write our own GC next to Go's GC" section to this book and to instead reuse Go's GC. Garbage collection itself is a huge topic and adding the dimension of working around an existing GC blows it out of the scope of this book. But still, I hope that this section gave you a rough idea of what a GC does and which problems it solves. Maybe you even know now what to do if you were to translate the interpreter we built here into another host language without garbage collection.

And with that... we're done! Our interpreter works. All that's left for us is to extend it and make it more useful by adding more data types and functions.

CHAPTER 4

EXTENDING THE INTERPRETER

4.1 - DATA TYPES & FUNCTIONS

Even though our interpreter works amazingly well and has some mind-blowing features, like first-class functions and closures, the only data types we had available as users of Monkey were integers and booleans. That's not especially useful and a lot less than what we're used to from other programming languages. In this chapter we're going to change that. We're going to add new data types to our interpreter.

The great thing about this endeavor is that it takes us through the whole interpreter again. We will add new token types, modify the lexer, extend the parser and finally add support for the data types to our evaluator and the object system.

Even better is that the data types we're going to add are already present in Go. That means that we only need to make them available in Monkey. We don't need to implement them from scratch, which is pretty handy, since this book isn't called "Implementing Common Data Structures In Go" and we can concentrate on our interpreter.

In addition to that we're also going to make the interpreter much more powerful by adding some new functions. Of course, as users of our interpreter we could define functions ourselves just fine, but those were limited in what they could do. These new ones, called built-in functions, will be much more powerful, since they have access to the inner workings of the Monkey programming language.

The first thing we're going to do is add a data type we all know: the string. Nearly every programming language has it and Monkey shall have it too.

4.2 - Strings

In Monkey strings are a sequence of characters. They are first-class values, can be bound to identifiers, used as arguments in functions calls and be returned by functions. They look just like the strings in many other programming languages: characters enclosed by double quotes.

Besides the data type itself, in this section we'll also add support for string concatenation by supporting the infix operator + for strings.

At the end, we'll be able to do this:

```
$ go run main.go
Hello mrnugget! This is micro, your own programming language!
Feel free to type in commands
>> let firstName = "Thorsten";
>> let lastName = "Ball";
>> let fullName = fn(first, last) { first + " " + last };
>> fullName(firstName, lastName);
Thorsten Ball
```

Supporting Strings in our Lexer

The first thing we have to do is add support for string literals to our lexer. The basic structure of strings is this:

```
"<sequence of characters>"
```

That's not too hard, right? A sequence of characters enclosed by double quotes.

What we want from our lexer is a single token for each string literal. So in the case of `"Hello World"` we want a single token, instead of tokens for `"`, `Hello`, `World` and `"`. A single token for string literals makes handling them in our parser a lot easier and we move the bulk of the work to one small method in the lexer.

Of course, the approach using multiple tokens is also valid and maybe beneficial in some cases/parsers. We could use `"` surrounding `token.IDENT` tokens. But in our case, we'll mirror the `token.INT` integer tokens we already have and carry the string literal itself around in the `.Literal` field of the token.

And with that being clear, it's time to work on our tokens and our lexer again. We haven't touched those since the first chapter, but I'm sure we'll do just fine.

The first thing we need to do is add a new `STRING` token type to our `token` package:

```
// token/token.go

const (
// [...]
    STRING = "STRING"
// [...]
)
```

With that in place we can add a test case for our lexer to see if strings are properly supported. To do that we just extend the `input` in our `TestNextToken` test function:

```
// lexer/lexer_test.go

func TestNextToken(t *testing.T) {
    input := `let five = 5;
let ten = 10;

let add = fn(x, y) {
  x + y;
};

let result = add(five, ten);
!-/*5;
5 < 10 > 5;

if (5 < 10) {
    return true;
} else {
    return false;
}

10 == 10;
10 != 9;
"foobar"
"foo bar"
`

    tests := []struct {
        expectedType    token.TokenType
        expectedLiteral string
    }{
// [...]
        {token.STRING, "foobar"},
        {token.STRING, "foo bar"},
        {token.EOF, ""},
    }
// [...]
}
```

The input now has two more lines containing the string literals we want to turn into tokens. There's "foobar" to make sure that lexing of string literals works and "foo bar" to make sure that it still works even with whitespace inside a literal.

Of course, the tests fail, because we haven't changed anything in the Lexer yet:

```
$ go test ./lexer
--- FAIL: TestNextToken (0.00s)
  lexer_test.go:122: tests[73] - tokentype wrong. expected="STRING",\
    got="ILLEGAL"
FAIL
FAIL    monkey/lexer    0.006s
```

Fixing the tests is easier than you might think. All we need to do is add a case branch for " to the switch statement in our Lexer and add a small helper method:

```
// lexer/lexer.go

func (l *Lexer) NextToken() token.Token {
// [...]

    switch l.ch {
// [...]
    case '"':
        tok.Type = token.STRING
        tok.Literal = l.readString()
// [...]
    }

// [...]
}

func (l *Lexer) readString() string {
    position := l.position + 1
    for {
        l.readChar()
        if l.ch == '"' || l.ch == 0 {
            break
        }
    }
    return l.input[position:l.position]
}
```

There's really nothing mysterious about these changes. A new case branch and a helper function called readString that calls readChar until it encounters either a closing double quote or the end of the input.

If you think that this is too easy, feel free to make readString report an error instead of simply returning when it reaches the end of the input. Or you can add support for character escaping so that string literals like `"hello \"world\""`, `"hello\n world"` and `"hello\t\t\tworld"` work.

Meanwhile, our tests are passing:

```
$ go test ./lexer
ok      monkey/lexer    0.006s
```

Great! Our lexer now knows how to handle string literals. It's time to teach the parser how to do the same.

PARSING STRINGS

In order for our parser to turn `token.STRING` into a string literal AST node we need to define said node. Thankfully the definition couldn't be simpler. It looks really similar to `ast.IntegerLiteral`, except that the `Value` field now contains a `string` instead of an `int64`.

```go
// ast/ast.go

type StringLiteral struct {
    Token token.Token
    Value string
}

func (sl *StringLiteral) expressionNode()      {}
func (sl *StringLiteral) TokenLiteral() string { return sl.Token.Literal }
func (sl *StringLiteral) String() string       { return sl.Token.Literal }
```

Of course, string literals are expressions and not statements. They evaluate to the string.

With that definition we can write a small test case that makes sure the parser knows how to handle `token.STRING` tokens and outputs `*ast.StringLiterals`:

```go
// parser/parser_test.go

func TestStringLiteralExpression(t *testing.T) {
    input := `"hello world";`

    l := lexer.New(input)
    p := New(l)
    program := p.ParseProgram()
    checkParserErrors(t, p)

    stmt := program.Statements[0].(*ast.ExpressionStatement)
    literal, ok := stmt.Expression.(*ast.StringLiteral)
    if !ok {
```

```go
        t.Fatalf("exp not *ast.StringLiteral. got=%T", stmt.Expression)
    }

    if literal.Value != "hello world" {
        t.Errorf("literal.Value not %q. got=%q", "hello world", literal.Value)
    }
}
```

Running the tests results in a well known type of parser error:

```
$ go test ./parser
--- FAIL: TestStringLiteralExpression (0.00s)
  parser_test.go:888: parser has 1 errors
  parser_test.go:890: parser error: "no prefix parse function for STRING found"
FAIL
FAIL    monkey/parser   0.007s
```

We've seen that many times before and we know how to fix it. All we have to do is register a new `prefixParseFn` for `token.STRING` tokens. This parse function then returns an `*ast.StringLiteral`:

```go
// parser/parser.go

func New(l *lexer.Lexer) *Parser {
// [...]
    p.registerPrefix(token.STRING, p.parseStringLiteral)
// [...]
}

func (p *Parser) parseStringLiteral() ast.Expression {
    return &ast.StringLiteral{Token: p.curToken, Value: p.curToken.Literal}
}
```

Three new lines! That's all it takes to make the tests pass:

```
$ go test ./parser
ok      monkey/parser   0.007s
```

So now our lexer turns string literals into `token.STRING` tokens and the parser turns those into `*ast.StringLiteral` nodes. We're now ready to make changes to our object system and the evaluator.

EVALUATING STRINGS

Representing a string in our object system is as easy as representing integers. And the biggest reason why it's so easy is that we reuse Go's `string` data type. Imagine adding a data type to the guest language that can't be represented with built-in data structures of the host language. E.g.: strings in C. That's a lot more work. But instead, all we have to do is define a new object that holds a string:

```
// object/object.go

const (
// [...]
    STRING_OBJ = "STRING"
)

type String struct {
    Value string
}

func (s *String) Type() ObjectType { return STRING_OBJ }
func (s *String) Inspect() string  { return s.Value }
```

Now we need to extend our evaluator so it turns `*ast.StringLiteral` in `object.String` objects. The test to make sure that this works is tiny:

```
// evaluator/evaluator_test.go

func TestStringLiteral(t *testing.T) {
    input := `"Hello World!"`

    evaluated := testEval(input)
    str, ok := evaluated.(*object.String)
    if !ok {
        t.Fatalf("object is not String. got=%T (%+v)", evaluated, evaluated)
    }

    if str.Value != "Hello World!" {
        t.Errorf("String has wrong value. got=%q", str.Value)
    }
}
```

The call to `Eval` doesn't return an `*object.String` yet but `nil`:

```
$ go test ./evaluator
--- FAIL: TestStringLiteral (0.00s)
  evaluator_test.go:317: object is not String. got=<nil> (<nil>)
FAIL
FAIL    monkey/evaluator        0.007s
```

Getting this test to pass needs even fewer lines than in the parser. Just two:

```
// evaluator/evaluator.go

func Eval(node ast.Node, env *object.Environment) object.Object {
// [...]
```

```go
    case *ast.StringLiteral:
        return &object.String{Value: node.Value}

// [...]
}
```

That makes the tests pass and we can now use strings in our REPL:

```
$ go run main.go
Hello mrnugget! This is the Monkey programming language!
Feel free to type in commands
>> "Hello world!"
Hello world!
>> let hello = "Hello there, fellow Monkey users and fans!"
>> hello
Hello there, fellow Monkey users and fans!
>> let giveMeHello = fn() { "Hello!" }
>> giveMeHello()
Hello!
```

We now have full support for strings in our interpreter! Sweet! Or should I say...

```
>> "This is amazing!"
This is amazing!
```

STRING CONCATENATION

Having the string data type available is great. But we can't do much with strings yet, besides creating them. Let's change that! In this section we're going to add string concatenation to our interpreter. And we'll do that by adding support for the + infix operator with string operands.

What we want is perfectly described by this test:

```go
// evaluator/evaluator_test.go

func TestStringConcatenation(t *testing.T) {
    input := `"Hello" + " " + "World!"`

    evaluated := testEval(input)
    str, ok := evaluated.(*object.String)
    if !ok {
        t.Fatalf("object is not String. got=%T (%+v)", evaluated, evaluated)
    }

    if str.Value != "Hello World!" {
        t.Errorf("String has wrong value. got=%q", str.Value)
```

```
    }
}
```

We can also extend our `TestErrorHandling` function to make sure that we only add support for the + operator and nothing more:

```
// evaluator/evaluator_test.go

func TestErrorHandling(t *testing.T) {
    tests := []struct {
        input           string
        expectedMessage string
    }{
// [...]
        {
            `"Hello" - "World"`,
            "unknown operator: STRING - STRING",
        },
// [...]
    }

// [...]
}
```

This test case is already green and acts more as specification and regression testing than as a guide for an implementation. But our concatenation test is failing:

```
$ go test ./evaluator
--- FAIL: TestStringConcatenation (0.00s)
  evaluator_test.go:336: object is not String. got=*object.Error\
    (&{Message:unknown operator: STRING + STRING})
FAIL
FAIL    monkey/evaluator        0.007s
```

The place where we need to make changes is `evalInfixExpression`. Here we need to add a new branch to the existing switch statement that's evaluated when both operands are strings:

```
// evaluator/evaluator.go

func evalInfixExpression(
    operator string,
    left, right object.Object,
) object.Object {
    switch {
// [...]
    case left.Type() == object.STRING_OBJ && right.Type() == object.STRING_OBJ:
        return evalStringInfixExpression(operator, left, right)
// [...]
```

```
    }
}
```

The `evalStringInfixExpression` is the most minimal implementation possible:

```go
// evaluator/evaluator.go

func evalStringInfixExpression(
    operator string,
    left, right object.Object,
) object.Object {
    if operator != "+" {
        return newError("unknown operator: %s %s %s",
            left.Type(), operator, right.Type())
    }

    leftVal := left.(*object.String).Value
    rightVal := right.(*object.String).Value
    return &object.String{Value: leftVal + rightVal}
}
```

The first thing here is the check for the correct operator. If it's the supported `+` we unwrap the string objects and construct a new string that's a concatenation of both operands.

If we want to support more operators for strings this is the place where to add them. Also, if we want to support comparison of strings with the `==` and `!=` we'd need to add this here too. Pointer comparison doesn't work for strings, at least not in the way we want it to: with strings we want to compare values and not pointers.

And that's it! Our tests pass:

```
$ go test ./evaluator
ok      monkey/evaluator        0.007s
```

We can now use string literals, pass them around, bind them to names, return them from functions and also concatenate them:

```
>> let makeGreeter = fn(greeting) { fn(name) { greeting + " " + name + "!" } };
>> let hello = makeGreeter("Hello");
>> hello("Thorsten");
Hello Thorsten!
>> let heythere = makeGreeter("Hey there");
>> heythere("Thorsten");
Hey there Thorsten!
```

Alright! I'd say strings are now working very well in our interpreter. But we can still add something else to work with them...

4.3 - BUILT-IN FUNCTIONS

In this section we're going to add built-in functions to our interpreter. They're called "built-in", because they're not defined by a user of the interpreter and they're not Monkey code - they are built right into the interpreter, into the language itself.

These built-in functions are defined by us, in Go, and bridge the world of Monkey with the world of our interpreter implementation. A lot of language implementations provide such functions to offer functionality to the language's user that's not provided "inside" the language.

Here's an example: a function that returns the current time. In order to get the current time one could ask the kernel (or another computer, etc.). Asking and talking to the kernel is normally done via something called system calls. But if the programming language doesn't offer users to make such system calls themselves, then the language implementation, be it the compiler or the interpreter, has to provide something to make these system calls on behalf of the users instead.

So, again, the built-in functions we're going to add are defined by us, the implementers of the interpreter. The user of the interpreter can call them, but we define them. What these functions can do, we leave open. The only restriction they have is that they need to accept zero or more `object.Object` as arguments and return an `object.Object`.

```
// object/object.go

type BuiltinFunction func(args ...Object) Object
```

That's the type definition of a callable Go function. But since we need to make these `BuiltinFunctions` available to our users we need to fit them into our object system. We do that by wrapping them:

```
// object/object.go

const (
// [...]
    BUILTIN_OBJ = "BUILTIN"
)

type Builtin struct {
    Fn BuiltinFunction
}

func (b *Builtin) Type() ObjectType { return BUILTIN_OBJ }
func (b *Builtin) Inspect() string  { return "builtin function" }
```

There's not much to `object.Builtin`, as you can see. It's clearly just a wrapper.

But in combination with `object.BuiltinFunction` it's enough to get us started.

LEN

The first built-in function we're going to add to our interpreter is `len`. Its job is to return the number of characters in a string. It's impossible to define this function as a user of Monkey. That's why we need it to be built-in. What we want from `len` is this:

```
>> len("Hello World!")
12
>> len("")
0
>> len("Hey Bob, how ya doin?")
21
```

I think that makes the idea behind `len` pretty clear. So clear in fact, that we can easily write a test for it:

```go
// evaluator/evaluator_test.go

func TestBuiltinFunctions(t *testing.T) {
    tests := []struct {
        input    string
        expected interface{}
    }{
        {`len("")`, 0},
        {`len("four")`, 4},
        {`len("hello world")`, 11},
        {`len(1)`, "argument to `len` not supported, got INTEGER"},
        {`len("one", "two")`, "wrong number of arguments. got=2, want=1"},
    }

    for _, tt := range tests {
        evaluated := testEval(tt.input)

        switch expected := tt.expected.(type) {
        case int:
            testIntegerObject(t, evaluated, int64(expected))
        case string:
            errObj, ok := evaluated.(*object.Error)
            if !ok {
                t.Errorf("object is not Error. got=%T (%+v)",
                    evaluated, evaluated)
                continue
            }
            if errObj.Message != expected {
```

```
                t.Errorf("wrong error message. expected=%q, got=%q",
                    expected, errObj.Message)
            }
        }
    }
}
```

So here we have a few test cases that run `len` through its paces: an empty string, a normal string and a string containing whitespace. It really shouldn't matter if there's whitespace in the string, but you'll never know, so I put the test case in. The last two test cases are more interesting: we want to make sure that `len` returns an `*object.Error` when called with an integer or with the wrong number of arguments.

If we run the tests we can see that calling `len` gives us an error, but not the one expected in our test case:

```
$ go test ./evaluator
--- FAIL: TestBuiltinFunctions (0.00s)
  evaluator_test.go:389: object is not Integer. got=*object.Error\
    (&{Message:identifier not found: len})
  evaluator_test.go:389: object is not Integer. got=*object.Error\
    (&{Message:identifier not found: len})
  evaluator_test.go:389: object is not Integer. got=*object.Error\
    (&{Message:identifier not found: len})
  evaluator_test.go:371: wrong error message.\
    expected="argument to `len` not supported, got INTEGER",\
    got="identifier not found: len"
FAIL
FAIL    monkey/evaluator        0.007s
```

`len` can't be found, which isn't that baffling considering that we haven't defined it yet.

In order to do that, the first thing we have to do is provide a way for built-in functions to be found. One option is to add them to the top-level `object.Environment`, that gets passed into `Eval`. But instead we're going to keep a separate environment of built-in functions:

```
// evaluator/builtins.go

package evaluator

import "monkey/object"

var builtins = map[string]*object.Builtin{
    "len": &object.Builtin{
        Fn: func(args ...object.Object) object.Object {
```

```
                return NULL
            },
        },
}
```

In order to make use of that, we need to edit our `evalIdentifier` function to lookup built-in functions as a fallback when the given identifier is not bound to a value in the current environment:

```go
// evaluator/evaluator.go

func evalIdentifier(
    node *ast.Identifier,
    env *object.Environment,
) object.Object {
    if val, ok := env.Get(node.Value); ok {
        return val
    }

    if builtin, ok := builtins[node.Value]; ok {
        return builtin
    }

    return newError("identifier not found: " + node.Value)
}
```

So now `len` is found when looking up the `len` identifier, calling it doesn't work yet:

```
$ go run main.go
Hello mrnugget! This is the Monkey programming language!
Feel free to type in commands
>> len()
ERROR: not a function: BUILTIN
>>
```

Running the tests gives us the same error. We need to teach our `applyFunction` about `*object.Builtin` and `object.BuiltinFunction`:

```go
// evaluator/evaluator.go

func applyFunction(fn object.Object, args []object.Object) object.Object {
    switch fn := fn.(type) {

    case *object.Function:
        extendedEnv := extendFunctionEnv(fn, args)
        evaluated := Eval(fn.Body, extendedEnv)
        return unwrapReturnValue(evaluated)

    case *object.Builtin:
        return fn.Fn(args...)
```

```go
    default:
        return newError("not a function: %s", fn.Type())
    }
}
```

Besides moving the existing lines around, what changed here is the addition of the case `*object.Builtin` branch, in which we call the `object.BuiltinFunction`. Doing so is as easy as using the `args` slice as arguments and calling the function.

Of note is that we don't need to `unwrapReturnValue` when calling a built-in function. That's because we never return an `*object.ReturnValue` from these functions.

Now the tests are rightfully complaining about `NULL` being returned when calling `len`:

```
$ go test ./evaluator
--- FAIL: TestBuiltinFunctions (0.00s)
  evaluator_test.go:389: object is not Integer. got=*object.Null (&{})
  evaluator_test.go:389: object is not Integer. got=*object.Null (&{})
  evaluator_test.go:389: object is not Integer. got=*object.Null (&{})
  evaluator_test.go:366: object is not Error. got=*object.Null (&{})
  evaluator_test.go:366: object is not Error. got=*object.Null (&{})
FAIL
FAIL    monkey/evaluator        0.007s
```

That means that calling `len` works though! It's just that it returns only `NULL`. But fixing this is as easy as writing any other Go function:

```go
// evaluator/builtins.go

import (
    "monkey/object"
    "unicode/utf8"
)

var builtins = map[string]*object.Builtin{
    "len": &object.Builtin{
        Fn: func(args ...object.Object) object.Object {
            if len(args) != 1 {
                return newError("wrong number of arguments. got=%d, want=1",
                    len(args))
            }

            switch arg := args[0].(type) {
            case *object.String:
                return &object.Integer{Value: int64(len(arg.Value))}
            default:
                return newError("argument to `len` not supported, got %s",
```

```
                        args[0].Type())
                }
            },
        },
}
```

The most important part of this function is the call to Go's `len` and the returning of a newly allocated `object.Integer`. Besides that we have error checking that makes sure that we can't call this function with the wrong number of arguments or with an argument of an unsupported type. And alas, our tests pass:

```
$ go test ./evaluator
ok      monkey/evaluator        0.007s
```

That means we can take `len` on a test drive in our REPL:

```
$ go run main.go
Hello mrnugget! This is the Monkey programming language!
Feel free to type in commands
>> len("1234")
4
>> len("Hello World!")
12
>> len("Woooooohooo!", "len works!!")
ERROR: wrong number of arguments. got=2, want=1
>> len(12345)
ERROR: argument to `len` not supported, got INTEGER
```

Perfect! Our first built-in function works and is ready to go.

4.4 - Array

The data type we're going to add to our Monkey interpreter in this section is the array. In Monkey an array is an ordered list of elements of possibly different types. Each element in the array can be accessed individually. Arrays are constructed by using their literal form: a comma separated list of elements, enclosed by brackets.

Initializing a new array, binding it to a name and accessing individual elements will look like this:

```
>> let myArray = ["Thorsten", "Ball", 28, fn(x) { x * x }];
>> myArray[0]
Thorsten
>> myArray[2]
28
>> myArray[3](2);
4
```

As you can see, Monkey arrays really don't care about the types of their elements. Every possible value in Monkey can be an element in an array. In this example `myArray` holds two strings, an integer and a function.

Accessing individual elements by their index in the array, as seen in the last three lines, is done with a new operator, called the index operator: `array[index]`.

In this section we'll also add support for arrays to our newly added `len` function and also add a few more built-in functions that work with arrays:

```
>> let myArray = ["one", "two", "three"];
>> len(myArray)
3
>> first(myArray)
one
>> rest(myArray)
[two, three]
>> last(myArray)
three
>> push(myArray, "four")
[one, two, three, four]
```

The basis for our implementation of the Monkey array in our interpreter will be a Go slice of type `[]object.Object`. That means that we don't have to implement a new data structure. We can just reuse Go's slice.

Sounds awesome? Good! The first thing we have to do is teach our lexer a few new tokens.

SUPPORTING ARRAYS IN OUR LEXER

In order to correctly parse array literals and the index operator, our lexer needs to be able to identify more tokens than it currently does. All the tokens we need in order to construct and use arrays in Monkey are `[`, `]` and `,`. The lexer already knows about `,` so we only need to add support for `[` and `]`.

The first step is to define these new token types in the `token` package:

```
// token/token.go

const (
// [...]

    LBRACKET = "["
    RBRACKET = "]"

// [...]
)
```

The second step is to extend the test suite of the lexer, which is easy, since we've done this many times before:

```
// lexer/lexer_test.go

func TestNextToken(t *testing.T) {
    input := `let five = 5;
let ten = 10;

let add = fn(x, y) {
  x + y;
};

let result = add(five, ten);
!-/*5;
5 < 10 > 5;

if (5 < 10) {
    return true;
} else {
    return false;
}

10 == 10;
10 != 9;
"foobar"
"foo bar"
[1, 2];
`

    tests := []struct {
        expectedType    token.TokenType
        expectedLiteral string
    }{
// [...]
        {token.LBRACKET, "["},
        {token.INT, "1"},
        {token.COMMA, ","},
        {token.INT, "2"},
        {token.RBRACKET, "]"},
        {token.SEMICOLON, ";"},
        {token.EOF, ""},
    }
// [...]
}
```

Again the `input` is extended to include new tokens (`[1, 2]` in this case) and new `tests` have been added to make sure the lexer's `NextToken` method really returns token.LBRACKET and token.RBRACKET.

Making the test pass is as easy as adding these *four* lines to our NextToken() method. Yes, just four:

```
// lexer/lexer.go

func (l *Lexer) NextToken() token.Token {
// [...]

    case '[':
        tok = newToken(token.LBRACKET, l.ch)
    case ']':
        tok = newToken(token.RBRACKET, l.ch)

// [...]
}
```

Alright! The tests are passing:

```
$ go test ./lexer
ok      monkey/lexer    0.006s
```

In our parser we'll now use token.LBRACKET and token.RBRACKET to parse arrays.

PARSING ARRAY LITERALS

As we saw before, an array literal in Monkey is a comma-separated list of expressions enclosed by an opening and a closing bracket.

```
[1, 2, 3 + 3, fn(x) { x }, add(2, 2)]
```

Yes, the elements in an array literal can be any type of expression. Integer literals, function literals, infix or prefix expressions.

If that sounds complicated, don't worry. We already know how to parse comma-separated lists of expressions - function call arguments are just that. And we also know how to parse something enclosed by matching tokens. In other words: let's get to it!

The first thing we have to do is define the AST node for array literals. Since we already have the essential pieces in place for this, the definition is rather self-explanatory:

```
// ast/ast.go

type ArrayLiteral struct {
    Token    token.Token // the '[' token
    Elements []Expression
```

```go
}

func (al *ArrayLiteral) expressionNode()      {}
func (al *ArrayLiteral) TokenLiteral() string { return al.Token.Literal }
func (al *ArrayLiteral) String() string {
    var out bytes.Buffer

    elements := []string{}
    for _, el := range al.Elements {
        elements = append(elements, el.String())
    }

    out.WriteString("[")
    out.WriteString(strings.Join(elements, ", "))
    out.WriteString("]")

    return out.String()
}
```

The following test function makes sure that parsing array literals results in a `*ast.ArrayLiteral` being returned. (I also added a test function for empty array literals to make sure that we don't run into nasty edge-cases)

```go
// parser/parser_test.go

func TestParsingArrayLiterals(t *testing.T) {
    input := "[1, 2 * 2, 3 + 3]"

    l := lexer.New(input)
    p := New(l)
    program := p.ParseProgram()
    checkParserErrors(t, p)

    stmt, ok := program.Statements[0].(*ast.ExpressionStatement)
    array, ok := stmt.Expression.(*ast.ArrayLiteral)
    if !ok {
        t.Fatalf("exp not ast.ArrayLiteral. got=%T", stmt.Expression)
    }

    if len(array.Elements) != 3 {
        t.Fatalf("len(array.Elements) not 3. got=%d", len(array.Elements))
    }

    testIntegerLiteral(t, array.Elements[0], 1)
    testInfixExpression(t, array.Elements[1], 2, "*", 2)
    testInfixExpression(t, array.Elements[2], 3, "+", 3)
}
```

Just to make sure that the parsing of expressions really works the test input contains two different infix operator expressions, even though integer or boolean literals would be enough. Other than that the test is pretty boring and asserts that the parser really returns an *ast.ArrayLiteral with the correct number of elements.

In order to get the tests to pass we need to register a new prefixParseFn in our parser, since the opening token.LBRACKET of an array literal is in prefix position.

```
// parser/parser.go

func New(l *lexer.Lexer) *Parser {
// [...]

    p.registerPrefix(token.LBRACKET, p.parseArrayLiteral)

// [...]
}

func (p *Parser) parseArrayLiteral() ast.Expression {
    array := &ast.ArrayLiteral{Token: p.curToken}

    array.Elements = p.parseExpressionList(token.RBRACKET)

    return array
}
```

We've added prefixParseFns before, so that part's not really exciting. What's interesting here is the new method called parseExpressionList. This method is a modified and generalized version of parseCallArguments, which we used before in parseCallExpression to parse a list of comma separated arguments:

```
// parser/parser.go

func (p *Parser) parseExpressionList(end token.TokenType) []ast.Expression {
    list := []ast.Expression{}

    if p.peekTokenIs(end) {
        p.nextToken()
        return list
    }

    p.nextToken()
    list = append(list, p.parseExpression(LOWEST))

    for p.peekTokenIs(token.COMMA) {
        p.nextToken()
        p.nextToken()
        list = append(list, p.parseExpression(LOWEST))
    }
```

```
    if !p.expectPeek(end) {
        return nil
    }

    return list
}
```

Again, we've seen this before under the name `parseCallArguments`. The only change is that this new version now accepts an `end` parameter that tells the method which token signifies the end of the list. The updated `parseCallExpression` method, in which we used `parseCallArguments` before, now looks like this:

```
// parser/parser.go

func (p *Parser) parseCallExpression(function ast.Expression) ast.Expression {
    exp := &ast.CallExpression{Token: p.curToken, Function: function}
    exp.Arguments = p.parseExpressionList(token.RPAREN)
    return exp
}
```

The only change is the call to `parseExpressionList` with `token.RPAREN` (which signifies the end of the arguments list). We could reuse a relatively big method by changing a few lines. Great! And the best of all? The tests are passing:

```
$ go test ./parser
ok      monkey/parser   0.007s
```

We can mark "parsing array literals" as "done".

PARSING INDEX OPERATOR EXPRESSIONS

To fully support arrays in Monkey we not only need to be able to parse array literals but also index operator expressions. Maybe the name "index operator" doesn't ring a bell, but I bet you know what it is. Index operator expressions look like this:

```
myArray[0];
myArray[1];
myArray[2];
```

That's the basic form at least, but there are many. Take a look at these examples to spot the structure underlying them all:

```
[1, 2, 3, 4][2];

let myArray = [1, 2, 3, 4];
myArray[2];
```

```
myArray[2 + 1];

returnsArray()[1];
```

Yep, you're totally correct! The basic structure is this one:

```
<expression>[<expression>]
```

That seems simple enough. We can define a new AST node, called `ast.IndexExpression`, that reflects this structure:

```go
// ast/ast.go

type IndexExpression struct {
    Token token.Token // The [ token
    Left  Expression
    Index Expression
}

func (ie *IndexExpression) expressionNode()      {}
func (ie *IndexExpression) TokenLiteral() string { return ie.Token.Literal }
func (ie *IndexExpression) String() string {
    var out bytes.Buffer

    out.WriteString("(")
    out.WriteString(ie.Left.String())
    out.WriteString("[")
    out.WriteString(ie.Index.String())
    out.WriteString("])")

    return out.String()
}
```

It's important to note that both `Left` and `Index` are just `Expressions`. `Left` is the object that's being accessed and we've seen that it can be of any type: an identifier, an array literal, a function call. The same goes for `Index`. It can be any expression. Syntactically it doesn't make a difference which one it is, but semantically it has to produce an integer.

The fact that both `Left` and `Index` are expressions makes the parsing process easier, because we can use our `parseExpression` method to parse them. But first things first! Here is the test case that makes sure our parser knows how to return an `*ast.IndexExpression`:

```go
// parser/parser_test.go

func TestParsingIndexExpressions(t *testing.T) {
    input := "myArray[1 + 1]"
```

```go
    l := lexer.New(input)
    p := New(l)
    program := p.ParseProgram()
    checkParserErrors(t, p)

    stmt, ok := program.Statements[0].(*ast.ExpressionStatement)
    indexExp, ok := stmt.Expression.(*ast.IndexExpression)
    if !ok {
        t.Fatalf("exp not *ast.IndexExpression. got=%T", stmt.Expression)
    }

    if !testIdentifier(t, indexExp.Left, "myArray") {
        return
    }

    if !testInfixExpression(t, indexExp.Index, 1, "+", 1) {
        return
    }
}
```

Now, this test only asserts that the parser outputs the correct AST for a single expression statement containing an index expression. But equally important is that the parser handles the precedence of the index operator correctly. The index operator has to have the highest precedence of all operators yet. Making sure of that is as easy as extending our existing `TestOperatorPrecedenceParsing` test function:

```go
// parser/parser_test.go

func TestOperatorPrecedenceParsing(t *testing.T) {
    tests := []struct {
        input    string
        expected string
    }{
// [...]
        {
            "a * [1, 2, 3, 4][b * c] * d",
            "((a * ([1, 2, 3, 4][(b * c)])) * d)",
        },
        {
            "add(a * b[2], b[1], 2 * [1, 2][1])",
            "add((a * (b[2])), (b[1]), (2 * ([1, 2][1])))",
        },
    }
// [...]
}
```

The additional (and) in the String() output of *ast.IndexExpression help us when writing these tests, since they make the precedence of the index operator visible. In these added test cases we expect that the precedence of the index operator is higher than the precedence of call expressions or even the * operator in infix expressions.

The tests fail because the parser doesn't know anything about index expressions yet:

```
$ go test ./parser
--- FAIL: TestOperatorPrecedenceParsing (0.00s)
  parser_test.go:393: expected="((a * ([1, 2, 3, 4][(b * c)])) * d)",\
    got="(a * [1, 2, 3, 4])([(b * c)] * d)"
  parser_test.go:968: parser has 4 errors
  parser_test.go:970: parser error: "expected next token to be ), got [ instead"
  parser_test.go:970: parser error: "no prefix parse function for , found"
  parser_test.go:970: parser error: "no prefix parse function for , found"
  parser_test.go:970: parser error: "no prefix parse function for ) found"
--- FAIL: TestParsingIndexExpressions (0.00s)
  parser_test.go:835: exp not *ast.IndexExpression. got=*ast.Identifier
FAIL
FAIL    monkey/parser   0.007s
```

Even though the tests complain about a missing prefixParseFn what we want is an infixParseFn. Yes, index operator expressions do not really have a single operator between operands on each side. But in order to parse them without a lot of trouble it's of advantage to act like they do, just like we did with call expressions. Specifically, that means treating the [in myArray[0] as the infix operator, myArray as the left operand and 0 as the right operand.

Doing this makes the implementation fit really nicely into our parser:

```
// parser/parser.go

func New(l *lexer.Lexer) *Parser {
// [...]

    p.registerInfix(token.LBRACKET, p.parseIndexExpression)

// [...]
}

func (p *Parser) parseIndexExpression(left ast.Expression) ast.Expression {
    exp := &ast.IndexExpression{Token: p.curToken, Left: left}

    p.nextToken()
    exp.Index = p.parseExpression(LOWEST)
```

```go
    if !p.expectPeek(token.RBRACKET) {
        return nil
    }

    return exp
}
```

Neat! But that doesn't fix our tests:

```
$ go test ./parser
--- FAIL: TestOperatorPrecedenceParsing (0.00s)
  parser_test.go:393: expected="((a * ([1, 2, 3, 4][(b * c)])) * d)",\
    got="(a * [1, 2, 3, 4])([(b * c)] * d)"
  parser_test.go:968: parser has 4 errors
  parser_test.go:970: parser error: "expected next token to be ), got [ instead"
  parser_test.go:970: parser error: "no prefix parse function for , found"
  parser_test.go:970: parser error: "no prefix parse function for , found"
  parser_test.go:970: parser error: "no prefix parse function for ) found"
--- FAIL: TestParsingIndexExpressions (0.00s)
  parser_test.go:835: exp not *ast.IndexExpression. got=*ast.Identifier
FAIL
FAIL    monkey/parser   0.008s
```

That's because the whole idea behind our Pratt parser hinges on the idea of precedences and we haven't defined the precedence of our index operator yet:

```go
// parser/parser.go
const (
    _ int = iota
// [...]
    INDEX       // array[index]
)

var precedences = map[token.TokenType]int{
// [...]
    token.LBRACKET: INDEX,
}
```

It's important that the definition of `INDEX` is the last line in the `const` block. That gives `INDEX` the highest value of all defined precedence constants, thanks to the `iota`. The added entry in `precedences` gives `token.LBRACKET` this highest precedence of all, `INDEX`. And, well, it does wonders:

```
$ go test ./parser
ok      monkey/parser   0.007s
```

Lexer done, parser done. See you in the evaluator!

EVALUATING ARRAY LITERALS

Evaluating array literals is not hard. Mapping Monkey arrays to Go's slices makes life pretty, pretty sweet. We don't have to implement a new data structure. We only need to define a new `object.Array` type, since that's what the evaluation of array literals produces. And the definition of `object.Array` is simple, since arrays in Monkey are simple: they are just a list of objects.

```
// object/object.go

const (
// [...]
    ARRAY_OBJ = "ARRAY"
)

type Array struct {
    Elements []Object
}

func (ao *Array) Type() ObjectType { return ARRAY_OBJ }
func (ao *Array) Inspect() string {
    var out bytes.Buffer

    elements := []string{}
    for _, e := range ao.Elements {
        elements = append(elements, e.Inspect())
    }

    out.WriteString("[")
    out.WriteString(strings.Join(elements, ", "))
    out.WriteString("]")

    return out.String()
}
```

I think you'll agree with me when I say that the most complicated thing about this definition is the `Inspect` method. And even that one is pretty easy to understand.

Here is the evaluator test for array literals:

```
// evaluator/evaluator_test.go

func TestArrayLiterals(t *testing.T) {
    input := "[1, 2 * 2, 3 + 3]"

    evaluated := testEval(input)
    result, ok := evaluated.(*object.Array)
    if !ok {
```

```
        t.Fatalf("object is not Array. got=%T (%+v)", evaluated, evaluated)
    }

    if len(result.Elements) != 3 {
        t.Fatalf("array has wrong num of elements. got=%d",
            len(result.Elements))
    }

    testIntegerObject(t, result.Elements[0], 1)
    testIntegerObject(t, result.Elements[1], 4)
    testIntegerObject(t, result.Elements[2], 6)
}
```

We can reuse some existing code to get this test to pass, just like we did in our parser. And again the code we're reusing was originally written for call expressions. Here is the case branch that evaluates `*ast.ArrayLiterals` and produces array objects:

```
// evaluator/evaluator.go

func Eval(node ast.Node, env *object.Environment) object.Object {
// [...]

    case *ast.ArrayLiteral:
        elements := evalExpressions(node.Elements, env)
        if len(elements) == 1 && isError(elements[0]) {
            return elements[0]
        }
        return &object.Array{Elements: elements}
    }

// [...]
}
```

Isn't that one of the great joys of programming? Reusing existing code without having to turn it into a super generic, over-engineered spaceship.

The tests are passing and we can use array literals in our REPL to produce arrays:

```
$ go run main.go
Hello mrnugget! This is the Monkey programming language!
Feel free to type in commands
>> [1, 2, 3, 4]
[1, 2, 3, 4]
>> let double = fn(x) { x * 2 };
>> [1, double(2), 3 * 3, 4 - 3]
[1, 4, 9, 1]
>>
```

Amazing, isn't it? But what we can't do yet is accessing single elements of the array by using the index operator.

EVALUATING INDEX OPERATOR EXPRESSIONS

Great news: much harder than evaluating index expressions is parsing them. And we already did that. The only problem left is the possibility of off-by-one errors when accessing and retrieving the elements in an array. But for that we'll just add a few tests to our test suite:

```
// evaluator/evaluator_test.go

func TestArrayIndexExpressions(t *testing.T) {
	tests := []struct {
		input    string
		expected interface{}
	}{
		{
			"[1, 2, 3][0]",
			1,
		},
		{
			"[1, 2, 3][1]",
			2,
		},
		{
			"[1, 2, 3][2]",
			3,
		},
		{
			"let i = 0; [1][i];",
			1,
		},
		{
			"[1, 2, 3][1 + 1];",
			3,
		},
		{
			"let myArray = [1, 2, 3]; myArray[2];",
			3,
		},
		{
			"let myArray = [1, 2, 3]; myArray[0] + myArray[1] + myArray[2];",
			6,
		},
		{
```

```
			"let myArray = [1, 2, 3]; let i = myArray[0]; myArray[i]",
			2,
		},
		{
			"[1, 2, 3][3]",
			nil,
		},
		{
			"[1, 2, 3][-1]",
			nil,
		},
	}

	for _, tt := range tests {
		evaluated := testEval(tt.input)
		integer, ok := tt.expected.(int)
		if ok {
			testIntegerObject(t, evaluated, int64(integer))
		} else {
			testNullObject(t, evaluated)
		}
	}
}
```

Okay, I'll admit, these tests might seem excessive. A lot of the things we're testing implicitly here have already been tested elsewhere. But the test cases are so easy to write! And they are so readable! I love these tests.

Take note of the desired behaviour these tests specify. They contain something we haven't talked about yet: when we use an index that's out of the arrays bounds, we'll return `NULL`. Some languages produce an error in such a case and some return a null value. I choose to return `NULL`.

As expected the tests are failing. And not only that, they're blowing up:

```
$ go test ./evaluator
--- FAIL: TestArrayIndexExpressions (0.00s)
  evaluator_test.go:492: object is not Integer. got=<nil> (<nil>)
  evaluator_test.go:492: object is not Integer. got=<nil> (<nil>)
  evaluator_test.go:492: object is not Integer. got=<nil> (<nil>)
  evaluator_test.go:492: object is not Integer. got=<nil> (<nil>)
  evaluator_test.go:492: object is not Integer. got=<nil> (<nil>)
  evaluator_test.go:492: object is not Integer. got=<nil> (<nil>)
panic: runtime error: invalid memory address or nil pointer dereference
[signal SIGSEGV: segmentation violation code=0x1 addr=0x28 pc=0x70057]
[redacted: backtrace here]
FAIL    monkey/evaluator        0.011s
```

So how do we fix this and evaluate index expressions? As we've seen, the left operand of the index operator can be any expression and the index itself can be any expression. That means we need to evaluate both before we can evaluate the "indexing" itself. Otherwise we'd try to access elements of an identifier or a function call, which doesn't work.

Here is the case branch for `*ast.IndexExpression` that makes these desired calls to `Eval`:

```
// evaluator/evaluator.go

func Eval(node ast.Node, env *object.Environment) object.Object {
// [...]

    case *ast.IndexExpression:
        left := Eval(node.Left, env)
        if isError(left) {
            return left
        }
        index := Eval(node.Index, env)
        if isError(index) {
            return index
        }
        return evalIndexExpression(left, index)

// [...]
}
```

And here is the `evalIndexExpression` function it uses:

```
// evaluator/evaluator.go

func evalIndexExpression(left, index object.Object) object.Object {
    switch {
    case left.Type() == object.ARRAY_OBJ && index.Type() == object.INTEGER_OBJ:
        return evalArrayIndexExpression(left, index)
    default:
        return newError("index operator not supported: %s", left.Type())
    }
}
```

An if-conditional would do the job of the switch statement here just fine, but we're going to add another case branch later in this chapter. Besides the error handling (for which I also added a test) nothing really interesting happens in this function. The meat of the operation is in `evalArrayIndexExpression`:

```
// evaluator/evaluator.go

func evalArrayIndexExpression(array, index object.Object) object.Object {
    arrayObject := array.(*object.Array)
```

```
    idx := index.(*object.Integer).Value
    max := int64(len(arrayObject.Elements) - 1)

    if idx < 0 || idx > max {
        return NULL
    }

    return arrayObject.Elements[idx]
}
```

Here we actually retrieve the element with the specified index from the array. Besides the little type assertion and conversion dances this function is pretty straightforward: it checks if the given index is out of range and if that's the case it returns NULL, otherwise the desired element. Just like we specified in our tests, which are now passing:

```
$ go test ./evaluator
ok      monkey/evaluator        0.007s
```

Okay, now take a deep breath, relax and take a look at this:

```
$ go run main.go
Hello mrnugget! This is the Monkey programming language!
Feel free to type in commands
>> let a = [1, 2 * 2, 10 - 5, 8 / 2];
>> a[0]
1
>> a[1]
4
>> a[5 - 3]
5
>> a[99]
null
```

Retrieving elements from an array works! Sweet! I can only repeat myself here: it's amazing how easy it was to implement this language feature, isn't it?

ADDING BUILT-IN FUNCTIONS FOR ARRAYS

We are now able to construct arrays by using array literals. And we can access single elements by using index expressions. Just those two things alone make arrays quite useful to have. But in order to make them even more useful, we need to add a few built-in functions that make working with them more convenient. In this sub-section we're going to do exactly that.

I won't be showing any test code and test cases in this section. The reason is that these particular tests take up space without adding anything new. Our "framework" for testing built-in functions is already in place with `TestBuiltinFunctions` and the added tests follow the existing scheme. You can find them in the accompanying code.

Our goal is to add new built-in functions. But the first thing we actually have to do is not adding a new one but changing an existing function. We need to add support for arrays to `len`, which only supported strings until now:

```
// evaluator/builtins.go

var builtins = map[string]*object.Builtin{
    "len": &object.Builtin{
        Fn: func(args ...object.Object) object.Object {
            if len(args) != 1 {
                return newError("wrong number of arguments. got=%d, want=1",
                    len(args))
            }

            switch arg := args[0].(type) {
            case *object.Array:
                return &object.Integer{Value: int64(len(arg.Elements))}
            case *object.String:
                return &object.Integer{Value: int64(len(arg.Value))}
            default:
                return newError("argument to `len` not supported, got %s",
                    args[0].Type())
            }
        },
    },
// [...]
}
```

The only change is the added `case` branch for `*object.Array`. And with that out of the way, we're ready to start adding new functions. Yay!

The first of these new built-in functions is `first`. `first` returns the first element of the given array. Yes, calling `myArray[0]` does the same thing. But `first` is arguably prettier. Here is its implementation:

```
// evaluator/builtins.go

var builtins = map[string]*object.Builtin{
// [...]

    "first": &object.Builtin{
        Fn: func(args ...object.Object) object.Object {
            if len(args) != 1 {
                return newError("wrong number of arguments. got=%d, want=1",
                    len(args))
```

```go
        }
        if args[0].Type() != object.ARRAY_OBJ {
            return newError("argument to `first` must be ARRAY, got %s",
                args[0].Type())
        }

        arr := args[0].(*object.Array)
        if len(arr.Elements) > 0 {
            return arr.Elements[0]
        }

        return NULL
    },
  },
}
```

Great! That works! And what comes after `first`? You're correct, the next function we're going to add is called `last`.

The purpose of `last` is to return the last element of the given array. In index operator terms it returns `myArray[len(myArray)-1]`. And as it turns out, implementing `last` is not much harder than implementing `first` - who would have thought that? Here it is:

```go
// evaluator/builtins.go

var builtins = map[string]*object.Builtin{
// [...]

    "last": &object.Builtin{
        Fn: func(args ...object.Object) object.Object {
            if len(args) != 1 {
                return newError("wrong number of arguments. got=%d, want=1",
                    len(args))
            }
            if args[0].Type() != object.ARRAY_OBJ {
                return newError("argument to `last` must be ARRAY, got %s",
                    args[0].Type())
            }

            arr := args[0].(*object.Array)
            length := len(arr.Elements)
            if length > 0 {
                return arr.Elements[length-1]
            }

            return NULL
        },
```

```
    },
}
```

The next function we're going to add would be called `cdr` in Scheme. In some other languages it's sometimes called `tail`. We're going to call it `rest`. `rest` returns a new array containing all elements of the array passed as argument, *except the first one*. Here's what using it looks like:

```
>> let a = [1, 2, 3, 4];
>> rest(a)
[2, 3, 4]
>> rest(rest(a))
[3, 4]
>> rest(rest(rest(a)))
[4]
>> rest(rest(rest(rest(a))))
[]
>> rest(rest(rest(rest(rest(a)))))
null
```

Its implementation is simple, but keep in mind that we're returning a *newly allocated* array. We're not modifying the array passed to `rest`:

```
// evaluator/builtins.go

var builtins = map[string]*object.Builtin{
// [...]

    "rest": &object.Builtin{
        Fn: func(args ...object.Object) object.Object {
            if len(args) != 1 {
                return newError("wrong number of arguments. got=%d, want=1",
                    len(args))
            }
            if args[0].Type() != object.ARRAY_OBJ {
                return newError("argument to `rest` must be ARRAY, got %s",
                    args[0].Type())
            }

            arr := args[0].(*object.Array)
            length := len(arr.Elements)
            if length > 0 {
                newElements := make([]object.Object, length-1, length-1)
                copy(newElements, arr.Elements[1:length])
                return &object.Array{Elements: newElements}
            }

            return NULL
        },
```

```
    },
}
```

The last array function we're going to build into our interpreter is called `push`. It adds a new element to the end of the array. But, and here's the kicker, it doesn't modify the given array. Instead it allocates a new array with the same elements as the old one plus the new, pushed element. Arrays are immutable in Monkey. Here is `push` in action:

```
>> let a = [1, 2, 3, 4];
>> let b = push(a, 5);
>> a
[1, 2, 3, 4]
>> b
[1, 2, 3, 4, 5]
```

And here is its implementation:

```
// evaluator/builtins.go

var builtins = map[string]*object.Builtin{
// [...]

    "push": &object.Builtin{
        Fn: func(args ...object.Object) object.Object {
            if len(args) != 2 {
                return newError("wrong number of arguments. got=%d, want=2",
                    len(args))
            }
            if args[0].Type() != object.ARRAY_OBJ {
                return newError("argument to `push` must be ARRAY, got %s",
                    args[0].Type())
            }

            arr := args[0].(*object.Array)
            length := len(arr.Elements)

            newElements := make([]object.Object, length+1, length+1)
            copy(newElements, arr.Elements)
            newElements[length] = args[1]

            return &object.Array{Elements: newElements}
        },
    },
}
```

TEST-DRIVING ARRAYS

We now have array literals, the index operator and a few built-in functions to work with arrays. It's time to take them for a spin. Let's see what they can do.

With `first`, `rest` and `push` we can build a `map` function:

```
let map = fn(arr, f) {
  let iter = fn(arr, accumulated) {
    if (len(arr) == 0) {
      accumulated
    } else {
      iter(rest(arr), push(accumulated, f(first(arr))));
    }
  };

  iter(arr, []);
};
```

And with `map` we can do things like this:

```
>> let a = [1, 2, 3, 4];
>> let double = fn(x) { x * 2 };
>> map(a, double);
[2, 4, 6, 8]
```

Isn't this amazing? There's more! Based on the same built-in functions we can also define a `reduce` function:

```
let reduce = fn(arr, initial, f) {
  let iter = fn(arr, result) {
    if (len(arr) == 0) {
      result
    } else {
      iter(rest(arr), f(result, first(arr)));
    }
  };

  iter(arr, initial);
};
```

And `reduce`, in turn, can be used to define a `sum` function:

```
let sum = fn(arr) {
  reduce(arr, 0, fn(initial, el) { initial + el });
};
```

And it works like a charm:

```
>> sum([1, 2, 3, 4, 5]);
15
```

As you probably know, I'm not a fan of patting oneself on the back, but let me just say this: holy monkey! Look at what our interpreter can do! A `map` function?! `reduce`?! We've come a long, long way!

And that's not even all of it! There's a lot more we can do now and I urge you to explore the possibilities the array data type and the few built-in functions give us. But you know what you should do first? Take some time off, brag about this to your friends and family, enjoy the praise and compliments. And when you come back, we'll add another data type.

4.5 - Hashes

The next data type we're going to add is called "hash". A hash in Monkey is what's sometimes called hash, map, hash map or dictionary in other programming languages. It maps keys to values.

In order to construct a hash in Monkey one uses the hash literal: a comma-separated list of key-value pairs that's enclosed by curly braces. Each key-value pair uses a colon to differentiate between the key and the value. Here is what using a hash literal looks like:

```
>> let myHash = {"name": "Jimmy", "age": 72, "band": "Led Zeppelin"};
>> myHash["name"]
Jimmy
>> myHash["age"]
72
>> myHash["band"]
Led Zeppelin
```

In this example `myHash` contains three key-value pairs. The keys are all strings. And, as you can see, we can use index operator expressions to get values out of the hash again, just like we can with arrays. Except that in this example the index values are strings, which don't work with arrays. And that's not even the only data type that's usable as a hash key:

```
>> let myHash = {true: "yes, a boolean", 99: "correct, an integer"};
>> myHash[true]
yes, a boolean
>> myHash[99]
correct, an integer
```

That's also valid. In fact, besides string, integer and boolean literals we can use any expression as index in index operator expressions:

```
>> myHash[5 > 1]
yes, a boolean
```

```
>> myHash[100 - 1]
correct, an integer
```

As long as these expressions evaluate to either strings, integers or booleans they are usable as hash keys. Here `5 > 1` evaluates to `true` and `100 - 1` evaluates to `99`, both of which are valid and mapped to values in `myHash`.

Rather unsurprisingly our implementation will use Go's `map` as the underlying data structure for Monkey hashes. But since we want to use strings, integers and booleans interchangeably as keys, we need to build something on top of plain old `map` to make it work. We'll come to that when we extend our object system. But first we have to turn hash literals into tokens.

Lexing Hash Literals

How do we turn hash literals into tokens? Which tokens do we need to recognize and output in our lexer so that we can later work with them in the parser? Here is the hash literal from above again:

```
{"name": "Jimmy", "age": 72, "band": "Led Zeppelin"}
```

Besides the string literals there are four characters in use here that are important: `{`, `}`, `,` and `:`. We already know how to lex the first three. Our lexer turns these into `token.LBRACE`, `token.RBRACE` and `token.COMMA` respectively. That means, all that's left for us to do in this section is to turn `:` into a token.

And for that we first need to define the necessary token type in the `token` package:

```
// token/token.go

const (
// [...]
    COLON = ":"
// [...]
)
```

Next we're going to add a new test for the `NextToken` method of `Lexer` that expects a `token.COLON`:

```
// lexer/lexer_test.go

func TestNextToken(t *testing.T) {
    input := `let five = 5;
let ten = 10;

let add = fn(x, y) {
  x + y;
};
```

```
let result = add(five, ten);
!-/*5;
5 < 10 > 5;

if (5 < 10) {
    return true;
} else {
    return false;
}

10 == 10;
10 != 9;
"foobar"
"foo bar"
[1, 2];
{"foo": "bar"}
`

    tests := []struct {
        expectedType    token.TokenType
        expectedLiteral string
    }{
// [...]
        {token.LBRACE, "{"},
        {token.STRING, "foo"},
        {token.COLON, ":"},
        {token.STRING, "bar"},
        {token.RBRACE, "}"},
        {token.EOF, ""},
    }

// [...]
}
```

We could get away with adding a single `:` to the test input, but using a hash literal as we did here provides a little more context when later reading and eventually debugging the test.

Turning `:` into `token.COLON` is as easy as it gets:

```
// lexer/lexer.go

func (l *Lexer) NextToken() token.Token {
// [...]
    case ':':
        tok = newToken(token.COLON, l.ch)
// [...]
}
```

Only two new lines and the lexer now spits out `token.COLON`:

```
$ go test ./lexer
ok      monkey/lexer    0.006s
```

Boom! The lexer now returns `token.LBRACE`, `token.RBRACE`, `token.COMMA` and the new `token.COLON`. That's all we need in order to parse to hash literals.

Parsing Hash Literals

Before we start working on our parser or even writing a test, let's look at the basic syntactic structure of a hash literal:

```
{<expression> : <expression>, <expression> : <expression>, ... }
```

It's a comma-separated list of pairs. Each pair consists of two expressions. One produces the hash key and one produces the value. The key is separated from the value with a colon. The list is enclosed by a pair of curly braces.

When we turn this into an AST node, we have to keep track of the key-value pairs. Now how would we do that? We'll use a `map`, yes, but of what type are the keys and the values in this `map`?

We said earlier that the only admissible data types for hash keys are strings, integers and booleans. But we can't enforce that in the parser. Instead we'll have to validate hash key types in the evaluation stage and generate possible errors there.

That's because a lot of different expressions can produce strings, integers or booleans. Not just their literal forms. Enforcing the data type of hash keys in the parsing stage would prevent us from doing something like this:

```
let key = "name";
let hash = {key: "Monkey"};
```

Here `key` evaluates to `"name"` and is thus totally valid as a hash key, even though it's an identifier. In order to allow this, we need to allow any expression as a key and any expression as a value in a hash literal. At least in the parsing stage. Following that our `ast.HashLiteral` definition looks like this:

```
// ast/ast.go

type HashLiteral struct {
    Token token.Token // the '{' token
    Pairs map[Expression]Expression
}

func (hl *HashLiteral) expressionNode()       {}
func (hl *HashLiteral) TokenLiteral() string { return hl.Token.Literal }
```

```go
func (hl *HashLiteral) String() string {
	var out bytes.Buffer

	pairs := []string{}
	for key, value := range hl.Pairs {
		pairs = append(pairs, key.String()+":"+value.String())
	}

	out.WriteString("{")
	out.WriteString(strings.Join(pairs, ", "))
	out.WriteString("}")

	return out.String()
}
```

Now that we're clear about the structure of hash literals and have `ast.HashLiteral` defined, we can write tests for our parser:

```go
// parser/parser_test.go

func TestParsingHashLiteralsStringKeys(t *testing.T) {
	input := `{"one": 1, "two": 2, "three": 3}`

	l := lexer.New(input)
	p := New(l)
	program := p.ParseProgram()
	checkParserErrors(t, p)

	stmt := program.Statements[0].(*ast.ExpressionStatement)
	hash, ok := stmt.Expression.(*ast.HashLiteral)
	if !ok {
		t.Fatalf("exp is not ast.HashLiteral. got=%T", stmt.Expression)
	}

	if len(hash.Pairs) != 3 {
		t.Errorf("hash.Pairs has wrong length. got=%d", len(hash.Pairs))
	}

	expected := map[string]int64{
		"one":   1,
		"two":   2,
		"three": 3,
	}

	for key, value := range hash.Pairs {
		literal, ok := key.(*ast.StringLiteral)
		if !ok {
			t.Errorf("key is not ast.StringLiteral. got=%T", key)
```

```
        }

        expectedValue := expected[literal.String()]

        testIntegerLiteral(t, value, expectedValue)
    }
}
```

And of course, we also have to be sure that we parse an empty hash literal correctly, because such edge-cases are the root of all hair loss in programming:

```
// parser/parser_test.go

func TestParsingEmptyHashLiteral(t *testing.T) {
    input := "{}"

    l := lexer.New(input)
    p := New(l)
    program := p.ParseProgram()
    checkParserErrors(t, p)

    stmt := program.Statements[0].(*ast.ExpressionStatement)
    hash, ok := stmt.Expression.(*ast.HashLiteral)
    if !ok {
        t.Fatalf("exp is not ast.HashLiteral. got=%T", stmt.Expression)
    }

    if len(hash.Pairs) != 0 {
        t.Errorf("hash.Pairs has wrong length. got=%d", len(hash.Pairs))
    }
}
```

I also added two more tests that are similar to `TestHashLiteralStringKeys` but use integers and booleans as hash keys and make sure the parser turns those into `*ast.IntegerLiteral` and `*ast.Boolean` respectively. And then there is a fifth test function that makes sure the values in a hash literal can be any expression, even operator expressions. It looks like this:

```
// parser/parser_test.go

func TestParsingHashLiteralsWithExpressions(t *testing.T) {
    input := `{"one": 0 + 1, "two": 10 - 8, "three": 15 / 5}`

    l := lexer.New(input)
    p := New(l)
    program := p.ParseProgram()
    checkParserErrors(t, p)

    stmt := program.Statements[0].(*ast.ExpressionStatement)
```

```go
    hash, ok := stmt.Expression.(*ast.HashLiteral)
    if !ok {
        t.Fatalf("exp is not ast.HashLiteral. got=%T", stmt.Expression)
    }

    if len(hash.Pairs) != 3 {
        t.Errorf("hash.Pairs has wrong length. got=%d", len(hash.Pairs))
    }

    tests := map[string]func(ast.Expression){
        "one": func(e ast.Expression) {
            testInfixExpression(t, e, 0, "+", 1)
        },
        "two": func(e ast.Expression) {
            testInfixExpression(t, e, 10, "-", 8)
        },
        "three": func(e ast.Expression) {
            testInfixExpression(t, e, 15, "/", 5)
        },
    }

    for key, value := range hash.Pairs {
        literal, ok := key.(*ast.StringLiteral)
        if !ok {
            t.Errorf("key is not ast.StringLiteral. got=%T", key)
            continue
        }

        testFunc, ok := tests[literal.String()]
        if !ok {
            t.Errorf("No test function for key %q found", literal.String())
            continue
        }

        testFunc(value)
    }
}
```

So how are all of these test functions doing? Not so well, to be honest. We get a lot of failures and parser errors:

```
$ go test ./parser
--- FAIL: TestParsingEmptyHashLiteral (0.00s)
  parser_test.go:1173: parser has 2 errors
  parser_test.go:1175: parser error: "no prefix parse function for { found"
  parser_test.go:1175: parser error: "no prefix parse function for } found"
--- FAIL: TestParsingHashLiteralsStringKeys (0.00s)
  parser_test.go:1173: parser has 7 errors
```

```
  parser_test.go:1175: parser error: "no prefix parse function for { found"
[... more errors ...]
--- FAIL: TestParsingHashLiteralsBooleanKeys (0.00s)
  parser_test.go:1173: parser has 5 errors
  parser_test.go:1175: parser error: "no prefix parse function for { found"
[... more errors ...]
--- FAIL: TestParsingHashLiteralsIntegerKeys (0.00s)
  parser_test.go:967: parser has 7 errors
  parser_test.go:969: parser error: "no prefix parse function for { found"
[... more errors ...]
--- FAIL: TestParsingHashLiteralsWithExpressions (0.00s)
  parser_test.go:1173: parser has 7 errors
  parser_test.go:1175: parser error: "no prefix parse function for { found"
[... more errors ...]
FAIL
FAIL    monkey/parser   0.008s
```

It might sound unbelievable but there's good news: it only takes one function to make all of these tests pass. One `prefixParseFn`, to be exact. Since the `token.LBRACE` of a hash literal is in prefix position, just like the `token.LBRACKET` of an array literal, we can define a `parseHashLiteral` method as a `prefixParseFn`:

```go
// parser/parser.go

func New(l *lexer.Lexer) *Parser {
// [...]
    p.registerPrefix(token.LBRACE, p.parseHashLiteral)
// [...]
}

func (p *Parser) parseHashLiteral() ast.Expression {
    hash := &ast.HashLiteral{Token: p.curToken}
    hash.Pairs = make(map[ast.Expression]ast.Expression)

    for !p.peekTokenIs(token.RBRACE) {
        p.nextToken()
        key := p.parseExpression(LOWEST)

        if !p.expectPeek(token.COLON) {
            return nil
        }

        p.nextToken()
        value := p.parseExpression(LOWEST)

        hash.Pairs[key] = value

        if !p.peekTokenIs(token.RBRACE) && !p.expectPeek(token.COMMA) {
```

```
            return nil
        }
    }

    if !p.expectPeek(token.RBRACE) {
        return nil
    }

    return hash
}
```

It may look intimidating, but there is nothing in `parseHashLiteral` we haven't seen before. It only loops over key-value expression pairs by checking for a closing `token.RBRACE` and calling `parseExpression` two times. That and the filling of `hash.Pairs` are the most important parts of this method. It does its job well:

```
$ go test ./parser
ok      monkey/parser   0.006s
```

All of our parser tests pass! And judging by the numbers of tests we added, we can be reasonably sure that our parser now knows how to parse hash literals. That means we're now coming to the most interesting part of adding hashes to our interpreter: representing them in the object system and evaluating hash literals.

HASHING OBJECTS

Besides extending the lexer and parser, adding a new data type also means representing it in the object system. We successfully did that for integers, strings and arrays. But whereas implementing these other data types just meant defining a struct that has a `.Value` field with the correct type, hashes require a little bit more effort. Let me explain why.

Let's say we defined a new `object.Hash` type like this:

```
type Hash struct {
  Pairs map[Object]Object
}
```

That's the most obvious choice for implementing a `Hash` data type based on Go's `map`. But with this definition, how would we fill the `Pairs` map? And more importantly, how would we get values back out of it?

Consider this piece of Monkey code:

```
let hash = {"name": "Monkey"};
hash["name"]
```

Let's say we are evaluating these two lines and are using the object.Hash definition from above. When evaluating the hash literal in the first line we take every key-value pair and put it in the map[Object]Object map, resulting in .Pairs having the following mapping: an *object.String with .Value being "name" mapped to an *object.String with .Value being "Monkey".

So far, so good. But the problem arises in the second line where we use an index expression to try to access the "Monkey" string.

In this second line the "name" string literal of the index expression evaluates to a new, freshly allocated *object.String. And even though this new *object.String also contains "name" in its .Value field, just like the other *object.String in Pairs, we can't use the new one to retrieve "Monkey".

The reason for this is that they're pointers pointing to different memory locations. The fact that the content of the memory locations they point to is the same ("name") doesn't matter. Comparing these pointers would tell us that they're not equal. That means using the newly created *object.String as a key doesn't get us "Monkey". That's how pointers and comparison between them works in Go.

Here is an example that demonstrates the problem we'd face with the object.Hash implementation from above:

```
name1 := &object.String{Value: "name"}
monkey := &object.String{Value: "Monkey"}

pairs := map[object.Object]object.Object{}
pairs[name1] = monkey

fmt.Printf("pairs[name1]=%+v\n", pairs[name1])
// => pairs[name1]=&{Value:Monkey}

name2 := &object.String{Value: "name"}

fmt.Printf("pairs[name2]=%+v\n", pairs[name2])
// => pairs[name2]=<nil>

fmt.Printf("(name1 == name2)=%t\n", name1 == name2)
// => (name1 == name2)=false
```

As a solution to this problem we could iterate over every key in .Pairs, check if it's an *object.String and compare its .Value to the .Value of the key in the index expression. We'd find the matching value this way, but this method turns the lookup time for a given key from O(1) into O(n), defeating the entire purpose of using hashes in the first place.

Another option is to define Pairs as a map[string]Object and then use the .Value of *object.String as the keys. That works, but not for integers and booleans.

No, what we need is a way to generate hashes for objects that we can easily compare and use as hash keys in our `object.Hash`. We need to be able to generate a hash key for an `*object.String` that's comparable and equal to the hash key of another `*object.String` with the same `.Value`. The same goes for `*object.Integer` and `*object.Boolean`. But the hash keys for an `*object.String` must never be equal to the hash key for an `*object.Integer` or an `*object.Boolean`. Between types the hash keys always have to differ.

We can express the desired behaviour in a set of test functions in our object system:

```go
// object/object_test.go

package object

import "testing"

func TestStringHashKey(t *testing.T) {
    hello1 := &String{Value: "Hello World"}
    hello2 := &String{Value: "Hello World"}
    diff1 := &String{Value: "My name is johnny"}
    diff2 := &String{Value: "My name is johnny"}

    if hello1.HashKey() != hello2.HashKey() {
        t.Errorf("strings with same content have different hash keys")
    }

    if diff1.HashKey() != diff2.HashKey() {
        t.Errorf("strings with same content have different hash keys")
    }

    if hello1.HashKey() == diff1.HashKey() {
        t.Errorf("strings with different content have same hash keys")
    }
}
```

That's exactly what we want from a `HashKey()` method. And not just for `*object.String` but for `*object.Boolean` and `*object.Integer`, which is why the same test function exists for both of them too.

To stop the tests from blowing up we need to implement the `HashKey()` method on each of the three types:

```go
// object/object.go

import (
// [...]
    "hash/fnv"
)
```

```go
type HashKey struct {
    Type  ObjectType
    Value uint64
}

func (b *Boolean) HashKey() HashKey {
    var value uint64

    if b.Value {
        value = 1
    } else {
        value = 0
    }

    return HashKey{Type: b.Type(), Value: value}
}

func (i *Integer) HashKey() HashKey {
    return HashKey{Type: i.Type(), Value: uint64(i.Value)}
}

func (s *String) HashKey() HashKey {
    h := fnv.New64a()
    h.Write([]byte(s.Value))

    return HashKey{Type: s.Type(), Value: h.Sum64()}
}
```

Every `HashKey()` method returns a `HashKey`. As you can see in its definition, `HashKey` is nothing fancy. The `Type` field contains an `ObjectType` and thus effectively "scopes" `HashKey`s to different object types. The `Value` field holds the actual hash, which is just an integer. Since it's just two integers we can easily compare a `HashKey` to another `HashKey` by using the == operator. And that also makes `HashKey` usable as a key in a Go `map`.

The problem we demonstrated earlier is solved by using this newly defined `HashKey` and the `HashKey()` methods:

```go
name1 := &object.String{Value: "name"}
monkey := &object.String{Value: "Monkey"}

pairs := map[object.HashKey]object.Object{}
pairs[name1.HashKey()] = monkey

fmt.Printf("pairs[name1.HashKey()]=%+v\n", pairs[name1.HashKey()])
// => pairs[name1.HashKey()]=&{Value:Monkey}
```

```go
name2 := &object.String{Value: "name"}

fmt.Printf("pairs[name2.HashKey()]=%+v\n", pairs[name2.HashKey()])
// => pairs[name2.HashKey()]=&{Value:Monkey}

fmt.Printf("(name1 == name2)=%t\n", name1 == name2)
// => (name1 == name2)=false

fmt.Printf("(name1.HashKey() == name2.HashKey())=%t\n",
  name1.HashKey() == name2.HashKey())
// => (name1.HashKey() == name2.HashKey())=true
```

That's *exactly* what we want! The `HashKey` definition and the `HashKey()` method implementations solve the problems we had with our naive `Hash` definition. They also make the tests pass:

```
$ go test ./object
ok      monkey/object   0.008s
```

Now we can define `object.Hash` and use this new `HashKey` type:

```go
// object/object.go

const (
// [...]
    HASH_OBJ = "HASH"
)

type HashPair struct {
    Key   Object
    Value Object
}

type Hash struct {
    Pairs map[HashKey]HashPair
}

func (h *Hash) Type() ObjectType { return HASH_OBJ }
```

This adds both the definition of `Hash` and `HashPair`. `HashPair` is the type of the values in `Hash.Pairs`. You might be wondering why we use that and not just define `Pairs` as a `map[HashKey]Object`.

The reason is the `Inspect()` method of `Hash`. When we later print a Monkey hash in our REPL, we want to print the values contained in the hash as well as its keys. And just printing the `HashKeys` is not really useful. So we keep track of the objects that generated the `HashKeys` by using `HashPairs` as values, where we save the original key object and the value object its mapped to. That way we can call the `Inspect()` methods of the key objects to generate the `Inspect()` output for *object.Hash. Here is said Inspect() method:

```go
// object/object.go

func (h *Hash) Inspect() string {
    var out bytes.Buffer

    pairs := []string{}
    for _, pair := range h.Pairs {
        pairs = append(pairs, fmt.Sprintf("%s: %s",
            pair.Key.Inspect(), pair.Value.Inspect()))
    }

    out.WriteString("{")
    out.WriteString(strings.Join(pairs, ", "))
    out.WriteString("}")

    return out.String()
}
```

The Inspect() method is not the only reason why it's good to keep track of the objects that generated the HashKey. That would also be necessary if we were to implement something like a range function for Monkey hashes, which iterates over keys and values in the hash. Or if we want to add a firstPair function that returns the first key and value of a given hash as an array. Or if we want... You get the drift. Keeping track of keys is highly useful, even though for now only the Inspect() method benefits.

And that's it! That's the whole implementation of object.Hash. But there's a small thing we ought to do while we still have the object package open:

```go
// object/object.go

type Hashable interface {
    HashKey() HashKey
}
```

We can use this interface in our evaluator to check if the given object is usable as a hash key when we evaluate hash literals or index expressions for hashes.

At the moment it's only implemented by *object.String, *object.Boolean and *object.Integer.

Granted, there's one more thing we could do before moving on: we could optimize the performance of the HashKey() methods by caching their return values, but that sounds like a nice exercise for the performance-minded reader.

EVALUATING HASH LITERALS

We're about to start evaluating hash literals and I'll be completely honest with you: the hardest part about adding hashes to our interpreter is over. It's smooth sailing from here on out. So, let's enjoy the ride, relax and write a test:

```
// evaluator/evaluator_test.go

func TestHashLiterals(t *testing.T) {
    input := `let two = "two";
    {
        "one": 10 - 9,
        two: 1 + 1,
        "thr" + "ee": 6 / 2,
        4: 4,
        true: 5,
        false: 6
    }`

    evaluated := testEval(input)
    result, ok := evaluated.(*object.Hash)
    if !ok {
        t.Fatalf("Eval didn't return Hash. got=%T (%+v)", evaluated, evaluated)
    }

    expected := map[object.HashKey]int64{
        (&object.String{Value: "one"}).HashKey():   1,
        (&object.String{Value: "two"}).HashKey():   2,
        (&object.String{Value: "three"}).HashKey(): 3,
        (&object.Integer{Value: 4}).HashKey():      4,
        TRUE.HashKey():                             5,
        FALSE.HashKey():                            6,
    }

    if len(result.Pairs) != len(expected) {
        t.Fatalf("Hash has wrong num of pairs. got=%d", len(result.Pairs))
    }

    for expectedKey, expectedValue := range expected {
        pair, ok := result.Pairs[expectedKey]
        if !ok {
            t.Errorf("no pair for given key in Pairs")
        }

        testIntegerObject(t, pair.Value, expectedValue)
    }
}
```

This test function shows what we want from `Eval` when it encounters a `*ast.HashLiteral`: a fresh `*object.Hash` with the correct number of `HashPairs` mapped to the matching `HashKeys` in its `Pairs` attribute.

And it also shows another requirement we have: strings, identifiers, infix operator expressions, booleans and integers - they should all be usable as keys. Any expression really. As long as it produces an `object` that implements the `Hashable` interface it should usable as a hash key.

Then there are the values. They can be produced by any expression, too. We test for this here by asserting that `10 - 9` evaluates to `1`, `6 / 2` to `3` and so on.

As expected the test fails:

```
$ go test ./evaluator
--- FAIL: TestHashLiterals (0.00s)
  evaluator_test.go:522: Eval didn't return Hash. got=<nil> (<nil>)
FAIL
FAIL    monkey/evaluator        0.008s
```

We know how to get it to pass, though. We need to extend our `Eval` function with another `case` branch for `*ast.HashLiterals`:

```go
// evaluator/evaluator.go

func Eval(node ast.Node, env *object.Environment) object.Object {
// [...]

    case *ast.HashLiteral:
        return evalHashLiteral(node, env)

// [...]
}
```

The `evalHashLiteral` function here may look intimidating, but trust me, it doesn't bite:

```go
// evaluator/evaluator.go

func evalHashLiteral(
    node *ast.HashLiteral,
    env *object.Environment,
) object.Object {
    pairs := make(map[object.HashKey]object.HashPair)

    for keyNode, valueNode := range node.Pairs {
        key := Eval(keyNode, env)
        if isError(key) {
            return key
```

```
        }

        hashKey, ok := key.(object.Hashable)
        if !ok {
            return newError("unusable as hash key: %s", key.Type())
        }

        value := Eval(valueNode, env)
        if isError(value) {
            return value
        }

        hashed := hashKey.HashKey()
        pairs[hashed] = object.HashPair{Key: key, Value: value}
    }

    return &object.Hash{Pairs: pairs}
}
```

When iterating over the `node.Pairs` the `keyNode` is the first to be evaluated. Besides checking if the call to `Eval` produced an error we also make a type assertion about the evaluation result: it needs to implement the `object.Hashable` interface, otherwise it's unusable as a hash key. That's exactly why we added the `Hashable` definition.

Then we call `Eval` again, to evaluate `valueNode`. If that call to `Eval` also doesn't produce an error, we can add the newly produced key-value pair to our `pairs` map. We do this by generating a `HashKey` for the aptly-named `hashKey` object with a call to `HashKey()`. Then we initialize a new `HashPair`, pointing to both `key` and `value` and add it to `pairs`.

And that's all it takes. The tests are now passing:

```
$ go test ./evaluator
ok      monkey/evaluator        0.007s
```

That means we can already start using hash literals in our REPL:

```
$ go run main.go
Hello mrnugget! This is the Monkey programming language!
Feel free to type in commands
>> {"name": "Monkey", "age": 0, "type": "Language", "status": "awesome"}
{age: 0, type: Language, status: awesome, name: Monkey}
```

That's awesome! But we can't get elements out of the hash yet, which kinda diminishes their usefulness:

```
>> let bob = {"name": "Bob", "age": 99};
>> bob["name"]
```

```
ERROR: index operator not supported: HASH
```

That's what we're going to fix now.

EVALUATING INDEX EXPRESSIONS WITH HASHES

Remember that switch statement we added to `evalIndexExpression` in our evaluator? And do you also remember when I told you that we're going to add another `case` branch? Well, here we are!

But first of all we need to add a test function that makes sure accessing values in a hash via an index expression works:

```go
// evaluator/evaluator_test.go

func TestHashIndexExpressions(t *testing.T) {
	tests := []struct {
		input    string
		expected interface{}
	}{
		{
			`{"foo": 5}["foo"]`,
			5,
		},
		{
			`{"foo": 5}["bar"]`,
			nil,
		},
		{
			`let key = "foo"; {"foo": 5}[key]`,
			5,
		},
		{
			`{}["foo"]`,
			nil,
		},
		{
			`{5: 5}[5]`,
			5,
		},
		{
			`{true: 5}[true]`,
			5,
		},
		{
			`{false: 5}[false]`,
			5,
```

```
        },
    }

    for _, tt := range tests {
        evaluated := testEval(tt.input)
        integer, ok := tt.expected.(int)
        if ok {
            testIntegerObject(t, evaluated, int64(integer))
        } else {
            testNullObject(t, evaluated)
        }
    }
}
```

Just like in `TestArrayIndexExpressions` we're making sure using index operator expressions produces the correct value - only this time with hashes. The different test cases here use string, integer or boolean hash keys when retrieving values out of a hash. So, in essence, what the test really asserts is that the `HashKey` methods implemented by various data types are called correctly.

And to make sure that using an object as hash key that does not implement `object.Hashable` produces an error, we can add another test to our `TestErrorHandling` test function:

```
// evaluator/evaluator_test.go

func TestErrorHandling(t *testing.T) {
    tests := []struct {
        input           string
        expectedMessage string
    }{
// [...]
        {
            `{"name": "Monkey"}[fn(x) { x }];`,
            "unusable as hash key: FUNCTION",
        },
    }

// [...]
}
```

Running `go test` now results in the expected failures:

```
$ go test ./evaluator
--- FAIL: TestErrorHandling (0.00s)
  evaluator_test.go:228: no error object returned. got=*object.Null(&{})
--- FAIL: TestHashIndexExpressions (0.00s)
  evaluator_test.go:611: object is not Integer. got=*object.Null (&{})
  evaluator_test.go:611: object is not Integer. got=*object.Null (&{})
```

```
    evaluator_test.go:611: object is not Integer. got=*object.Null (&{})
    evaluator_test.go:611: object is not Integer. got=*object.Null (&{})
    evaluator_test.go:611: object is not Integer. got=*object.Null (&{})
FAIL
FAIL    monkey/evaluator        0.007s
```

That means we're ready to add another case branch to the switch statement in `evalIndexExpression`:

```go
// evaluator/evaluator.go

func evalIndexExpression(left, index object.Object) object.Object {
    switch {
    case left.Type() == object.ARRAY_OBJ && index.Type() == object.INTEGER_OBJ:
        return evalArrayIndexExpression(left, index)
    case left.Type() == object.HASH_OBJ:
        return evalHashIndexExpression(left, index)
    default:
        return newError("index operator not supported: %s", left.Type())
    }
}
```

The new case branch calls a new function: `evalHashIndexExpression`. And we already know how `evalHashIndexExpression` has to work, since we successfully tested the usage of the `object.Hashable` interface before - in our tests and when evaluating hash literals. So no surprises here:

```go
// evaluator/evaluator.go

func evalHashIndexExpression(hash, index object.Object) object.Object {
    hashObject := hash.(*object.Hash)

    key, ok := index.(object.Hashable)
    if !ok {
        return newError("unusable as hash key: %s", index.Type())
    }

    pair, ok := hashObject.Pairs[key.HashKey()]
    if !ok {
        return NULL
    }

    return pair.Value
}
```

Adding `evalHashIndexExpression` to the switch statement made the tests pass:

```
$ go test ./evaluator
ok      monkey/evaluator        0.007s
```

We can now successfully retrieve values from our hashes! Don't believe me? Think the tests are lying to us? I faked the test output? It can't be? The whole book is full of li.. what? No, watch this.

```
$ go run main.go
Hello mrnugget! This is the Monkey programming language!
Feel free to type in commands
>> let people = [{"name": "Alice", "age": 24}, {"name": "Anna", "age": 28}];
>> people[0]["name"];
Alice
>> people[1]["age"];
28
>> people[1]["age"] + people[0]["age"];
52
>> let getName = fn(person) { person["name"]; };
>> getName(people[0]);
Alice
>> getName(people[1]);
Anna
```

4.6 - The Grand Finale

Our Monkey interpreter is now fully functional. It supports mathematical expressions, variable bindings, functions and the application of those functions, conditionals, return statements and even advanced concepts like higher-order functions and closures. And then there are the different data types: integers, booleans, strings, arrays and hashes. We can be proud of ourselves.

But… and here comes the but… our interpreter still does not pass the most basic of all programming language tests: printing something. Yes, our Monkey interpreter can't communicate with the outside world. Even programming language scoundrel like Bash and Brainfuck manage to do that. It's clear what we have to do. We have to add one last built-in function: `puts`.

`puts` prints the given arguments on new lines to STDOUT. It calls the `Inspect()` method on the objects passed in as arguments and prints the return value of these calls. The `Inspect()` method is part of the `Object` interface, so every entity in our object system supports it. Using `puts` should look kinda like this:

```
>> puts("Hello!")
Hello!
>> puts(1234)
1234
>> puts(fn(x) { x * x })
fn(x) {
```

```
    (x * x)
}
```

And puts is a variadic function. It takes an unlimited number of arguments and prints each on a separate line:

```
>> puts("hello", "world", "how", "are", "you")
hello
world
how
are
you
```

Of course, puts is all about printing things and not producing a value, so we need to make sure that it returns NULL:

```
>> let putsReturnValue = puts("foobar");
foobar
>> putsReturnValue
null
```

That also means that our REPL will print the null in addition to the output we expect from puts. So it will look like this:

```
>> puts("Hello!")
Hello!
null
```

Now that's more than enough information and specification to complete this last quest of ours. Are you ready?

Here it is, here's what this section has been building up to, here is the complete, working implementation of puts:

```go
// evaluator/builtins.go

import (
    "fmt"
    "monkey/object"
    "unicode/utf8"
)

var builtins = map[string]*object.Builtin{
// [...]
    "puts": &object.Builtin{
        Fn: func(args ...object.Object) object.Object {
            for _, arg := range args {
                fmt.Println(arg.Inspect())
            }
```

```
                return NULL
            },
        },
}
```

And with that, we did it. We're done. Even if you were wary of our little celebrations and shrugged them off before, now's the time to go looking for a funny party hat and put it on.

In chapter three we brought the Monkey programming language to life. It started to breathe. With our last change, we made it talk. Now, Monkey is finally a real programming language:

```
$ go run main.go
Hello mrnugget! This is the Monkey programming language!
Feel free to type in commands
>> puts("Hello World!")
Hello World!
null
>>
```

THE LOST CHAPTER

Nearly half a year after publishing the first version of *Writing An Interpreter In Go*, I decided to add another chapter. It's called *The Lost Chapter: A Macro System For Monkey* and available for free. You can read or download it as an eBook at https://interpreterbook.com/lost.

RESOURCES

BOOKS

- Abelson, Harold and Sussman, Gerald Jay with Sussman, Julie. 1996. **Structure and Interpretation of Computer Programs, Second Edition**. MIT Press.
- Appel, Andrew W.. 2004. **Modern Compiler Implementation in C**. Cambridge University Press.
- Cooper, Keith D. and Torczon Linda. 2011. **Engineering a Compiler, Second Edition**. Morgan Kaufmann.
- Grune, Dick and Jacobs, Ceriel. 1990. **Parsing Techniques. A Practical Guide.**. Ellis Horwood Limited.
- Grune, Dick and van Reeuwijk, Kees and Bal Henri E. and Jacobs, Ceriel J.H. Jacobs and Langendoen, Koen. 2012. **Modern Compiler Design, Second Edition**. Springer
- Nisan, Noam and Schocken, Shimon. 2008. **The Elements Of Computing Systems**. MIT Press.

PAPERS

- Ayock, John. 2003. **A Brief History of Just-In-Time**. In **ACM Computing Surveys, Vol. 35, No. 2, June 2003**
- Ertl, M. Anton and Gregg, David. 2003. **The Structure and Performance of Efficient Interpreters**. In **Journal Of Instruction-Level Parallelism 5 (2003)**
- Ghuloum, Abdulaziz. 2006. **An Incremental Approach To Compiler Construction**. In **Proceedings of the 2006 Scheme and Functional Programming Workshop**.
- Ierusalimschy, Robert and de Figueiredo, Luiz Henrique and Celes Waldemar. **The Implementation of Lua 5.0**. https://www.lua.org/doc/jucs05.pdf

- Pratt, Vaughan R. 1973. **Top Down Operator Precedence**. Massachusetts Institute of Technology.
- Romer, Theodore H. and Lee, Dennis and Voelker, Geoffrey M. and Wolman, Alec and Wong, Wayne A. and Baer, Jean-Loup and Bershad, Brian N. and Levy, Henry M.. 1996. **The Structure and Performance of Interpreters**. In **ASPLOS VII Proceedings of the seventh international conference on Architectural support for programming languages and operating systems**.
- Dybvig, R. Kent. 2006. **The Development of Chez Scheme**. In **ACM ICFP '06**

WEB

- Jack W. Crenshaw - Let's Build a Compiler! - http://compilers.iecc.com/crenshaw/tutorfinal.pdf
- Douglas Crockford - Top Down Operator Precedence - http://javascript.crockford.com/tdop/tdop.html
- Bob Nystrom - Expression Parsing Made Easy - http://journal.stuffwithstuff.com/2011/03/19/pratt-parsers-expression-parsing-made-easy/
- Shriram Krishnamurthi and Joe Gibbs Politz - Programming Languages: Application and Interpretation - http://papl.cs.brown.edu/2015/
- A Python Interpreter Written In Python - http://aosabook.org/en/500L/a-python-interpreter-written-in-python.html
- Dr. Dobbs - Bob: A Tiny Object-Oriented Language - http://www.drdobbs.com/open-source/bob-a-tiny-object-oriented-language/184409401
- Nick Desaulniers - Interpreter, Compiler, JIT - https://nickdesaulniers.github.io/blog/2015/05/25/interpreter-compiler-jit/
- Peter Norvig - (How to Write a (Lisp) Interpreter (in Python)) - http://norvig.com/lispy.html
- Fredrik Lundh - Simple Town-Down Parsing In Python - http://effbot.org/zone/simple-top-down-parsing.htm
- Mihai Bazon - How to implement a programming language in JavaScript - http://lisperator.net/pltut/
- Mary Rose Cook - Little Lisp interpreter - https://www.recurse.com/blog/21-little-lisp-interpreter
- Peter Michaux - Scheme From Scratch - http://peter.michaux.ca/articles/scheme-from-scratch-introduction
- Make a Lisp - https://github.com/kanaka/mal
- Matt Might - Compiling Scheme to C with closure conversion - http://matt.might.net/articles/compiling-scheme-to-c/
- Rob Pike - Implementing a bignum calculator - https://www.youtube.com/watch?v=PXoG0WX0r_E

- Rob Pike - Lexical Scanning in Go - https://www.youtube.com/watch?v=HxaD_trXwRE

SOURCE CODE

- The Wren Programming Language - https://github.com/munificent/wren
- Otto - A JavaScript Interpreter In Go - https://github.com/robertkrimen/otto
- The Go Programming Language - https://github.com/golang/go
- The Lua Programming Language (1.1, 3.1, 5.3.2) - https://www.lua.org/versions.html
- The Ruby Programming Language - https://github.com/ruby/ruby
- c4 - C in four functions - https://github.com/rswier/c4
- tcc - Tiny C Compiler - https://github.com/LuaDist/tcc
- 8cc - A Small C Compiler - https://github.com/rui314/8cc
- Fedjmike/mini-c - https://github.com/Fedjmike/mini-c
- thejameskyle/the-super-tiny-compiler - https://github.com/thejameskyle/the-super-tiny-compiler
- lisp.c - https://gist.github.com/sanxiyn/523967

FEEDBACK

If you spot a typo, find something wrong with the code, have a suggestion to make or just a question, feel free to send me an email:

me@thorstenball.com

CHANGELOG

28 JUNE 2017 - 1.4

- Section 1.4:
  - Use a local variable to save the `literal` when creating `token.EQ` and `token.NOT_EQ`
- Section 2.3:
  - Fix a small typo
- Section 2.4:
  - Change incorrect mention of `peekPosition` in lexer to correct `readPosition`
- Section 2.6:
  - Fix duplicate test input in `TestOperatorPrecedenceParsing` here and in the following sections where it's referenced
- Section 3.9:
  - In the first example the expression `5 * 5` was used and the text explained that this should evaluate to `10`, which is wrong. It should evaluate to `25`, of course.
- The Lost Chapter:
  - Added a new section at the end of the book about *The Lost Chapter: A Macro System For Monkey* and where it can be found.

26 JANUARY 2017 - 1.3

- License of the code:
  - The `code` folder and its content are now licensed under the MIT license. See the `LICENSE` file and/or the `README.md` file.
- Section 1.1:
  - Make clear that whitespace is only significant in the sense that it separates tokens, but not its length.
- Section 1.3:

    - Small wording change
    - Fix wrong reference to `NextToken` when `readChar` was meant
- Section 2.8:
    - Fix the `parseBlockStatement` method so it doesn't run into an endless loop when parsing incomplete input
- Section 4.2:
    - Fix the `readString` method so it doesn't run into an endless loop when a string in the input is not terminated with a closing double quote
- Section 4.4:
    - Fix a typo in the error message of the builtin `push` function

20 DECEMBER 2016 - 1.2

- Section 2.8:
    - Add a missing semicolon to the test input in `TestLetStatements`
- Section 4.4:
    - Fix the failing test for the builtin `push` function. Error was introduced with the last update. This change only occurrs in the code accompanying the book and only in subfolder `04`.

8 DECEMBER 2016 - 1.1

Besides fixed typos and spelling errors:

- Introduction
    - Change the "How To Use This Book" subsection to include a link to the downloadable archive of the accompanying code
- Section 1.4:
    - Add hint about accompanying code
    - Show the last, fully extended version of the test `input` for `TestNextToken`
- Section 2.6:
    - The failing test output for `TestParsingPrefixExpressions` in the book text was wrong. It's corrected to match the actual output one gets when building the parser from scratch
    - Fix wording that didn't match the described test output
    - Remove `token.LPAREN` from the `precedences` table here. It somehow slipped in at this point, but should only be added later on in section 2.8, where tests are supposed to fail because it's missing
- Section 2.8:
    - Fix wrong test expectation (`"x"` changed to `"y"`) in `TestLetStatement`
    - Change `parser_parser_test.go` to `parser_test.go`

- Better show how to use `testLiteralExpression` in `TestParsingInfixExpressions`
- Fix outdated test output for failing `TestOperatorPrecedenceParsing`, `TestIfExpression`, `TestIfElseExpression`, `TestFunctionLiteralParsing`

- Section 3.10:
  - Change the `Inspect()` method of `*object.Function` to use `fn` instead of `function` and newlines in output
  - Remove needless semicolons in example
- Section 3.5:
  - Change from if/else to "if and return" in `nativeBoolToBooleanObject`
- Section 3.6:
  - Update the version of `testNullObject` to be the one in the accompanying code, with a correct call to `t.Errorf`
- Section 4.4:
  - Name the `token.Token` field of `ast.ArrayLiteral`
  - Fix possible panic through nil error in "first", "last", "rest", and "push" functions by adding separate check
- Section 4.5:
  - Name the `token.Token` field of `ast.HashLiteral`
  - Replace `null` in output with missing error message when trying to access hash via index expression before it's implemented
- Section 4.6:
  - Change the expected output using `puts` with a function literal to match the updated `Inspect()` of `*object.Function`
  - Explain the `null`s in the expected output of `put` better

23 NOVEMBER 2016 - 1.0

- Initial Release

32559477R00145

Printed in Great Britain
by Amazon